Secularism and Freedom of Religion in Italy

The display of religious symbols in the public space has been the subject of much debate. This book provides an overview of the presence of religious symbols in Italian public institutions from a legal standpoint.

The situation is analysed from the perspective of the principles of *laicità/* secularism, as defined by the Constitutional Court, and freedom of religion. It is argued that while the display of religious symbols in public institutions has been widely investigated doctrinally, the wearing of religious symbols in Italy has generally been neglected. Key cases are examined in light of national jurisprudence as well as intervention by the European Court of Human Rights and relevant judgments from foreign courts regarding this issue. Finally, the work considers the presence of religious symbols that transcend national borders, as in the case of arts, sport, and advertising. A comparison is made with the French system which takes a very different approach. The book outlines possible ways forward in light of the growing interculturality of European societies.

It will be a valuable resource for academics, researchers, and policy-makers working in the areas of Law and Religion and Comparative Law.

Maria Cristina Ivaldi is Full Professor of Law and Religion in the Department of Political Sciences at the University of Campania Luigi Vanvitelli, where she teaches courses on Law and Religion in Multicultural Societies, Religious Cultural Heritage, and Pilgrimage and Religious Tourism.

ICLARS Series on Law and Religion

Series Editors:
Silvio Ferrari, *University of Milan, Italy*
Russell Sandberg, *Cardiff University, UK*
Pieter Coertzen, *University of Stellenbosch, South Africa*
W. Cole Durham, *Jr., Brigham Young University, USA, and*
Tahir Mahmood, *Amity International University, India*

The *ICLARS Series on Law and Religion* is a new series designed to provide a forum for the rapidly expanding field of research in law and religion. The series is published in association with the International Consortium for Law and Religion Studies, an international network of scholars and experts of law and religion founded in 2007 with the aim of providing a place where information, data and opinions can easily be exchanged among members and made available to the broader scientific community. The series aims to become a primary source for students and scholars while presenting authors with a valuable means to reach a wide and growing readership.

Other titles in this series:

Religious Freedom and COVID-19: A European Perspective
A European Perspective
Edited by Jelle Creemers and Tatiana Kopaleishvili

Human Dignity, Religion and the Law
Pluralism and Reasonable Accommodation of Religious Practices
Edited by Mark Hill KC and María-José Valero-Estarellas

Freedom of Religion and Religious Diversity
State Accommodation of Religious Minorities
Edited by Md Jahid Hossain Bhuiyan and Ann Black

Fundamental Rights, Religion and Human Dignity
A Constitutional Journey
Edited by Javier Martínez-Torrón and Li-ann Thio

Secularism and Freedom of Religion in Italy
Religious Symbols in the Public Space
Maria Cristina Ivaldi

For more information about this series, please visit: www.routledge.com/ICLARS-Series-on-Law-and-Religion/book-series/ICLARS

Secularism and Freedom of Religion in Italy

Religious Symbols in the Public Space

Maria Cristina Ivaldi

Routledge
Taylor & Francis Group
LONDON AND NEW YORK

First published 2025
by Routledge
4 Park Square, Milton Park, Abingdon, Oxon OX14 4RN

and by Routledge
605 Third Avenue, New York, NY 10158

Routledge is an imprint of the Taylor & Francis Group, an informa business

British Library Cataloguing-in-Publication Data
A catalogue record for this book is available from the British Library

Library of Congress Cataloging-in-Publication Data
Names: Ivaldi, Maria Cristina, author.
Title: Secularism and freedom of religion in Italy : religious symbols in the public space / Maria Cristina Ivaldi.
Description: Abingdon, Oxon [UK] ; New York, NY : Routledge, 2025. | Series: ICLARS series on law and religion | Includes bibliographical references and index.
Identifiers: LCCN 2024044196
Subjects: LCSH: Freedom of religion—Italy. | Signs and symbols—Italy—Religious aspects. | Secularism—Italy.
Classification: LCC KKH2693 .I93 2025 | DDC 342.4508/52137—dc23/eng/20240919
LC record available at https://lccn.loc.gov/2024044196

ISBN: 978-0-367-19737-7 (hbk)
ISBN: 978-1-032-96854-4 (pbk)
ISBN: 978-0-429-24295-3 (ebk)

DOI: 10.4324/9780429242953

Typeset in Galliard
by Apex CoVantage, LLC

In loving memory of Aldo and Vilma

Contents

About the author

Maria Cristina Ivaldi is Full Professor of Law and Religion in the Department of Political Sciences at the University of Campania Luigi Vanvitelli, where she teaches courses on Law and Religion in Multicultural Societies, Religious Cultural Heritage, and Pilgrimage and Religious Tourism.

Her fields of interest are religious freedom and the status of religious groups in the Italian, French, and Algerian legal systems, with special attention to the living law as emphasised by jurisprudence. She currently focuses her research on Law and Religion within the Council of Europe and the European Union frameworks, blasphemy and religious vilification in the arts and advertising, and the religious factor in *lex sportiva*, notably in football regulations. She is the author of essays and books on these topics.

She is a member of the ADEC, the Italian Association of Academics of the Legal Discipline of the Religious Phenomenon; ICLARS, the International Consortium for Law and Religion Studies; and EuARe, the European Academy of Religion.

Acknowledgements

I express my heartfelt gratitude to my family, who have provided immense support, particularly in recent months. Thank you, Antonio. Thank you, Ivan. I ask you to forgive me for the time I have taken from you.

I express my gratitude to my friends and colleagues in the discipline who encouraged me to persevere in this "enterprise" despite the overwhelming academic obligations I faced. I also thank them for the fruitful scholarly discussion that has always characterised our meetings.

I extend my heartfelt appreciation to the many affable individuals who regularly enrich my experience in the Department of Political Science at the University of Campania Luigi Vanvitelli. My department is also a home away from home.

I would like to express my gratitude to those who have consistently and unwaveringly believed in me, particularly the esteemed Professor Nicoletta De Luca, who was the first to challenge me to delve into the field of Law and Religion studies, and whom I hold dear in my memories.

Abbreviations

A	author
AD	*Anno Domini*
ADI	Assemblies of God in Italy (*Assemblee di Dio in Italia*)
AIART	Italian Association of Radio and Television Listeners (*Associazione Italiana Ascoltatori Radio e Televisione*)
AMI	Association of Italian Muslims (*Associazione dei Musulmani Italiani*)
art./arts.	article/articles
BayAGO	General Rules of Procedure for the Authorities of the Free State of Bavaria (*Allgemeine Geschäftsordnung für die Behörden des Freistaates Bayern*)
BayEUG	Bavarian Law on Education and Teaching (*Bayerisches Gesetz über das Erziehungs- und Unterrichtswesen*)
BC	Before Christ
BayVerfGH	Bavarian Constitutional Court (*Bayerischen Verfassungsgerichtshofs*)
BVerfG	German Federal Constitutional Court (*BundesVerfassungsGericht*)
BVerwG	German Federal Administrative Court (*BundesVerwaltungsGericht*)
CE	French Council of State (*Conseil d'État*)
CEI	Italian Bishops' Conference (*Conferenza episcopale italiana*)
CELI	Evangelical Lutheran Church in Italy (*Chiesa Evangelica Luterana in Italia*)
CGUE	Court of Justice of the European Union
col./cols.	column/columns
Const.	Constitution
COREIS	Islamic Religious Community (*Comunità Religiosa Islamica*)
CSM	Superior Council of the Judiciary (*Consiglio Superiore della Magistratura*)
d.lgs.	legislative decree (*decreto legislativo*)

d.P.R.	decree of the President of the Republic (*decreto del Presidente della Repubblica*)
ECHR	European Convention of Human Rights
ECtHR	European Court of Human Rights
e.g.	*exempli gratia* (for example)
esp.	especially
etc.	*et cetera*
EU	European Union
FFF	French Football Federation (*Féderation Française de Football*)
GG	German Basic Law (*GrundGesezt*)
IAP	Institute of Advertising Self-Discipline (*Istituto di autodisciplina pubblicitaria*)
IBSG	Italian Buddhist Institute Soka Gakkai (*Istituto Buddista Italiano Soka Gakkai*)
ICCPR	International Covenant on Civile and Political Rights
i.e.	*id est* (in other words)
m.d.	ministerial decree (*decreto ministeriale*)
N.A.	No author
para./paras.	paragraph/paragraphs
r.d.	royal decree (*regio decreto*)
resp.	respectively
SCC	Supreme Court of Cassation (*Suprema Corte di Cassazione*)
subpara./subparas.	subparagraph/subparagraphs
TAR	Regional Administrative Court (*Tribunale amministrativo egionale*)
TFEU	Treaty on the Functioning of the European Union
TUEL	Consolidated text of laws on the organisation of local authorities (*Testo unico delle leggi sull'ordinamento degli enti locali*)
TULPS	Consolidated law on public security (*Testo unico delle leggi di pubblica sicurezza*)
UAAR	Union of Atheists Agnostics Rationalists (*Unione Atei Agnostici Razionalisti*)
UBI	Italian Buddhist Union (*Unione Buddhista Italiana*)
UCEBI	Evangelical Baptist Christian Union of Italy (*Unione Cristiana Evangelica Battista d'Italia*)
UCEI	Union of Jewish Communities in Italy (*Unione delle Comunità ebraiche in Italia*)
UCOII	Union of Italian Islamic Communities (*Unione delle Comunità Islamiche Italiane*)
UDHR	Universal Declaration of Human Rights
US	United States

USCIRF	United States Commission on International Religious Freedom
VfGH	Austrian Constitutional Court (*VerfassungsGerichtsHof*)
Vv.Aa.	*Variae Auctores*

Notes to the reader

The attempt to make the subject matter more accessible to an audience that, while perhaps comprising mainly legal scholars, may nevertheless know little about Italian Law and Religion in all its particularities determined several preliminary choices.

The most relevant of these choices is to primarily refer to the bibliographies of foreign or Italian authors in English. Undoubtedly, the renowned ECtHR *Lautsi I* and *Lautsi II* rulings have also brought the Italian perspective on symbol-related matters to the forefront of discussions among religious scholars.

However, the issue of symbols – including those worn by believers – does not exhaust the many other "symbolic" issues that remain legal grey areas in the Italian system. The issues discussed here strive to give the best possible account of events that have not yet been adequately resolved in Italy.

For this reason, I have made the deliberate choice to give precedence to citing doctrinal sources that can be easily accessed on the internet. The intention is to provide reference points for individuals who desire to deepen their comprehension of the subject matter.

Regrettably, the reader will encounter increased difficulty in locating the numerous court orders referenced in the text. Except for the access portal to Italian law (www.normattiva.it), there is no generalised database of jurisprudence. While the decisions of the Constitutional Court and Administrative Justice (Council of State and Regional Administrative Courts) are easily usable, the same cannot be said for civil and criminal case law on the merits. Sometimes I have been forced to indicate a paper-only publication or to refer to non-institutional sites for viewing a given ruling. Equally inadequate is the service provided with respect to the Court endowed with the task of nomofilachy (*nomofilachia*), namely, the Supreme Court of Cassation. Only its pronouncements made after 2019 can be accessed publicly and without any charge, although not in their entirety.

All links cited in the notes were carefully double-checked when the monograph was released.

For reference, a compilation of the principal legal portals used, listed in order of appearance, can be found at the end of the bibliography.

Introduction

The presence of religious symbols in the public space represents one of the issues being given the most attention by national[1] and European supranational[2] jurisprudences and doctrine.

While not claiming to be exhaustive, the purpose of this book is to offer an overview of the issue of religious symbols in Italy. It specifically focuses on their display by public institutions or by believers from a legal standpoint. The analysis examines these two profiles – with a particular emphasis on the former – in relation to the principle of *laicità* (secularism), as defined by the Constitutional Court since the late 1980s, and the freedom of religion or belief.

While the display of religious symbols in public institutions has been widely investigated in doctrine, the wearing of religious symbols by believers has received less attention, probably because it has given rise to fewer disputes in Italy.[3]

The assessment of prevailing case law and legal doctrines serves as the primary foundation for delineating the *status quo* of the law on religious matters both within the Italian legal system, with its various particularities, as well as within the broader framework of Western legal systems.

The study emphasises – even from a comparative viewpoint – the positive and negative aspects of the Italian solution, as it is embodied in living law, also in the perspective of *ius condendum*. This analysis is set against a backdrop of increasing non-belief and militant atheism on the one hand and religious and cultural diversity on the other.

This analysis refers primarily – though not exclusively – to the now significant production of Italian doctrine in the English language as well as to other

1 Our examination will commence with Italian jurisprudence decisions, and subsequently, we will delve into foreign jurisprudences, placing particular emphasis on the matter of symbols in public institutions.

2 In addition to the pronouncements specifically rendered on crucifixes by the Strasbourg Court, a selection of pronouncements of the European Court of Human Rights (ECtHR) and the Court of Justice of the European Union (CJEU), mainly concerning religious symbols worn by believers, will be considered when deemed appropriate.

3 Cf. *amplius infra* Chapter 3.

DOI: 10.4324/9780429242953-1

representative doctrine in the English language regarding Law and Religion in Italy.[4]

*****

Chapter 1 provides a general overview of the Italian legal system surrounding Law and Religion, formerly known as *Diritto ecclesiastico* (Ecclesiastical Law).[5]

The analysis exposes the underlying tensions frequently found within the Italian legal order and draws attention to the legislator's inertia in upholding constitutional rules.

Constitutional jurisprudence commonly assumes compliance with constitutional rules through the interpretation or declaration of unconstitutionality. This is the case with the delineation of the principle of *laicità* (secularism) by the Constitutional Court at the end of the 1980s, the guiding principles (namely, the *principio supremo dell'ordinamento giuridico*) of Law and Religion, and the principle of *laicità*, which was subsequently specified in its contents by the Court itself.

Chapter 2 emphasises the crucial issues surrounding religious symbols, including with regard to the concept of public space. In Italy, public space does not have the same significance as in other legal systems (e.g. France), especially regarding the admissibility of religious symbols worn by believers. This chapter thoroughly investigates the issue of religious symbols' display within public institutions. In Italy, the symbols in question are principally crucifixes, although questions have also arisen concerning the presence of nativity scenes in public spaces and liturgical celebrations or blessings in schools during key Catholic holidays.[6]

4 Cf. *in primis* M. Ventura, *Law and Religion in Italy*, Wolkers Kluvers, Alphen aan den Rijn, 2013, 234 pp. and A. Ferrari, *Religious Freedom in Italy. An Impossible Paradigm?*, De Gruyter, Berlin – Boston, 2023, VII–201 pp. as well as the many essays published by Silvio Ferrari, mentioned in the manuscript, concerning various aspects of Italian doctrine. With specific regard to the status of Islam, see F. Alicino, *Constitutional Democracy and Islam. The Legal Status of Muslims in Italy*, Routledge, Abingdon – New York, 2023, X–210 pp.

Correspondingly, see the volumes of the *European Consortium for Church and State Research*, which has published the proceedings of the annual conference since 1989 (www.churchstate.eu/publications/proceedings-meetings.html). Each conference focuses on a specific topic, with a dedicated section reserved for Italy. For the most recent volume, see L. Papadopoulou (ed.), *Islam and Human Rights in the European Union/Islam et droits de l'homme dans l'Union européenne*, Comares, Granada, 2022, *passim*, freely downloadable at www.churchstate.eu/pdf/NEW/tripa_Islam_human.pdf.

5 The Italian name still commonly still used for the study of the corpus of legal provisions related in many ways to religion, both with regard to the profile of state-church relationships and with regard to the individual or collective exercise of the right to religious freedom, regardless of the provisions' position in the system of sources of law.

6 These events are often mentioned in the local press but normally do not lead to judicial decisions. For a more in-depth discussion, see *infra* para. 4.2.

After an analysis of the well-known *Lautsi* case, additional examples of the crucifix in other public institutions that have been submitted to judgment are considered.[7] Finally, a brief survey is given of the approaches of other foreign courts to similar cases.[8]

In Chapter 3, religious symbols are considered as an expression of the religious freedom of believers. Generally, the wearing of religious symbols by individuals – even if they are public officials or in charge of a public service – does not give rise to significant controversy in Italy. To tackle this issue, no specific national legislation has been enacted on this point. Instead, recourse has been made to provisions already present in the legal system, even if they were enacted in other contexts. There have also been examples of cases in which the wearing of certain symbols (e.g. the *niqab*, *burqa*, or *kirpan*) has led to controversies entailing solutions that do not appear to be in line with the constitutional framework.

Comparative approaches are not neglected, especially with reference to the French approach to secularism and the regulation of the wearing of religious symbols by believers.

Following review of a significant ruling by the Supreme Court of Cassation concerning crucifixes in schools in recent years,[9] Chapter 4 briefly discusses another symbolic use of religion that can transcend national borders, namely, in arts and advertising.

Next, reference will be made to other issues of a symbolic nature that hinder the Italian legal system from fully implementing the constitutional dictate on religion and equality, such as those concerning places of worship, the lack of *intese* for specific religious denominations, and the replacement of legislation on admitted cults through the enactment of a general law on religious freedom.

This part of the study ends with an examination of the latest incidents related to the crucifix decided by jurisprudence as well as the *ius condendum* on the matter.

This is followed by a brief conclusion that attempts to synthesise the emerging trends – particularly on the subject of the presence of religious symbols within institutions – in relation to the more or less unimplemented constitutional framework on religion. The interpretations take into account the growing interculturality of European societies despite the lack of a common or convergent standard (common *v.* specific constitutional traditions).

7 Cf. *infra* para. 2.4. regarding the display of the crucifix in polling stations, courtrooms, and hospitals.

8 This includes foreign jurisprudence not only on crucifixes but also on other religious symbols such as the Ten Commandments, icons, statues, and Christian mangers. Cf. esp. *infra* para. 2.5 and 4.2.

9 *Infra* para. 4.1.

1 Overview of Law and Religion in Italy

Summary: 1.1. Brief historical background of the Italian legal system – 1.2. Conflicts between the constitutional level and the ordinary legislation on religion – 1.3. From the sacred character to the particular significance of Rome for Catholicism – 1.4. The Italian approach to *laicità* (secularism) – 1.5. The principle of *laicità* as used mainly by judges but without formal legal implementation

1.1 Brief historical background of the Italian legal system

A study from the perspective of law that intends to address the issue of the presence of religious symbols in the public space in Italy – primarily from the viewpoint of their presence in State institutions – must at least briefly address the historical evolution of the national legal system. After all, Italy is a relatively young country, being born on 17 March 1861 when Victor Emmanuel II was proclaimed King of Italy.[1] On this date, the Albertine Statute of 4 March 1848 and particularly its art. 1 became the fundamental text of the new state. It was a flexible *octroyée* constitution – i.e. granted unilaterally by the King – as it could be amended by the provision of ordinary laws, Albertine Statute which remained formally operative until the Republican Constitution came into force in 1948. Art. 1 of the Albertine Statute stated that "the Catholic, Apostolic and Roman Religion is the sole Religion of the State. The other cults now existing are tolerated in accordance with the law".[2]

1 Law of the Kingdom of Sardinia, 17 March 1861, no. 4671, which shortly afterwards – on 21 April 1861 – became the first law of the newly constituted Kingdom of Italy.

2 Cf. D. Jahier, *Il 1° articolo dello Statuto e la libertà religiosa in Italia. Monografia storico-giuridica*, Lattes & C., Torino – Genova, 1925, *passim*. It should be noted that in Italian – as in French law – the noun "cult" does not in itself have a negative meaning. On the contrary, the eventual use of adjectives such as "tolerated" confers a specific meaning, as exemplified in this case. Similar remarks apply to the expression "admitted cults", which is basically neutral when referring to all religious denominations, whereas it takes on a very different value when compared with the presence of a state religion, which expresses a preference.

DOI: 10.4324/9780429242953-2

In 1861, however, Italian unification was not yet complete, as a significant portion of the centre of the peninsula was still under the sovereignty of the Papal States.[3] Unity would only be accomplished almost 10 years later with the seizure of Rome and the famous breach of Porta Pia on 20 September 1870. This gave rise to the "Roman Question", which was temporarily resolved unilaterally by the Italian State by means of law 13 May 1871, no. 214, or the so-called law of guarantees.[4]

The "Roman Question" remained unresolved for almost 60 years until it was settled with the signing of the Lateran Pacts on 11 February 1929.[5] The Lateran Pacts – consisting of a Treaty, a Concordat, and four annexes – already *prima facie* provide insight into the complexity of the circumstances. Indeed, it is worth considering that, due to the Lateran Treaty, Italy finds itself with an enclave within its territory endowed with autonomous territorial sovereignty – the Vatican City State, whose absolute monarch is the Supreme Pontiff and who is also the head of the Holy See (or Apostolic See). Vatican City is also endowed with international sovereignty, deputed to the universal government of the Catholic Church.[6]

The Concordat, on the other hand, aimed at the bilateral regulation of the so-called *rex mistae*, i.e. topics of shared interest for the Church and the State, primarily those of marriage[7] and compulsory religious instruction in

3 It was a process that began around the middle of the 19th century and – through various steps, including Garibaldi's Expedition of the Thousand – led to the unification.

Simultaneously, a parallel process unfolded with the emergence of legislation emphasising jurisdictional authority. Notably, this legislation included extensive measures targeting the practice of ecclesiastical mortmain, whereby the Church amassed substantial land holdings and withdrew them from the economic market. Additionally, it advocated for the State to assume exclusive competencies in marriage, education, and welfare.

For a concise overview of the Italian historical background, consult M. Ventura, *Law and Religion in Italy*, p. 31 ff.

4 Cf. A.C. Jemolo, "Guarentigie (Legge delle)", in *Novissimo digesto italiano*, Utet, Torino, vol. VIII, 1962, p. 34.

5 The texts of the Lateran Pacts can be accessed at the following website: www.vatican.va/roman_curia/secretariat_state/archivio/documents/rc_seg-st_19290211_patti-lateranensi_it.html; enforced by law 27 May 1929, no. 810. For a commentary see M. Falco, "Accordi lateranensi", in *Nuovo digesto italiano*, UTET, Torino, 1937, vol. I, p. 86.

6 A.M. Petroncelli, "La Santa Sede e lo Stato Città del Vaticano", *Rivista Internazionale di Scienze Sociali e Discipline Ausiliarie*, vol. 3, no. 2, 1932, p. 169.

7 For example, consider the recognition of the civil effects for religious marriages and the exclusive jurisdiction of ecclesiastical courts and dicasteries in cases concerning the nullity of marriage and the dispensation of unconsummated marriages, as well as the attribution of effectiveness of the relative provisions in the Italian legal system. (art. 34, Concordat and, for Italy, law no. 847 from 27 May 1929, "Provisions for the implementation of the Concordat of 11 February 1929 between the Holy See and Italy, in the part concerning marriage").

state schools.[8] The recovery of the principle of the State religion through the reference in art. 1 of the Lateran Treaty to art. 1 of the Albertine Statute represents another important facet of the Lateran Treaty.[9]

The Lateran Pacts was followed by the unilateral, slightly later law 24 June 1929, no. 1159, "Provisions on the exercise of the cults admitted in the State and on marriage celebrated before the ministers of those cults".[10] In this case, "admitted cults" are those other than Catholicism (assumed to be the State religion) that were present in Italy at the time, with an entirely different meaning from that of the liberal legislation of the late 19th century. Cults were admitted "as long as they do not profess principles or follow rites contrary to public order or morals".[11] This law is based on state control of religion and, as will be seen in the following,[12] is still in force, albeit with some corrections made by the by the Constitutional Court's jurisprudence of the Republican era for denominations that have not entered into an *intesa* (bilateral agreement) with the State, pursuant to art. 8, para. 3, Const.[13]

The outcome of this neo-confessionalism, which had been anticipated by several provisions prior to the stipulation of the Lateran Pacts,[14] was the new Criminal Code enacted in 1930, in which the religion of the State received

8 Cf. art. 36, Concordat, under which "Italy considers the teaching of Christian doctrine according to the form received from the Catholic tradition to be the foundation and crowning achievement of public education". Rule implemented by law 5 June 1930, no. 824, "Religious Education in Classical, Scientific, Magisterial, Technical and Artistic Schools". As a result of this provision, compulsory teaching, which was already provided in elementary schools by royal decree (hereafter r.d.) 1 October 1923, no. 2185 "Regulation of school grades and curricula in primary education", was extended to other public schools of all levels. Nevertheless, art. 6, law no. 1159/1929 (which is discussed later in the text) allowed for dispensation from this teaching upon request for students belonging to one of the cults recognised by the State. This dispensation was not possible for adherents of non-admitted cults and, above all, for those who professed to be agnostics or atheists.

9 Art. 1, Treaty: "Italy recognizes and reaffirms the principle established in the first Article of the Statute of the Kingdom of 4 March 1848, according to which the Catholic, Apostolic and Roman Religion is the only religion of the State".

10 Law implemented by r.d. 28 February 1930, no. 289. For an almost contemporary review, see C. Magni, *Intorno al nuovo diritto dei culti acattolici ammessi in Italia*, Sassari, Gallizzi, 1931, *passim* and U. Della Seta, *La legge fondamentale sui Culti ammessi (Valutazione etica)*, Guanda, Modena, 1937, *passim*.

All laws and regulations cited in the following that are still in force can be accessed on the Italian law portal www.normattiva.it.

11 Art. 1, para. 1, law no. 1159/1929.

12 *Infra* para. 1.2.

13 *Infra* paras. 1.5. and 4.4.

14 In addition to the aforementioned law no. 2185/1923, which already addressed the teaching of Christian doctrine according to the Catholic tradition as the foundation and coronation of primary education in art. 1, see art. 2, (b), r.d. 15 July 1923, no. 3288 "Rules on the management and vigilance of newspapers and periodical publications", which referred to the Catholic religion as the religion of the State.

specific and distinct protection from that granted to admitted cults,[15] amounting to total dismissal of any claim to equal treatment.[16]

It should also be observed that the repeal of the so-called law of guarantees, particularly its art. 2, para. 4, which provided for freedom of discussion in religious matters, was replaced by art. 5 of law no. 1159/1929 which reproduces its wording. Additionally, art. 1, para. 2 permits free exercise of the admitted cults, including in public.[17] In reality, this is a largely formal recognition given that it operates within a totalitarian – as well as confessional – system.[18]

This is the historical background to the birth of the legal discipline that was until recently known as "Ecclesiastical Law".[19] This discipline can be dated to the final decades of the 19th century, inspired by the German doctrine, with

15 Through the modification of the liberal viewpoint that had served as the inspiration for Zanardelli's 1889 Criminal Code on religion. On this topic, M.C. Ivaldi, *La tutela penale in materia religiosa nella giurisprudenza*, Giuffrè, Milano, 2004, p. 1 ff.

It is worth noting that, for the Fascist legislator, the admitted cults were those known and present in the kingdom's territory. These included first and foremost those historically persisting in the peninsula since time immemorial, i.e. Waldensians and Jews. Jews were first authoritatively organised by the State legislator through r.d. 30 October 1930, no. 1731 "Rules on the Israelitic Communities and the Union of these Communities", implemented by the regulation referred to in r.d. 19 December 1931, no. 1561. They were then the target of so-called racial legislation from 1938 onwards. For an exhaustive list of these norms, see www.governo.it/sites/governo.it/files/leggi_antiebraiche_38_43.pdf.

Regarding Italian politics on religious matters in the colonies, see G. Anello, "Colonialismo giuridico italiano. Archeologia della subalternità legale nei contesti multiculturali" e F. Botti, "Oltre i culti ammessi. Prime note sulla gestione giuridica del pluralismo religioso nella legislazione coloniale italiana", resp., *Stato, Chiese e pluralismo confessionale*, Rivista telematica (www.statoechiese.it), November 2009, pp. 1–45 and July 2011, pp. 1–20.

16 A preference that is also inferred from art. 142 "Compulsory religious practices for prisoners", of r.d. 18 June 1931, no. 787 "Regulations for prevention and punishment institutions", which obliged "prisoners, who at the time of entering the establishment have not declared that they belong to another religious denomination", to follow the practices of Catholic worship and envisaged the presence of an oratory and a Catholic priest in each institute.

17 This provision was received negatively by the Holy See, which had already expressed disapproval of art. 5 of the law of guarantees. Cf. O. Giacchi, *La legislazione italiana sui culti ammessi*, Vita e Pensiero, Milano, 1934, pp. 10–11.

18 On the use of wide margins of discretion granted to the public authority by the law on admitted cults, see G. Peyrot, *Gli evangelici nei loro rapporti con lo Stato dal fascismo ad oggi*, Torre Pellice, Società di studi valdesi, 1977, p. 11.

Unsurprisingly, the publication of circular 9 April 1935, no. 600/158 (the so-called Buffarini-Guidi circular) followed shortly thereafter and prohibited Pentecostal worshipping under art. 2, law no. 1159/1929, "as it is expressed and embodied in religious practices contrary to the social order and harmful to the physical and psychic integrity of the race".

19 However, even in the very remote past (Edict of Constantine of AD 313), some scholars have spoken of ecclesiastical law as mainly referring to the profile of relations between civil and religious authorities, excluding the profile of *legislatio libertatis*.

early scholars including Francesco Scaduto[20] and Francesco Rufini.[21] Historically, in Italy this field constitutes – along with Canon Law – an autonomous scientific disciplinary field.[22] In very recent times, after extensive discussion among scholars, the name of the discipline has been changed to "Law and Religion".[23] For many scholars,[24] this syntagma seems to more completely and neutrally define the discipline's subject matter, including first and foremost studies relating to the legal regulation of religious phenomenon and ethical and cultural pluralism, as well as national and supranational law on religious freedom and belief and equality before the law, the relationship between civil and religious systems, canon law, other religious rights and their comparative and historical evolution, and Vatican law.[25]

As is partially predictable the term "law" denotes the whole range of norms (constitutional laws, ordinary laws, regional laws, *etc.*) dealing directly or indirectly with religious elements, including their interaction with the obligations Italy has as a result of its adhesion to supranational and international instruments.[26]

The present overview does not allow for an in-depth analysis into all the distinctive profiles of Italian "Law and Religion", defined as a middle science ("*scienza di mezzo*").[27] Nevertheless, the subject of religious symbols highlights several peculiarities of the Italian legal system in relation to religious matters.[28]

20 This author, with his lecture at the University of Palermo on 21 November 1884, is unanimously considered the foremost proponent of the birth of the new Ecclesiastical Law in Italy. *Amplius* M. D'Arienzo, "L'Università di Napoli e la prima cattedra di Diritto ecclesiastico in Italia, L'insegnamento di Francesco Scaduto", *Stato, Chiese e pluralismo confessionale*, Rivista telematica (www.statoechiese.it), no. 27, 2012, pp. 1–19.

21 F. Ruffini, *La libertà religiosa. I, Storia dell'idea*, Fratelli Bocca, Torino, 1901, p. 1 ff. and of the same A., *Corso di diritto ecclesiastico italiano. La libertà religiosa come diritto pubblico subiettivo*, Fratellli Bocca, Torino, 1924, p. 1 ff.

22 SSD IUS/11 – "*Diritto ecclesiastico e canonico*" now GIUR-07/A – "*Diritto e religione*".

23 Cf. the ministerial decree (hereafter m.d.), 2 May 2024, no. 639, "Determination of the scientific-disciplinary groups and their related declaratory clauses, as well as the rationalisation and updating of the scientific-disciplinary sectors and their allocation to the scientific-disciplinary groups", available with its annexes at www.mur.gov.it/it/atti-e-normativa/decreto-ministeriale-n-639-del-02-05-2024.

24 M. Ventura, "Diritto ecclesiastico e Europa. Dal *Church and State* al *Law and Religion*", in G.B. Varnier (ed.), *Il nuovo volto del diritto ecclesiastico italiano*, Rubbettino, Soveria Mannelli, 2004, p. 191.

25 For a comprehensive current definition, see annex A of the aforementioned m.d. no. 639/2024.

26 For an analytical analysis of the issues of relevance to the discipline, see F. Finocchiaro, *Diritto ecclesiastico*, update edited by A. Bettentini and G. Lo Castro, Zanichelli, Bologna, XIII ed., 2020, *passim*.

27 M. Tedeschi, *Sulla scienza del diritto ecclesiastico*, Giuffrè, Milano, 2007, p. 145.

28 For a reconstruction, see M. Ventura, *Law and Religion in Italy, passim* and, to a lesser extend, M.C. Ivaldi, "Law and Religion: The Peculiarities of the Italian Model – Emergin

1.2 Conflicts between the constitutional level and ordinary legislation on religion

Following the interlude of totalitarianism during the fascist era, the constituent legislator faced the challenging task of drafting a fundamental charter that would allow for the establishment of a democratic regime with full recognition of fundamental rights. Yet settlement of the religious factor has aroused significant debate, not so much regarding recognition of individual freedom and equality regardless of religion but rather in terms of the institutional structure of relations between the State and religious denominations.[29]

With relation to "Fundamental principles"[30] there are a number of rules that more or less directly address the religious factor. In art. 2, "[T]he Republic recognizes and guarantees the inviolable rights of the person, both as an individual and within the social formations where their personality is expressed",[31] and it also requires fulfilment of "fundamental duties of political, economic and social solidarity". The subsequent art. 3, para. 1, is also central and asserts that "[A]ll citizens possess equal social dignity and are equal before the law, without distinction of sex, race, language, religion and political orientation, personal and social conditions".[32]

Issues and Controversies", in S.D. Brunn (ed.), *The Changing World Religious Map. Sacred Places, Identities, Practices and Politics*, Springer, New York, 2015, p. 1275 ff.

29 For a general overview V. Falzone – F. Palermo – F. Cosentino (eds.), *La Costituzione della Repubblica italiana illustrata con i lavori preparatori*, Colombo, Roma, 1948, *passim*. Regarding the inherent norms of the religious factor: F. Margiotta Broglio, *Stato e confessioni religiose, 2 Teorie e ideologie*, La Nuova Italia, Firenze, 1976, p. 81 ff.

For a post-war historical-political reconstruction of the Church-State relationship, D.A. Wertman, "The Catholic Church: The Impact of Secularization", *West European Politics*, vol. 5, no. 2, 1982, p. 87; M. Donovan, "The Italian State: No Longer Catholic, No Longer Christian", in Z. Enyedi – J.T.S. Madeley (eds.), *Church and State in Contemporary Europe. The Chimera of Neutrality*, Routledge, Abingdon – New York, 2003, p. 95.

30 Arts. 1–12, Const. Several Italian institutional websites have English translations of the Constitution, including the website of the Presidency of the Republic (www.quirinale.it/allegati_statici/costituzione/costituzione_inglese.pdf).

Nevertheless, as stressed elsewhere in the book, some of these translations do not adequately reflect the legal meaning of the terms in the Italian original.

31 Social structures, groups, associations, and communities in which and through which the individual's personality is expressed and developed. Among these are, first and foremost, the family "as a natural society founded on marriage" (art. 29, Const.), but also trade unions (art. 39, Const.), political parties (art. 40, Const.), and religious denominations. Bodies that include all those entities belonging to the so-called Third Sector, i.e. the ensemble of private organisations operating for civic, solidarity, and socially useful ends and with non-profit purposes (cf. para. 4.3.3. on a stratagem sometimes used by Islamic associations for the exercise of worship).

Provision completed with the request for the fulfilment of the "fundamental duties of political, economic and social solidarity".

32 Article complemented by the provision in para. 2 on the "duty of the Republic to remove economic and social obstacles which, by limiting the freedom and equality of citizens, prevent the full development of the human person and the effective participation of all workers in the political, economic and social organization of the country".

Art. 7, Const., regulates the Catholic religion. It establishes that

> the State and the Catholic Church are, each within its own sphere, independent and sovereign.
>
> Their relations are governed by the Lateran Pacts. Changes to the Pacts that are accepted by both parties shall not require a constitutional amendment procedure.[33]

Art. 8, Const. is more specific. Para. 1 refers to all religious denominations, while the second and third paragraphs only concern denominations other than Catholicism, as can be inferred from the following:

> [A]ll religious denominations are equally free before the law.
>
> Religious denominations other than Catholicism have the right to organize themselves according to their own statute, provided they do not conflict with the Italian legal system.
>
> Their relations with the State shall be regulated by law based on *intese* with their respective representatives.[34]

Two important provisions concerning religious freedom both for individuals and middle social groups follow these two articles on "Fundamental principles", which help outline the principle of cooperation between the State and religious denominations.[35] Arts. 19 and 20 are located among the "Rights and Duties of Citizens".

Pursuant to art. 19,

> [E]veryone has the right to freely profess their religious beliefs in any form, individually or in association, to promote them and to practice their worship in private or public, provided that the religious rites are not contrary to public morals.[36]

33 Procedure laid down in art. 138, Const. For an in-depth analysis, see F. Finocchiaro, "Art. 7", in G. Branca (ed.), *Commentario della Costituzione, Articoli 1–12, Principi fondamentali*, Zanichelli – il Foro italiano, Bologna – Roma, 1975, p. 321.

34 It is worth emphasising that the English term "denomination" does not properly translate the Italian "*confessione*". The latter, literally translatable as "confession", is itself religiously connoted as it originated in Christianity in reference to the Augsburg Confession, presented by the Lutheran Church on 25 June 1530. With regard to para. 3, it must be stressed that the term "agreement" does not seem to convey the meaning of the word "*intesa*", even if the adjective "bilateral" is added, since this is an act that explains its effects only within the Italian legal system if it is implemented in law.

For an analysis, F. Finocchiaro, "Art. 8", in G. Branca (ed.), *Commentario della Costituzione, Articoli 1–12, Principi fondamentali*, Zanichelli – il Foro italiano, Bologna – Roma, 1975, p. 383.

35 With obvious reference to the previous art. 2, Const.

36 F. Finocchiaro, "Art. 19", in G. Branca (ed.), *Commentario della Costituzione, Articoli 13–20, Rapporti civili*, Zanichelli – il Foro italiano, Bologna – Roma, 1977, p. 238.

It is a wording that, *ex post*, appears different from that chosen to start the Universal Declaration of Human Rights of 1948[37] and the European Convention on Human Rights, signed in Rome on 4 November 1950.[38] These ultimately led to the much later Charter of Fundamental Rights of the European Union, drafted in 2000 but made binding only through the Treaty of Lisbon of 2007 and in force since 1 December 2009.[39] In art. 19, only freedom of religion is mentioned. Freedom of thought and conscience are omitted. Indeed, part of the doctrine and jurisprudence has considered attributing so-called negative religious freedom (i.e. the freedom of agnosticism and atheism) to the freedom of expression of thought provided for in art. 21, Const. This freedom was appropriately attributed by the Constitutional Court to art. 19, Const., in a famous ruling regarding the oath in trials, which originally required taking responsibility "before God".[40]

37 UDHR proclaimed by the United Nations General Assembly in Paris on 10 December 1948. Art. 18, "Everyone has the right to freedom of thought, conscience and religion; this right includes freedom to change his religion or belief, and freedom, either alone or in community with others and in public or private, to manifest his religion or belief in teaching, practice, worship and observance". Soft law provision later incorporated and specified in the International Covenant on Civil and Political Rights of 1966 (ICCPR) in art. 18.

The UDHR, which unmistakably acknowledges its personalist basis, owes much of its inspiration to the French philosopher and Catholic convert Jacques Maritain. On this topic, see W. Sweet, "Jacques Maritain and the Universal Declaration of Human Rights", in R. Domingo – J. Witte Jr. (eds.), *Christianity and Global Law*, Routledge, Abingdon – New York, 2020, p. 158 ff. On the essential contribution of Christian thought to European integration, with particular focus on the French statesman, see M.C. Ivaldi, "Robert Schuman padre della riconciliazione e della costruzione europea", *Stato, chiese e pluralismo confessionale*, Rivista telematica (www.statoechiese.it), gennaio 2010, p. 1.

38 Art. 9 (Freedom of thought, conscience and religion) ECHR, "1. Everyone has the right to freedom of thought, conscience and religion; this right includes freedom to change his religion or belief and freedom, either alone or in community with others and in public or private, to manifest his religion or belief, in worship, teaching practice and observance. 2. Freedom to manifest one's religion or beliefs shall be subject only to such limitations as are prescribed by law and are necessary in a democratic society in the interests of public safety, for the protection of public order, health or morals, or for the protection of the rights and freedoms of others".

39 Art. 10 (Freedom if thought, conscience and religion) EU Charter of Fundamental Rights, "1. Everyone has the right to freedom of thought, conscience and religion. This right includes freedom to change religion or belief and freedom, either alone or in community with others and in public or in private, to manifest religion or belief, in worship, teaching, practice and observance. 2. The right to conscientious objection is recognised, in accordance with the national laws governing the exercise of this right".

For the boundaries and conditions of application, see arts. 51–54. On the establishment of the protection of fundamental rights in the European Community (now European Union), see M.C. Ivaldi, *Il fattore religioso nel diritto dell'Unione europea tra riconoscimento giurisprudenziale e codificazione normativa*, Nuova Cultura, Roma, 2012, esp. p. 12 ff.

40 Constitutional Court, judgment 2 October 1979, no. 117. This marks a turnaround from the previous approach expressed in judgment 13 July 1960, no. 58 (all rulings of the Court are available at www.cortecostituzionale.it, where a selection of decisions translated into English can be found). In the last case, however, the parameter of constitutionality assumed was the

Art. 19, Const., therefore expressly provides for the right to profession, propaganda, and the exercise of worship, with the sole limit of respect for public order. The limit of balancing with other constitutional rights also applies to religious freedom.

Art. 20, Const., completes the framework for the protection of the religious factor by stipulating that

> the ecclesiastical character and the purpose of religion or worship of an association or institution cannot be the cause of special legislative limitations, nor of special tax burdens for its constitution, legal capacity and any form of activity.[41]

It is a rule that is increasingly valued by doctrine and jurisprudence because it is aimed at protecting the substantial freedom of religious groups.[42]

Regardless, it is important to acknowledge the various other norms that can be examined in relation to the religious factor, particularly those that pertain to personal freedom (art. 13), freedom of domicile (art. 14), freedom and confidentiality of correspondence (art. 15), freedom of movement (art. 16),

---

freedom to manifest thought (art. 21, para. 1, Const.) and not freedom of religion (art. 19, Const.).

This case arises from the refusal to swear as a witness in a criminal trial due to being an atheist because the oath formula requires taking responsibility "before God". The Court, whose opinion is that the oath formula "accords with the conscience of the Italian people, who are mostly believers, and therefore presupposes the oath-taker's belief in God, is suitable for any confession, including non-Catholic ones". The situation of non-belief, according to the judgment, falls outside the norm that requires the oath "because religious freedom, while constituting the main aspect of the broader freedom of conscience, does not encompass all manifestations of freedom of thought: atheism begins where religious life ends" ("*Considerato in diritto*", para. 7).

With this judgment, the Court embarked on a path leading to the reformulation of the oath regulations. In this reformulation, the legislator also collaborated – at least in the criminal domain – via the promulgation of a new code of procedure, introduced by the decree of the President of the Republic (hereafter d.P.R.), 22 September 1989, no. 447.

Incidentally, this aspect, specifically concerning the alleged violation of the rights of nonbelievers and therefore their so-called negative religious freedom, is complemented by the issue of the refusal to take an oath as an activity prohibited by one's faith, which is practiced by some denominations based on certain Gospel verses (Mattew, 5, 34–37, "You have heard that it was said to the people long ago, 'Do not break your oath, but fulfill to the Lord the vows you have made'. But I tell you, do not swear an oath at all: either by heaven, for it is God's throne; or by the earth, for it is his footstool; or by Jerusalem, for it is the city of the Great King. And do not swear by your head, for you cannot make even one hair white or black. All you need to say is simply 'Yes' or 'No'; anything beyond this comes from the evil one"). This is a matter that pertains specifically to conscientious objection, or the right to act in accordance with professed religious principles. For an analysis, P. Floris, "Ateismo e religione nell'ambito del diritto di libertà religiosa", *Il Foro italiano*, pt. II, 1981, col. 625.

41 F. Finocchiaro, "Art. 20", in G. Branca (ed.), *Commentario della Costituzione, Articoli 13–20, Rapporti civili*, Zanichelli – il Foro italiano, Bologna – Roma, 1977, p. 302.

42 More recently L. Decimo, *Le organizzazioni religiose nel prisma costituzionale dell'art. 20*, Editoriale Scientifica, Napoli, 2017, *passim*.

freedom of assembly (art. 17), freedom of association (art. 18), freedom of speech (art. 21), marriage (art. 29) and family matters (art. 30), and so on.

The Constitution, as a result, delineated a framework that did not allow for the perpetual presence of a confessional principle.

Nonetheless, a part of the doctrine interpreted the reference to the Lateran Pacts referred to in art. 7, which effectively crystallises the concordat system, as a sort of legitimisation of the dictates of art. 1 of the Treaty and the reference to the principle of the State Church in art. 1, Albertine Statute.[43]

Authoritative contrary voices conversely are not lacking,[44] despite the fact that in this process of legal system transformation there is a "freezing of the regulatory system and the institutional structures developed by fascism in matters of relations between the State and religious denominations".[45]

In any case, the Constitution grafted itself onto a legal *corpus* that was heavily influenced by the authoritarian matrix from which it originated. This raises the issue – particularly with respect to previous provisions that regulate the religious factor in various texts – of aligning to the new fundamental norms, especially the principle of equality enshrined in art. 3, Const.

However, it may have been possible, within specific parameters, to pursue the path of implicit repeal of regulations conflicting with the fundamental law based on the principle of the succession of laws over time.[46] The circumstances nevertheless have the potential to give rise to potentially hazardous legislative gaps.

All that remained was to await the implementation of a new body provided for by the Constitution that would allow, among other things, incidental judgment on the question of the legality of a law or an act having the force of law.[47] However, the Constitutional Court[48] did not deliver its first judgment until 1956.[49]

43 For all, see P.A. D'Avack, "Confessionismo", in *Enciclopedia del diritto*, Giuffrè, Milano, vol. VIII, 1961, p. 929.

44 V. Crisafulli "Art. 7 della Costituzione e 'vilipendio della religione dello Stato'", *Archivio penale*, 1950, pt. II, p. 419, according to which "no provision of the Constitution establishes, directly or indirectly, any official position to the Catholic religion".

45 Broglio, *Stato e confessioni religiose. 2/Teorie e ideologie*, p. 1.

46 Cf. art. 15, Preliminary provisions to the Civil Code ("*preleggi*") – which was also drafted during the Fascist era in 1942 – provide that "laws are not repealed except by subsequent laws, by express declaration of the legislature, or because of incompatibility between the new provisions and the previous ones, or because the new law regulates the entire matter already regulated by the previous law".

47 A question that must be raised in the course of judicial proceedings by a special order (the order of remittal). To do so, it is necessary for the *a quo* court to verify that the requirement of relevance – i.e. that the decision on the question proposed is necessary for the resolution of the trial – is met and that the question is not presented as manifestly unfounded.

48 On this institution, see Italia, Corte Costituzionale, *The Italian Constituional Court*, Colombo, Roma, 2019, p. 1 ff., also available online at www.cortecostituzionale.it/documenti/download/pdf/The_Italian_Constitutional_Court.pdf.

49 Constitutional Court, judgment 14 June 1956, no. 1. It is precisely on this occasion that the Constitutional Court has the occasion to clarify its exclusive jurisdiction over pre-constitutional provisions, distinguishing constitutional illegitimacy from the narrower institution of repeal *ex* art. 15, *Preleggi*.

This is an institution which, from the outset, has been called upon to rule on matters pertaining to the religious factor, thus giving rise to a jurisprudence with two key lines of action. The first aims to maximise the exercise of constitutionally guaranteed rights, particularly religious freedom. The second is characterised by its conservatism and seeks to uphold the prevailing norms that ensure a distinct position for the Catholic Church, as articulated in art. 7, Const., and as is the case in rulings on vilification or blasphemy.[50]

In this regard, it is notable that the aforementioned norms consistently designate the Catholic religion as the "Religion of the State".[51] These norms have been interpreted from the beginning as referring to Catholicism as the religion of the majority of the Italian population, introducing *ex adverso* more or less implicitly the concept of the religious minority.[52]

It is no coincidence that the subject of the Constitutional Court's censures is, among other things, the body of legislation relating to the so-called admitted cults, and especially the provisions imposing unjustified restrictions on freedom of worship and the organisation of religious denominations other than Catholic.[53]

1.3 From the sacred character to the particular significance of Rome for Catholicism

The upcoming chapters primarily focus on symbols found in public institutions and, to a lesser extent, symbols worn by believers. However, it is important to mention that the Italian legal system encompasses other symbolic issues that demand the attention of Law and Religion scholars.

One of the most significant issues originates precisely from bilateral texts that the State has signed with the Catholic Church since 1929. Art. 1, para. 2, Concordat, provides that

50 Arts. 402–406 and 724, Criminal Code. Cf. M.C. Ivaldi, *La tutela penale in materia religiosa nella giurisprudenza*, p. 62 ff.

51 With the sole exception represented by art. 405, Criminal Code, which originally spoke of "Disturbance of religious functions of Catholic worship".

52 On this topic, see D. Edigati – A. Tira (eds.), *Le minoranze religiose nel diritto italiano ed europeo. Esperienze del passato e problematiche contemporanee*, Giappichelli, Torino, 2021, *passim*. Concerning to the concept of minorities, please refer to the ATLAS project (Atlas of Religious or Belief Minority Rights) located at the website www.atlasminorityrights.eu.

53 Constitutional Court, judgment 24 November 1958, no. 59, declaring the partial unconstitutionality of art. 1, r.d. 28 February 1930, no. 289, insofar as it requires governmental authorisation for the opening of temples or oratories, for civil effects, and for the mere exercise of worship. The ruling also deemed art. 2 completely unconstitutional as it imposed certain conditions on the performance of religious ceremonies or acts of worship in the aforementioned buildings (art. 1), namely, that the meeting was chaired by a minister of religion whose appointment had been duly approved. It is of considerable importance to highlight that the pronouncement still employs the unconstitutional term "admitted cults" ("*Considerato in diritto*", para. 2).

> in consideration of the sacred character of the Eternal City, the Episcopal See of the Sovereign Pontiff, centre of the Catholic world and place of pilgrimage, the Italian Government will take care to impede in Rome whatsoever may be in opposition with its said character.[54]

Per the wording of the norm, the burden placed on Italian institutions refers to the entire perimeter of the Italian capital and thus goes well beyond the portion of urban territory immediately bordering the instituting Vatican City State or those places located elsewhere but affected by the presence of significant vestiges attributable to the city's Christian history.[55] Upon closer examination, it is evident that this rule embodied one of the corollaries of the confessional principle, which was revived in art. 1 of the Lateran Treaty.

The reason for recalling art. 1, para. 2, Concordat, here is precisely its application more than a decade after the promulgation of the Republican Constitution. This application set the tone for a process that would slowly lead to the revision of the 1929 Concordat itself.

The opportunity of the beginnings of this revision process was occasioned by the 1965 staging of Rolf Hochhuth's[56] *The Deputy*, directed by and starring Gian Maria Volonté. The play's plot is based on Pope Pius XII's silence regarding the Holocaust.[57] Under the provision of art. 1, para. 2, Concordat, the play was strictly prohibited by a prefectural decree.

This episode gave rise to a lively discussion that revealed the irreconcilable contrast between the provision and art. 21, Const., which establishes the right to free expression of thought.[58] It also engendered a heated parliamentary debate that contributed to the birth of the first concrete initiative of the Concordat's revision, namely, the motion presented by the Honourable Lelio Basso on 17 March 1965.[59]

Notably, Hochhuth's *The Deputy* has consistently provoked both passionate and conflicting responses, even in contemporary times. We refer most recently to Constantin Costa Gavras' film *Amen*, presented at the 2002 Berlin Film Festival. In this case, however, it is not so much the film that was discussed as the poster signed by Oliviero Toscani. The poster featured the photograph of

54 G. Caputo, *Il carattere sacro di Roma*, Giuffrè, Milano, 1971, *passim*.

55 *Amplius*, M. Madonna, *La città di Roma nel Concordato del 1929 e nell'Accordo del 1984. Dal "carattere sacro" al Particolare significato". Un itinerario storico giuridico*, Libellula, Tricase, LE, 2014, p. 1 ff., regarding development in the understanding of this provision.

56 The text, with the original title "*Der Stellvertreter. Ein christliches Trauespiel*", dates back to 1963.

57 The subject is based on the conflict of conscience of the real-life protagonist Kurt Gerstein – a chemical engineer and *Schutzstaffel* officer – who, upon realising the real use of "Ziklon B" as a toxic agent in the gas chambers of some of the death camps, tries to stop the Holocaust by unsuccessfully soliciting the intervention of Pius XII, the Vicar of Christ, to denounce what is happening in Germany.

58 On this subject, G. Moscon, "Separa e sarai rispettato", *Il ponte*, 1965, p. 144.

59 Cf. F. Margiotta Broglio, *Stato e confessioni religiose. 2/Teorie e ideologie*, pp. 19–20.

the two main actors framed by a Christian cross, transformed in the top three arms into a svastika.[60]

However, it would still take almost two decades – compared to compared to *The Deputy* affair in 1965 – before the Concordat was revised. In fact, following numerous revisions and negotiations, the process of reform took place a full 55 years after the enactment of the Lateran Pacts.[61] The name "Agreement between the Holy See and the Italian Republic amending the Lateran Concordat"[62] represented a new text that replaced the previous one, with important repercussions on discussions concerning the Italian attitude towards settlement of the religious factor.[63]

Furthermore, the socio-economic development of Italy in those decades had already produced strong transformations to the legal system toward a progressive secularisation, as can be inferred from the introduction of divorce,[64] the reform of family law,[65] and the legalisation of abortion.[66]

Even within the Catholic framework, however, the Second Vatican Ecumenical Council[67] had introduced a spirit of rejuvenation to the Church with its documents, with a special emphasis on religious freedom.[68] This renewal

60 The poster was condemned in France as an infamy for identifying Christianity with Nazism by the Archbishop of Paris, Jean-Marie Lustiger, and was reported to the judiciary by a Catholic group, while in Italy it was not displayed at the behest of Mikado, the film's distributor, causing protests from the director.

61 Cf. Italia, Presidenza del Consiglio dei Ministri, *La revisione del Concordato. Un accordo di libertà*, Istituto poligrafico della zecca dello Stato, Roma, 1986, pp. 421–477, where comparative tables with the text of the different drafts are available. On this topic, see C. Cardia, *La riforma del concordato. Dal confessinismo alla laicità dello Stato*, Einaudi, Torino, 1980, *passim*.

62 Available on the Vatican portal at www.vatican.va. Agreement ratified and executed by law 25 March 1985, no. 121. For more details, see S. Ferrari (ed.), *Concordato e Costituzione. Gli accordi del 1984 tra Italia e Santa Sede*, il Mulino, Bologna, *passim* e il Mulino, 1985 as well as R. Coppola (ed.), *Il nuovo accordo tra l'Italia e la Santa Sede*, Milano, Giuffrè, 1987, *passim*.

63 For a review in English, S. Ferrari, "The New Concordat between Church and State", *Italian Politics*, vol. 1, 1985 p. 134 and M. Giovannelli, "The Covenant between the Republic of Italy and the Vatican: A Retrospective Analysis after Fifteen Years", *Journal of Church and State*, vol. 42, no. 3, 2000, p. 529.

64 Law 1 December 1970, no. 898, "Discipline of the dissolution of marriage cases".

65 Law 19 May 1975, no. 151, "Reform of family law", which is based on equality between spouses.

66 Law 22 May 1978, no. 194, "Provisions for the social protection of maternity and the voluntary interruption of pregnancy".

For an in-depth study of the processes leading to the legislative innovations with a focus on the contrasts between civil society and religious society, see S. Lariccia, *Diritti civili e fattore religioso*, il Mulino, Bologna, 1978, p. 19 ff., esp. pp. 105–122 and 123–152.

67 Convened on 25 January 1959 by Pope John XXIII, it followed Vatican Council I, which had been interrupted in 1870 because of the aforementioned *Porta Pia* breach. It opened on 11 October 1962 and was closed by Pope John XXIII's successor Pope Paul VI on 8 December 1965.

The Vatican II documents are available, also in English at www.vatican.va/archive/hist_councils/ii_vatican_council/index_it.htm.

68 Cf. the "*Declaration or religious freedom* Dignitatis Humanae" of 7 December 1965.

was also pursued shortly before the Concordat revision through the promulgation of a new code for the Latin Church.[69]

Though there are numerous important issues,[70] it is worth focusing on one provision not directly contained in the Revision Agreement. In point 1 of the annexed Additional Protocol, with a redundant formula that is hard to understand, "The principle, originally referred to in the Lateran Pacts, of the Catholic religion as the sole religion of the Italian State is considered no longer in force".

As for the "Eternal City", the 1984 Agreement's art. 2, para. 4, resizes the provision already contained in the 1929 Concordat, limiting it to "acknowledg[ing] the particular significance that Rome, the Episcopal See of the Supreme Pontiff, has to Catholicism".[71]

Despite this change it was precisely because of this rule that protests were raised by the Holy See when the first World Pride event was held in Rome in 2000 alongside the Jubilee celebrations.[72]

1.4 The Italian approach to *laicità* (secularism)

Firstly, it is necessary to emphasise the circumstance that in Italy – unlike other legal systems[73] – there is no specific and explicit legal or constitutional recognition of the principle of separation, not to mention that of neutrality or secularism.

69 The *Codex iuris canonici*, promulgated by Pope John Paul II on 25 January 25, 1983, and in force since 27 November of the same year (www.vatican.va/archive/cod-iuris-canonici/cic_index_it.html), replaced the previous text of 1917, the first codification of canon law.

70 Cf. the reform of marriage (art. 8), also in light of the Constitutional Court rulings, 1 March 1971, nos. 30, 31, and 32, and religious education in public schools. In the latter regard, based on the assumption of recognition for the "value of the religious culture and considering that the principles of the Catholic Church are part of the historical heritage of the Italian people", despite the provision of the "right to choose whether or not to receive religious instruction" (art. 9, para. 2), the teaching of the Catholic religion in non-university public schools of all levels persists.

71 See also art. 9, para. 2 of the 1984 Agreement, which significantly states that "the Italian Republic, recognizing the value of the religious culture and considering that the principles of the Catholic Church are part of the historical heritage of the Italian people, shall continue to assure, within the framework of the scope of the schools, the teaching of Catholic religion in the public schools of every order and grade except for Universities". Teaching that is provided "with respect for the freedom of conscience and educational responsibility of the parents, everyone shall be granted the right to choose whether or not to receive religious instruction".

72 On this topic, see D. McNeil, "Rome, Global City? Church, State and the Jubilee 2000", *Political Geography*, vol. 22, no. 5, 2003, p. 535.

73 France first enacted the principle of separation, relegating the religious fact essentially to the private sphere (*loi 9 decembre 1905 concernant la séparation des Églises et de l'État*, the so-called *loi séparation*), and then recognised the principle of secularism in the Constitution in 1946. For the text of the laws and codes, see the legal website of French law at www.legifrance.gouv.fr.

In fact, for a long time, this absence has led scholars to consider secularity as a merely meta-legal principle[74] with a multitude of meanings given the many forms it can take depending on the context of reference.[75]

It was necessary to wait over 40 years after the Constitution entered into force for the Constitutional Court to formalise secularism ("*laicità*") as a "supreme principle of the constitutional order"[76] in its judgment 11 April 1989, no. 203.

The supreme principles are a category, first introduced at an embryonic level in the early 1970s,[77] endowed with "a higher worth than other norms or laws of constitutional value".[78]

The Court deduced the principle of *laicità* from systematic interpretation of the articles of the Constitution relating to religion, namely, arts. 2, 3, 7, 8, 19, and 20, Const. Taken together, these provisions "structure the supreme principle of the secularity of the State, which is one of the profiles of the form of State outlined in the Constitutional Charter of the Republic".[79]

Significantly, the Court specifies that the principle "implies not indifference of the State before religions but the State's guarantee to safeguard freedom of religion, in a regime of confessional and cultural pluralism".[80] In subsequent decisions, the Constitutional Court detailed the boundaries of secularism and included the principle of the distinction of orders,[81] clarifying that *laicità* "entails equidistance and impartiality with respect to all religious

74 On this topic, see *in primis*, L. Guerzoni, "Note preliminari per uno studio della laicità sotto il profilo giuridico", *Archivio giuridico Filippo Serafini*, 1967, p. 61 ff.

75 C. Cardia, "Stato laico", in *Enciclopedia del diritto*, Giuffrè, Milano, 1990, vol. XVIII, p. 847. In addition to French "*laïcité*, which is discussed on several occasions (cf. paras. 2.5., 3.5, and 4.2), and the references to US separatism (paras. 2.5 and 4.2.), it is also useful to refer to Soviet secularism (G. Codevilla, *Chiesa e impero in Russia. Dalla Rus' di Kiev alla Federazione russa*, Jaka Book, Milano, 2011) and Turkish "*laiklik*" (R. Bottoni, *Il principio di laicità in Turchia. Profili storico-giuridici*, Vita e Pensiero, Milano, 2012). These models express different conceptions of separatism and secularism.

76 The Court was compelled to address the constitutionality of norms on religious education derived from the 1984 Agreement.

77 Cf. the yet mentioned rulings nos. 30, 31 and 32 of 1971 as well as the judgment 2 February 1982, esp. "*Considerato in diritto*" para. 5. For an in-depth analysis, see F. Modugno, "I principi costituzionali supremi come parametro del giudizio di legittimità costituzionale", in F. Modugno – A.S. Agrò – A. Cerri (eds.), *Il principio di unità del controllo sulle leggi nella giurisprudenza della Corte Costituzionale*, Giappichelli, Torino, IV ed., 2002, p. 292.

78 Constitutional Court, judgment 11 April 1989, no. 203, "*Considerato in diritto*", para. 3, which also refers to the use of the category as a barrier to EU law conflicting with the aforementioned supreme principles.

79 Constitutional Court, judgment no. 203/1989, "*Considerato in diritto*", para 4.

80 Constitutional Court, judgment no. 203/1989, "*Considerato in diritto*", para 4.

81 Constitutional Court, judgment 8 October 1996, no. 334, "*Considerato in diritto*" para 3.2., which speaks of a distinction "characterising in its essence the fundamental or 'supreme' constitutional principle of the secular or non-denominational nature of the State". Ruling on the subject of the decisory oath.

denominations"[82] and characterises "in a pluralistic sense the form of our State, within which different faiths, cultures and traditions have to coexist, in equal freedom".[83]

1.5 The principle of *laicità* as used mainly by judges but without formal legal implementation

This is, in essence, the model of Italian *laicità*[84] that has been repeatedly taken up in constitutional jurisprudence,[85] particularly in matters of the criminal protection of religion, oaths, and the building of worship.[86]

Ordinary jurisprudence does not seem to have adequately used the principle in some cases, such as the administrative judgment[87] concerning crucifixes in public schools[88] and in the case of the wearing of symbols by believers.[89] Certainly, as discussed in the following, it has interpreted it in a very particular way.

Conversely, within the legislative sphere, there is enduring resistance among legislators to proactively address pivotal matters such as the criminal protection of religion, which is considered as one of the most meaningful cases.[90] Simultaneously, the implementation of constitutional provisions promoting religious pluralism may encounter challenges. This is particularly evident in the realm of art. 8, para. 3, Const., concerning bilateral relations between the State and non-Catholic denominations.

82 Constitutional Court, judgment 10 November 1997, no. 329, "*Considerato in diritto*", para 2, relating to art. 404, Criminal Code, or the so-called vilification of persons.

83 Constitutional Court, judgment 20 November 2000, no. 508, "*Considerato in diritto*", para. 3, on the exclusive protection against the vilification of the State religion in art. 402, Criminal Code.

84 For all, see F. Freni, *La libertà religiosa tra solidarietà e pluralismo. Analisi delle proposte sul modello di laicità "all'italiana"*, Jovene, Napoli, 2013, *passim*.

85 For an analysis of constitutional jurisprudence from the perspective of the Law and Religion scholar, see A. Albisetti, *Il diritto ecclesiastico nella giurisprudenza della Corte costituzionale*, Giuffrè, Milano, V ed., 2014, *passim* and S. Domianello, *Giurisprudenza costituzionale e fattore religioso. Le pronunce della Corte costituzionale in materia ecclesiastica*, Giuffrè, Milano, 1999, *passim*.

86 Cf. the vexed question of religious buildings, in which regional legislation on land governance is often not constitutionally compliant. On this topic see Constitutional Court judgments 19 April 1993, no. 195 (Regione Abruzzo); 23 February 2016, no. 63 (Regione Lombardia); 7 April 2017, no. 67 (Regione Veneto); 22 October 2019, no. 254 (Regione Lombardia). *Amplius infra* para 4.3.

87 J. Pasquali Cerioli, "La laicità nella giurisprudenza amministrativa: da principio supremo a 'simbolo religioso'", *Stato, Chiese e pluralismo confessionale*, Rivista telematica (ww.statochiese.it), marzo 2009, p. 1. *Infra* paras. 2.1 ff. and 4.2.

88 *Infra* para. 2.2.

89 *Infra* para. 3.4., regarding the Sikh *kirpan*.

90 Cf. M.C. Ivaldi, *La tutela penale in materia religiosa nella giurisprudenza*, resp. pp. 49 ff. and 117 ff.

This provision was initially implemented in 1984 through the *intesa* concluded with the Methodist Waldensian Table[91] but only after the revision of the Lateran Concordat.

Since then, the Italian Government has also concluded *intese* with non-Christian denominations, starting with the Union of Italian Jewish Communities signed on 27 February 1989,[92] followed by the 2007 *intese* with the Italian Buddhist Union and the Italian Hindu Union[93] and the 2012 *intesa* with the Italian Buddhist Institute Soka Gakkai (the second *intesa* with a Buddhist denomination).[94]

Although there is a general and perhaps excessive tendency towards bilateralism,[95] the pattern is different for some religious groups.[96] For example, none of the *intese* concluded in the 2000s with Jehovah's Witnesses has ever been approved by Parliament,[97] and they are therefore still subject, like Muslims,[98] to law no. 1159/1929. Although this law has been adapted by a series of Constitutional Court rulings, it outlines a regulatory framework influenced by an old-established jurisdictionalist imprint, especially regarding the appointment of ministers of religion and places of worship. It is specified that the very expression "admitted cults" in the title of law no. 1159/1929 should be read in a constitutionally oriented sense as referring to religious denominations other than Catholic. Nonetheless, this expression is utilised in this discussion to emphasise its long-standing existence.

Despite repeated attempts, approval of a general law on religious freedom has proven challenging.[99] This suggests a certain mistrust on the part of the

91 *Intesa* stipulated on 21 February 1984 and implemented by 11 August 1984, no. 449.
On the system of *intese* and the survival of the legislation on so-called admitted cults for religious denominations that have not entered into an "agreement" with the State, see the following, para. 4.4.

92 Enacted on 8 March 1989, under law no. 101.

93 *Intese* signed on 4 April 2007 and implemented by law nos. 246 and 247 of 31 December 2012, respectively.

94 *Intesa* 27 June 2015, implemented by law 28 June 2016, no. 130.

95 The purpose of establishing the institution of the *intesa* was intended to regulate the specific aspects of religious denominations rather than to exempt them from adhering to the 1929 legislation on admitted cults. This trend has resulted in less diversity in interpretations. In fact, scholars have even referred to them as "photocopy *intese*". Cf. A. Fabbri, "Le intese alla prova: nuovi attori e vecchi contenuti", *Cultura giuridica e diritto vivente*, vol. 7, 2020, p. 1.

96 As in the case of Jehovah's Witnesses and the various Islamic associations that cannot benefit from the financing system provided for the Catholic Church and denominations with *intese* and therefore from the distribution of the 8 per thousand of the State's tax revenues based, at least, on the choices expressed.

97 *Amplius infra* para. 4.4.

98 *Amplius infra* para. 4.4.

99 To access a chronology and commentary on the projects that occurred between 1990 and 2020, please refer to L. De Gregorio, "Laicità e progetti per una legge generale sulla libertà religiosa", *Stato, Chiese e pluralismo confessionale*, Rivista telematica (www.statoechiese.it), no. 21, 2020, p. 67 ff. as well as *infra* para. 4.4.

succeeding Italian governments towards particular religious groups, while the Catholic Church continuing to have a political role and influence.

Similar remarks can be made regarding legislative and administrative action, especially at the regional level.[100] Additionally, various issues concerning, for example, Muslim places of worship and the legal treatment of organised atheism are investigated.[101]

100 *Infra*, paras 3.2., and 4.3.
101 *Infra*, subpara. 4.4.1.

2 Religious symbols in public institutions: National and the European Court of Human Rights case law

Summary: 2.1. Preliminary remarks about religious symbols and their polysemic meaning: The notion of public space – 2.2. National jurisprudence on the display of the crucifix – 2.2.1. *The Lautsi case within the framework of domestic jurisprudence* – 2.3. The European Court of Human Rights' decisions on the exhibition of the crucifix in Italian schools – 2.3.1. *The Lautsi I* – 2.3.2. The *Lautsi II* – 2.4. Display of the crucifix in polling stations, courtrooms, and hospitals – 2.5. The stance of other courts or institutions in similar cases – 2.5.1. *The European contest* – 2.5.2. *Further foreign legal rulings concerning statues, crosses, and other religious symbols* – 2.5.3. *Notes on the theme of preserving the majority religious landscape*

2.1 Preliminary remarks about religious symbols and their polysemic meaning: The notion of public space

Following the meaning of the term provided by an authoritative Italian dictionary,[1] a symbol can be said to be

> any element (sign, gesture, object, animal, person) capable of arousing in the mind an idea other than that offered by its immediate perceptible aspect, but capable of evoking it through any of the aspects that characterise the element itself, which is therefore assumed to evoke in particular abstract entities difficult to express.

In semiotics,[2] the symbol is one of the three types of signs that can be identified,[3] along with the icon and index.

As a prelude to any further investigation, it is necessary to provide an approximate definition of what is meant by a symbol, particularly a religious

1 "Sìmbolo", Treccani, *vocabolario on line*, available at www.treccani.it/vocabolario/simbolo/.

2 The discipline that studies signs and how they make sense (signification).

3 Charles Sanders Peirce (10 September 1839–19 April 1914) is considered one of the fathers of modern semiotics (or the theory of the sign, understood as an act of communication). Cf. J. Hoopes (ed.), *Peirce on Signs: Writings on Semiotic by Charles Sanders Peirce*, The University of California Press, Chapel Hill – London, 1991, p. 141 ff.

DOI: 10.4324/9780429242953-3

symbol. Even this preliminary wording suggests that a symbol may have or represent several meanings (cultural, religious, ethnic, etc.) that are sometimes impossible to distinguish.

For the investigation *de qua*, however, it is less important to dwell on the study of symbols as a category. Rather, we start from the assumption that symbols have a polysemic character.[4] Put differently, a particular symbol can simultaneously encompass multiple meanings depending on its location and the context in which it is employed. In other words, the meaning of the same symbol may vary depending on whether one has regard to the "internal" perception of those who align themselves with the value horizon expressed by the symbol itself, or vice versa to the "external" perception by those who do not accord with it.

What characterises the religious symbol, or what is suitable for recalling a religious meaning, is the allusion to something that transcends the human dimension and refers to the divine.

Of course, whenever one tries to define what is religion is or what pertains to religion, one encounters several difficulties. This can be attributed to the significant inadequacy of state laws in defining the distinction between temporal and spiritual orders. The distinction between the two orders has been cultivated in Europe since the Middle Ages, drawing on the Gospel command "[R]ender unto Caesar the things that are Caesar's, and unto God the things that are God's";[5] in Italy, this is echoed in art. 7, para. 1, Const.[6]

Likewise, it is also worth recalling the definition of religious denomination, an expression used by the Italian Constitution to refer generically both to the Catholic Church and to other denominations,[7] within Italian jurisprudence as a reality that is external to that of the State.[8] Defining what pertains to religion has become even more problematic. This is clear in countries like France, where the principle of strict separation[9] and constitutional secularism[10] assumes an even more definitive and radical distinction between the two domains.

4 For an interesting attempt in this direction by the Italian doctrine of law and religion, see S. Testa Bappenheim, *I simboli religiosi nello spazio pubblico. Profili giuridici comparati*, Editoriale Scientifica, Napoli, 2019, p. 16 ff. as well as p. 96 ff., concerning the examination of symbols in modern philosophy conducted by Ernst-Wolfgang Böckenförde, John Rawls, and Jürgen Habermas.

5 Matthew, 22:21; for the other synoptic Gospels, Mark, 12:17 and Luke, 20:25.

6 Cf. the aforementioned provision under which "The State and the Catholic Church are, each within its own sphere, independent and sovereign" (*supra* para. 1.2.).

7 Art. 8, para. 1, Const.

8 This is a concept that has been defined, in content, by constitutional jurisprudence since the aforementioned judgment 27 April 1993, no. 195 (*supra* para. 1.5.) and then confirmed by the subsequent ruling on 16 July 16, 2002, no. 346. On this topic see S. Ferrari, "La nozione giuridica di confessione religiosa (come sopravvivere senza conoscerla)", in V. Parlato – G.B. Varnier (eds.), *Principio pattizio e realtà religiose minoritarie*, Giappichelli, Torino, 1995, p. 19.

9 Law on Separation of Church and State of 9 December 1905 (the so-called *loi séparation*).

10 Art. 1, French Constitution, "France Shall Be an Indivisible, Secular, Democratic and Social Republic".

However, in this context the secularism referred to in the standard embodies a particular form characterised by content that is distinct from the general definition. Hence, it is more appropriate to use the term in its original language – "*laïcité*" for France and "*laicità*" for Italy – as they both encompass separate conceptions of the same principle, as explained in the following.

Nevertheless, there are specific facts that, in applying the law practically, demand a definition of religion or religious denomination, that is implicitly or explicitly posited even within non-religious legal systems.[11]

The approximation in defining what a symbol is – and even more so what a religious symbol is – further stems from the fact that in order to ascribe a symbol to a specific value horizon, it is necessary to use the principles and parameters of the same horizon. These parameters differ from those of civil orders even though certain value horizons, such as Judeo-Christian horizons, have played a crucial role in their development, as seen in European and Western law.[12]

Thus, once again the legal scholar must refer to a conventional definition of symbol drawn in part from common feeling. This last statement is also a prerequisite for further consideration. In a cultural and social landscape characterised by homogeneity and shared values, religious symbols do not – in principle – lead to conflict.[13]

Issues emerge when there is a discrepancy in this collective understanding or when requests arise for the elimination of religious symbols. For example, individuals may not identify with the same beliefs (e.g. atheists or agnostics)

11 The occurrence of this situation has been observed repeatedly, mirroring the jurisprudence of the French Council of State. On this topic, M.C. Ivaldi, "The Meaning of 'Religion' in French Case Law. The Judgements of the *Conseil d'État*", *Stato, chiese e pluralismo confessionale*, Rivista telematica (www.statoechiese.it), no. 39, 2017, p. 110 ff.

12 Cf. S. Ferrari, "The Christian Roots of the Secular State", in Vv.Aa., *Droit et religion en Europe. Étude en l'honneur de Francis Messner*, Presses Universitaires de Strasbourg, 2014, p. 425.

The topic of Europe's confirmed Christian foundations was specifically addressed during the drafting of the "Treaty establishing a Constitution for Europe". The Treaty, signed in Rome on 29 October 2004, was never be enforced due to disagreement in ratification by certain states. *Amplius*: M.C. Ivaldi, *Il fattore religioso nel diritto dell'Unione europea tra riconoscimento giurisprudenziale e codificazione normativa*, p. 61 ff.

From a Catholic standpoint, see J. Ratzinger, *Europa. I suoi fondamenti oggi e domani*, San Paolo, Cinisello Balsamo, MI, 2004, *passim*.

13 See the example of France, whose conflicting relationship with religious symbols at an institutional level goes back a long time. Cf. art. 28, the *loi séparation* prohibits "in the future, to place or display any religious sign or emblem on public monuments or in any public place whatsoever, with the exception of buildings used for worship, burial grounds in cemeteries, funerary monuments, museums or exhibitions".

Symbols are unrecognised, even in controversial figurative representations, as seen in the Summer Olympics Games Poster 2024 created by French illustrator Ugo Gattoni, which depicts the St. Luis Cathedral of the Invalids without the cross (source: https://olympics.com/en/paris-2024/the-games/the-brand/iconic-posters). The representation shows a noticeable trend towards a deliberate erasure, including of symbols strongly associated with the historical French cultural landscape.

or may adopt alternative perspectives.[14] This can be observed in urban settings, particularly when there is a demand for incorporating non-traditional religious architecture.[15]

In Italy, the most significant problem that has arisen is not the religious symbols believers wear[16] but those affixed to public buildings. As indicated earlier,[17] the State has embraced the principle of secularism, according to a positive interpretation, and has elevated it to the status of a fundamental principle within its legal framework.

The discussion surrounding religious symbols is closely associated with the concept of public space. This concept can also assume specific interpretations and arrangements within different legal systems.[18] To begin with a general definition, public space is a designated location intended for shared and collective purposes. This includes both the institutional public space, comprising public buildings, such as schools, hospitals, and town halls, as well as the urban public space, comprising streets, squares, parks, and so on. The categorisation of "institutional public space" and "urban public space" plays a crucial role in specific legal frameworks,[19] as seen in countries like France.[20]

The public space is host to the most significant issues involving the manifestation of religion, mainly the "*speciem*" of individual or institutional display of religious symbols.

2.2 National jurisprudence on the display of the crucifix

When discussing symbols in public space, the Italian case that has gained the most widespread international recognition and analysis is the display of crucifixes in classrooms. Indeed, this question brought Italy before the European Court of Human Rights.

14 To gain insight into the challenges associated with human migration in Italy, consult F. Gravino, *Migrantes. Gli esodi contemporanei tra diritto e religioni*, ESI, Napoli, 2024, p. 1 ff.

15 This phenomenon can be witnessed in many cases, such as the widely known *Amplius infra* subpara. 2.5.3.

16 Cf. *infra* para. 3.1. ff.

17 Cf. *supra* para. 1.1. ff.

18 Concerning this issue, see S. Ferrari – S. Pastorelli (eds.), *Religion in Public Space. A European Perspective*, Routledge, Abingdon – New York, 2012, *passim*, esp. A. Ferrari, "Religion and Rethinking the Public-Private Divide: A Broken Promise in Europe?", in S. Ferrari – S. Pastorelli (eds.), *Religion in Public Space. A European Perspective*, Routledge, Abingdon – New York, 2012, p. 71, and G. Di Cosimo, "Gli spazi pubblici e la religione", *Stato, Chiese e pluralismo confessionale*, Rivista telematica (www.statoechiese.it), no. 6, 2020, p. 21.

19 Cf. S. Ferrari, "State-Supported Display of Religious Symbols in the Public Space", *Journal of Catholic Legal Studies*, vol. 52, no. 1, 2013, p. 17 ff.

20 *Amplius infra* paras. 2.5.1. and 4.2.

The display of the crucifix in classrooms is a field governed by a regulation dating back to the beginning of the 20th century[21] that remains in force. Together with other provisions such as those concerning the introduction of the criminal punishment of blasphemy under art. 232 of the Consolidated Law on Public Security of 1926,[22] this regulation marked the new confessionalisation of the Italian State (at that time still the Kingdom of Italy) as Catholic. This process was completed with the conclusion of the Lateran Pacts, with art. 1 of the corresponding Treaty establishing that

> Italy recognises and reaffirms the principle established in the first Article of the of the Statute of the Kingdom dated 4 March 1848, according to which the Catholic Apostolic Roman religion is the only religion of the State.

The crucifix was an issue that remained outside any bilateral negotiations both in 1929 and in 1984, the time of the Concordat's review.[23]

The aforementioned regulation during the Fascist era specifically refers to a crucifix or a cross adorned with a depiction of Christ, commonly utilised in the Catholic tradition, in contrast to the bare cross, more prevalent in Protestant practices.[24]

Non-believers have consistently played a significant role in the ongoing discussion regarding the display of the crucifix in the classroom, as opposed to non-Catholics. Non-believers have been mainly represented by the Union

21 Cf. r.d. 30 April 1924, no. 965, "Ordinamento interno delle Giunte e dei Regi istituti di istruzione media" whose art. 118 states that "Every institute has the national flag; every classroom, the image of the Crucifix and the portrait of the King" as well as r.d. 26 April 1928, no. 1297, "Approvazione del regolamento generale sui servizi dell'istruzione elementare" which, pursuant to art. 119 – referring in turn to Annex C "Tabella degli arredi e del materiale occorrente nelle varie classi e dotazione della scuola" – foresees the crucifix as first among the "furnishings" of each classroom.

These provisions are still in force according to legislative decree (hereafter d.lgs.) 16 April 1994, no. 297, "Testo unico delle disposizioni in materia di istruzione, relative alle scuole di ogni ordine e grado".

It should be noted that r.d. no. 965/1924 was first repealed by art. 24 (Annex A), d.lgs., 25 June 2008, no. 112, "Disposizioni urgenti per lo sviluppo economico, la semplificazione, la competitività, la stabilizzazione della finanza pubblica e la perequazione tributaria" to be subsequently restored pursuant to art. 3, para. 1 *bis*, d.lgs. 22 December 2008, no. 200, "Misure urgenti di semplificazione amministrativa" (converted with amendments into law 18 February 2009, no. 9).

22 Art. 232, "Testo unico delle leggi di pubblica sicurezza" (hereafter TULPS) 1926, punished obscenity, blasphemy, and offences if they are against the Catholic religion with an increased sanction until the new Criminal Code came into force. TULPS was later amended and supplemented by r.d. 18 June 1931, no. 773, in light of the new Criminal and Criminal Procedure Codes.

23 *Supra* paras. 1.1 and 1.2.

24 Briefly, the main difference between the cross and crucifix in Catholicism and Protestantism lies in their symbolism and their liturgical and devotional use. In Catholicism, the crucifix is a central symbol of the faith representing Christ's redemptive sacrifice. In Protestantism, the bare cross is preferred and symbolises Christ's resurrection and victory, emphasising hope and new life.

of Atheists Agnostics Rationalists (UAAR), an Italian association known for its militancy and campaigns such as "*Scrocifiggiamo l'Italia*", a "permanent awareness campaign for the removal of crucifixes from public buildings",[25] and "*Sbattezzo*", which aimed "to cancel the civil effects of baptism".[26] Since its establishment on 18 March 1991,[27] the association has consistently advocated for the complete recognition of the right to negative religious freedom and actively combatted discrimination. The UAAR fought to have the opportunity to enter into an *intesa* with the Italian State under art. 8, para. 3, Const. However, this article formally reserves this possibility only to entities that can be defined as religious denominations.[28]

The emergence of discussions regarding the legitimacy of the display of crucifixes during the 1980s is not a coincidence. In the course of these years, the Council of State initiated its first substantial intervention in referral, in accordance with the Ministry of Education's request.[29]

The Council of State, section II, opinion, 27 April 1988, no. 63,[30] referring to the r.d. nos. 965/1924 and 1297/1928 pointed out that "the Cross, aside from its meaning for believers, is a symbol of Christian civilisation and culture, of its historical root as a universal value independent of specific religious denomination".

Additionally, the Council of State affirmed that the provisions remain valid and cannot be implicitly repealed by the new bilateral regulations of 1984 or by the Italian Constitution, which became effective in 1948.

The Constitution,

> while ensuring equal freedom to all religious denominations, does not prescribe any prohibition on the display in public offices of a symbol that, like the crucifix, is part of the historical heritage by virtue of the principles it evokes.

25 Cf. www.uaar.it/uaar/campagne/scrocifiggiamo, where copious documentation is available.

26 See www.uaar.it/laicita/sbattezzo.

27 This entity was informally founded on 19 October 1987. Currently, it takes the shape of a social promotion association.

28 On this point see *infra* para. 4.4.1.

29 For a precedent, see Magistrate's Court (*Pretura*) of Rome, judgment 17 May 1986, which considered the crucifix as "furniture" to corroborate the legitimacy of the affixation (judgment not available online as it is for the older rulings mentioned in the following).

Furthermore, there is a specific passage in the decision that reads, "the presence of such furniture cannot be detrimental in any way to the cultural and ideological formation of the pupil, because, although the crucifix constitutes a symbol of the Christian religions (and not only of the Catholic one), it assumes importance for the Italian State, given the particular importance that the figure of Christ has assumed in the birth and evolution of Western civilization, as demonstrated, *inter alia*, by the high testimony of a man of secular culture like Benedetto Croce, who publicly acknowledged that [. . .] 'we cannot help but call ourselves Christians'".

30 Available at www.uaar.it/uaar/campagne/scrocifiggiamo/04.html.

Shortly afterwards, Constitutional Court ruling 11 April 1989, no. 203 was issued, defining the principle of secularism as "one profile of the form of State outlined in the Constitutional Charter of the Republic", derived from arts. 2, 3, 7, 8, 19, and 20, Const.[31]

Regardless, it was only in the 2000s that the matter gained prominence in Italian political, institutional, and legal discourse. The first measure to mention is the note from the Ministry of Education dated 3 October 2002, no. 2267, "Display of the Crucifix in School Classrooms", followed by directive no. 2666, issued on the same date,[32] which instructs the competent offices to issue provisions ensuring that "the display of the Crucifix in school classrooms is assured" and that

> each educational institution [. . .] provides a dedicated space, outside of service obligations and hours, for moments of reflection and meditation for members of the school community who desire it.

The UAAR challenged this directive with an extraordinary complaint to the President of the Republic[33] invoking four grounds of illegitimacy, alleging the Ministry's lack of competence, violation of the constitutional principles of *laicità*, freedom of religion and teaching, and the principle of impartiality.

The Council of State ruled that the proposed complaints should not be upheld. According to the Council of State, Section II, opinion 15 February 2006, no. 4575/03-2482/04,[34] although secularism of the State constitutes a fundamental principle in all Western democratic systems and is therefore also part of the legal heritage, the same principle of secularism cannot be undermined by the display of crucifixes in classrooms.[35]

For the Council of State,

> the crucifix is indeed also a historical and cultural symbol; it represents a sign of national identity; it represents [. . .] one of the formative paths of our Country and in general of a large part of Europe (some national

31 *Supra* para. 1.4.

32 Both the note and the directive are available at https://archivio.pubblica.istruzione.it/normativa/2002/dir31002.shtml. Cf. the passage in the note referring to the opinion of the State Advocacy Office of Bologna, 16 July 2002, which, recalling opinion no. 63/1988 issued by the Council of State, concludes that "the provisions envisaging the display of crucifixes in classrooms are still in force" and that "the display of crucifixes is not considered being in breach of the principle of religious freedom".

33 Administrative remedy originally regulated by presidential decree (hereafter d.P.R.) 24 November 1971, no. 1199. This mechanism offers an alternative to judicial review, allowing for the contestation of final administrative acts to protect rights or legitimate interests in response to actions carried out by the public administration. Pursuant to art. 69, law 18 June 2009, no. 69, Disposizioni per lo sviluppo economico, la semplificazione, la competitività nonché in materia di processo civile" the institute was amended.

34 Also available at www.uaar.it/uaar/campagne/scrocifiggiamo/53.pdf.

35 Council of State, opinion no 4575/03-2482/04, para. 2.

banners of Northern Europe contain the sign of the cross and it is not by chance, perhaps, that they have been the object of recent episodes of retaliation in countries of Islamic religion), whose Christianity or Catholicism cannot be cancelled out, first and foremost as a sociological datum, by the recalled principle of secularism, to which Christianity is accompanied as an element of integration and development and certainly not as an element of contraposition or, even less, of discrimination.[36]

This statement calls attention to the presence of religious symbolism, including symbols from various religions, in multiple banners[37] and in the flag representing the European institutions. This flag was adopted initially by the Council of Europe and subsequently by the European Union.[38]

Likewise, for the Council of State, precisely "because of its symbolic character, it [the crucifix] cannot be considered in the same way as any school furniture".[39]

There is a noteworthy legal case from the early 2000s that pertains to the Italian province. The Italian Muslim father of children attending a primary school in Ofena (L'Aquila, Abruzzo) requested removal of the crucifix in the classroom.[40] Alternatively, he proposed hanging a small picture containing a sura from the Koran (*sura* 112) on the wall.

Initially, the monocratic Court of L'Aquila, seized on a cautionary measure under art. 700, Code of Civil Procedure, by order of 22 October 2003, reaffirmed the secular character of the Republic and its institutions. The Court thus imposed the removal of any religious symbols from the school building.[41]

36 Council of State, opinion no 4575/03-2482/04, para. 3.

37 Cf. the 2014 factsheets published by Pew Research Centre and the review of A.E. Theodorou, "64 Countries Have Religious Symbols on Their National Flags", 25 November 2014, available at https://assets.pewresearch.org/wp-content/uploads/sites/11/2014/11/NationalSymbol_CodedText_FINAL.pdf and www.pewresearch.org/short-reads/2014/11/25/64-countries-have-religious-symbols-on-their-national-flags/.

38 As Arsène Heitz, the author of the selected sketch, later emphasised. On this topic, M.C. Ivaldi, *Il fattore religioso nel diritto dell'Unione europea*, pp. 71–72.

39 Council of State, opinion no 4575/03-2482/04, para. 6.

40 Reference is made to Adel Smith, the protagonist of other events with judicial aftermaths concerning the crucifix in various ways (*infra* para. 2.4.) and former founder of an association called the Union of Muslims of Italy.

41 It is worth mentioning that shortly after the measure was published, a three-meter-high cross was erected in the square in front of the school, reportedly at the request of then mayor Anna Rita Coletti, as documented in the press.

The order references the previously mentioned 1986 ruling (nt. 29) regarding the crucifix and expresses criticism on the basis that the judicial body did not fully comprehend "the fundamental nature of the issue, overlooking the potential violation of an absolute right constitutionally protected", and instead emphasised the organisational aspect of the education service in its decision. Court of L'Aquila, order 22 October 2003, "*Diritto*", para. 2.1., available at www.costituzionalismo.it/wp-content/uploads/crocifisso_scuola.pdf.

This episode provoked a fervent national debate[42] and prompted resolution 6 November 2003, no. 8–0006, released by the VII Culture Commission of the Chamber of Deputies.[43] For the VII Commission, "to proceed with the removal of the crucifix from classrooms is a fact of absolute gravity that contradicts and offends the culture and sensibility of a large part of the Italian population". The crucifix is "the emblem of values such as freedom of the individual and the person, respect for all religious faiths, and the separation of 'God and Caesar' the foundation of the *laicità* of the state". The Commission added that there is "no logical connection between the demise of the Catholic religion as the state religion and the presence of the crucifix in classrooms".

The VII Commission also obliged the Government to avoid

> proceed[ing] with actions that are detrimental to the feelings and culture shared by a large majority of the Italian population, such as the removal of the crucifix, [and] to undertake an awareness-raising effort to make everyone understand why the crucifix is a symbol of values that underpin our national, European and Western identity.

According to the VII Commission, the crucifix, "far from offending cultural and religious pluralism, is and has been, on the contrary, the oldest and strongest symbol of love and defence of everyone's freedom".

Thereafter, the Court of L'Aquila, in collegial composition, noting the lack of jurisdiction of the ordinary court, revoked the previous precautionary order in its order of 19 November 2003.[44]

The Supreme Court of Cassation, United Civil Sections, order 10 July, 2006, no. 15614, confirmed the measure.[45]

However, part of the order holds that the crucifix cannot "because of its eschatological value and as a fundamental symbol of the Christian religion, be considered in the same way as any component of school furniture". The order therefore also foreshadows a possible

> evolution on the legislative level due to the increasingly pressing needs to protect religious, ethnic and cultural minorities in a system inspired by the values of tolerance, solidarity, non-discrimination and respect for pluralism.

42 Measure blocked by the proposed appeal of the State Attorney's Office.

43 At https://leg14.camera.it/_dati/leg14/lavori/bollet/200311/1106/pdf/07.pdf.

44 The text of the order is not available online.

45 Available at www.uaar.it/uaar/campagne/scrocifiggiamo/55.html/. The Supreme Court of Cassation (hereafter SCC) specifies that disputes concerning the legitimacy of the display of crucifixes in classrooms, based on ministerial regulations and circulars concerning the methods of providing public service, fall under the exclusive jurisdiction of the administrative judge even in the absence of an express legal provision imposing the obligation.

2.2.1 The Lautsi *case within the framework of domestic jurisprudence*

The analysis continues with the *Lautsi* case regarding the crucifix in public schools from the viewpoint of national jurisprudence. This jurisprudence has informed several interventions at the political and governmental levels, highlighting the ideological nature of the Italian debate.

The affair originating with the request of the parents of two minors attending a middle school in Abano Terme (Padova), Italy, for the removal of the crucifix. Undoubtedly, this is the most renowned case international worldwide. The Board of the Vittorino da Feltre Comprehensive Institute refused the request in the minutes of 27 May 2002, resolving to keep religious symbols on display on the school premises.

This issue passed through all tiers of the judicial system before being brought to the attention of the Strasbourg Court.

The Regional Administrative Court (hereafter TAR) of Veneto, Section I, by order 14 January 2004, no. 56, raised a question of constitutionality regarding the provisions censured.[46]

The main point of the order is the inadmissibility of the Constitutional Court conducting direct reviews of regulatory rules. The TAR Veneto, however, based its request on the grounds of so-called indirect control, which is allowed in cases in which a provision of law is applied through the specifications expressed by the regulatory legislation, the contents of which supplement the precept of the primary provision.[47]

According to the rather weak and unconvincing arguments of the TAR Veneto, this indirect relationship exists through arts. 159 and 190, d.lgs. 16 April 1994, no. 297, "Consolidated text of the laws in force in the field of education, relating to schools of all levels".[48]

The question for the TAR Veneto was therefore relevant and well-founded given the "unequivocal confessional significance" of the crucifix and its contradiction with the supreme principle of *laicità* as established by the Constitutional Court in numerous jurisprudential interventions.

The imposed display of the crucifix "cannot find justification even in its undoubted diffusion". This circumstance

> can, at most, justify in single schools, according to specific evaluations, the observance of religious traditions – such as those linked to Christmas or Easter – but not the generalised, presence of the crucifix.[49]

The Constitutional Court, by order 13 December 2004, no. 389, declared the manifest inadmissibility of the question raised by the TAR precisely because

46 Accessible at www.uaar.it/uaar/campagne/scrocifiggiamo/29.html/.

47 For a precedent see Constitutional Court, judgment 30 December 1994, no. 456.

48 Arts. 159 and 190, d.lgs. no. 267/1994 that place the costs of "furnishings" for elementary and middle schools on municipalities.

49 On Christmas or Easter celebrations, see *infra* para. 4.2.

it concerns regulatory rules. The argument was also discussed in depth at a conference of Constitutional Law scholars held in Ferrara on 28 May of that year.[50]

After the suspension, the TAR Veneto, Section III, judgment 22 March 2005, no. 1110,[51] dismissed the demand for the removal of crucifixes from classrooms, claiming the jurisdiction of the administrative court since the matter concerns the expression of an organisational power that belongs to the school administration.[52]

Significantly, the TAR Veneto ruling affirms that the crucifix cannot "be considered as a piece of furniture" but rather is a symbol "that invokes meanings other than its materiality".[53] This leaves the verification of whether "in the light of the applicable rules, mainly of constitutional status", the meanings that this symbol evokes "are or are not consistent with its display in a public school"[54] up to the administrative judge.

After a reconstruction of the principle of *laicità* as formulated by constitutional jurisprudence, references to supranational and international legislation on freedom of religion, and the same foreign jurisprudence on the subject, the TAR concluded that

> from a vision perspective, in the central and consistent core of the Christian faith, despite the Inquisition, anti-Semitism and the Crusades, it is easy to identify the principles of human dignity, tolerance, freedom, including religious freedom, and thus ultimately the foundation of the same secularism of the State.[55]

The Council of State, Section VI, judgment 13 February 2006, no. 556, reached a similar conclusion, declaring the appeal against the first instance measure unfounded.[56]

For the Council of State, the concept of *laicità*, although not expressly appearing in the Constitution, assumes – as reflected in the jurisprudence of

50 This proceeding was published in R. Bin et al. (eds.), *La laicità crocifissa? Il nodo costituzionale dei simboli religiosi nei luoghi pubblici*, Giappichelli, Torino, 2004, *passim*. The volume contains potential solutions to the *vexata quaestio*, including the proposal made by S. Ceccanti, "E se la Corte andasse in Baviera?", *ivi*, p. 1 ff. The proposal was submitted by the Author with the bill no. 1947/2009 shortly after the publication of the *Lautsi I* (*infra* subpara. 2.3.1.).

51 Available at www.uaar.it/uaar/campagne/scrocifiggiamo/41.html.

52 TAR Veneto, judgment no. 110/2005, "*Diritto*", para. 2.1.

53 TAR Veneto, judgment no. 110/2005, "*Diritto*", para. 6.1.

54 TAR Veneto, judgment no. 110/2005, "*Diritto*", para. 6.1.

55 TAR Veneto, judgment no. 110/2005, "*Diritto*", para. 11.6.

56 The most recent decisions and opinions of the Council of State can be viewed at www.giustizia-amministrativa.it/web/guest/dcsnprras well as the pronouncements of the various regional administrative courts, unless otherwise indicated.

the Constitutional Court – the quality of a supreme principle and assumes legal relevance from arts. 2, 3, 7, 8, 19, and 20 Const.

Laicità is therefore a linguistic symbol that must be correlated with content that can vary over time and space and that thus holds a relative character. Indeed, "although it presupposes and requires everywhere the distinction between the temporal and the spiritual dimension [. . .] it is related to the specific institutional organisation of each State".[57]

The crucifix is also a symbol that takes on different meanings depending on where it is displayed. In a non-religious venue, such as a school, it would not constitute a cultic symbol, *tout court*, since

> its display will be justified and will assume a religiously non-discriminatory significance if it is capable of recalling in a concise form immediately perceptible and intuitable [. . .] civilly relevant values.

Such values include those "underlying and inspiring our constitutional order, the foundation of our civil coexistence" and thus assume "a highly educational symbolic function, regardless of the religion professed by pupils".

For the Council of State, the crucifix is suitable for concisely expressing

> the religious origin of the values of tolerance, mutual respect, enhancement of the person, affirmation of his rights, regard for his freedom, autonomy of conscience vis-à-vis authority, human solidarity, and rejection of all discrimination, which characterize Italian civilization.

Hence, according to the Council of State – ruling out the possibility that the crucifix could constitute an ornament – the crucifix would serve the function of highlighting the religious foundation of these values "enshrined for all, regardless of the affiliation to the religion that inspired and advocated them" and which "delineate secularism in the current state order".

2.3 The European Court of Human Rights' decisions on the exhibition of the crucifix in Italian schools

This affair did not stop at the national level. Instead, the losing parties brought the matter before the Strasbourg Court, arousing the interest of foreign legal scholars that has commented extensively on both the first ruling in 2009 and especially the Grand Chamber's opposite ruling in 2011,[58] not least because

57 Council of State, Section VI, judgment no. 556/2006, para. 3, from which all the verbatim quotations that follow are taken.

58 For a reconstruction of the whole procedural affair in Italian doctrine, see A. Pin, "Public Schools, Italian Crucifix, and the European Court of Human Rights: The Italian Separation of Church and State", *Emory International Law Review*, no. 25, 2011, p. 97 ff.; F. Astengo,

the Strasbourg Court has usually been called upon to judge the issue of religious symbols worn by believers.[59]

The following two subparagraphs initially delve into the supranational case law that highlights the European Court of Human Rights' endeavour to establish a common understanding of neutrality. However, this notion was subsequently superseded by the Grand Chambre in favour of Italy's recognised margin of appreciation.[60]

2.3.1 The **Lautsi I**

The ECtHR, Second Section, judgment, 3 November 2009, *Lautsi and others v. Italy* (appl. no. 30814/2006), upheld the plaintiffs' claims, unanimously concluding that Italy should be condemned as there was a violation of parents' right to educate their children according to their convictions and the pupils' right to freedom of religion,[61] with payment of non-pecuniary damages.[62]

The Court deemed that

> the compulsory display of a symbol of a particular faith in the exercise of public authority in relation to specific situations subject to governmental supervision, particularly in classrooms, restricts the right of schoolchildren to believe or not believe.[63]

For the ECtHR, the compulsory display of the crucifix "infringes those rights because the restrictions are incompatible with the State's duty to respect neutrality in the exercise of public authority, particularly in the field of education".[64]

"Freedom of Religion Crucified? Secularism and Italian Schools before the European Court of Human Rights", *Politique européenne*, no. 3, 2013, p. 12.

For commentary from international scholar, see J. Temperman (ed.), *The Lautsi Papers: Multidisciplinary Reflections on Religious Symbols in the Public School Classroom*, Brill – Nijhof, Leiden, 2012, *passim*. XXVIII–444 pp.

59 Regarding the various statements about religious symbols worn by believers, please refer to the *Guide on Article 9 of the European Convention on Human Rights*. The Court also ruled regarding the cross as a symbol worn by believers in the judgment ECtHR Fourth Section, 27 May 2013, *Eweida and others v. the United Kingdom* (appls. nos. 48420/10, 59842/10, 51671/10 and 36516/10), esp. regarding the applicants Eweida and Chaplin. *Amplius infra* para 3.5.

All ECtHR measures can be viewed at the HUDOC database (www.echr.coe.int/hudoc-database).

60 Fourth Section, 27 May 2013, *Eweida and others v. the United Kingdom* (appls. nos. 48420/10, 59842/10, 51671/10 and 36516/10), esp. regarding the applicants Eweida and Chaplin. *Amplius infra* para 3.5.

61 Condemnation for infringement of art. 2 of the Additional Protocol to the European Convention on Human Rights (right to education), read in connection with art. 9 of the same Convention (freedom of thought, conscience, and religion).

62 For an analysis, G. Andreescu – L. Andreescu, "The European Court of Human Rights's Lautsi Decision: Context, Contents, Consequences", *Journal for the Study of Religions and Ideologies*, vol. 9, no. 26, 2010, p. 47.

63 ECtHR, Second Section, 3 November 2009, *Lautsi I*, para. 57.

64 ECtHR, Second Section, 3 November 2009, *Lautsi I*, para. 57.

The decision' s *ratio* lies in the ECtHR's development of a particular understanding of the principle of neutrality that is not made explicit in the European Convention on Human Rights (hereafter ECHR).[65] The ECtHR stated that "the State has a duty to uphold confessional neutrality in public education, where school attendance is compulsory regardless of religion, and which must seek to inculcate in pupils the habit of critical thought".[66]

Among the positive reactions to the *Lautsi I* case, besides those of a part of the academia,[67] is that of the Methodist Waldensian Church, which stated in Decision no. 44[68] at its 2010 synod that it

> welcomes the ruling of the European Court of Human Rights (ECtHR) in Strasbourg on 3 November 2009, which held that the display of crucifixes in Italian classrooms (Lautsi v. Italy case) was in breach of parents' right to educate their children in line with their religious and philosophical convictions and of the principle of the secular nature of schools.[69]

Decision no. 44 "deplores the instrumental use that has been made, and continues to be made, of the crucifix by heads of public offices and, most recently, also through orders issued by certain mayors" and "regrets that the Italian Government, instead of complying with the ECtHR's decision, has appealed to the Grand Chamber of the Court itself", holding that "the crucifix cannot be considered a 'symbol of Italian civilisation and culture'".

During the XVI Legislature, a little more than a month after the *Lautsi I* ruling, a draft law was submitted to the Presidency of the Senate on 18 December 2009, under no. 1977,[70] titled "General rules on the display of crucifixes in classrooms on the basis of the principle of autonomy of educational institutions, by analogy with Bavarian and Castilian legislation".[71]

The concept of requiring legislative intervention is rooted in the nature of the regulatory sources that both historically and currently govern the display of crucifixes in public schools, as well as the repeated disregard of these rules by different educational institutions.[72]

65 ECtHR, Second Section, 3 November 2009, *Lautsi I*, para. 47.
66 ECtHR, Second Section, 3 November 2009, *Lautsi I*, para. 56.
67 Cf. S. Mancini, "The Crucifix Rage: Supranational Constitutionalism Bumps Against the Counter-Majoritarian Difficulty", *European Constitutional Law Review*, vol. 6, no. 1, 2010, p. 6; M. Croce, "La 'sana laicità' capitola a Strasburgo: la Corte europea diritti dell'uomo giudice di costituzionalità sulle fonti non primarie?", *Il Foro italiano*, pt. IV, 2010, col. 67.
68 Synod held in Torre Pellice (TO), from 22 to August 2010.
69 The 2010 Waldensian Synod Decision no. 44 can be accessed at www.chiesavaldese.org/aria_cms.php?page=235.
70 Available at www.senato.it/leg/16/BGT/Schede/Ddliter/34717.htm.
71 For a brief examination of foreign jurisprudence on symbols in institutions, see *infra* para. 2.5.
72 For more recent attempts, see *infra* paras. 2.3.2 and 4.5.

The explanatory report states that the value of religious culture to the heritage of the Italian people is already embodied in national legislation.[73] A headteacher's decision to display the crucifix in a classroom is based on this notion as well as the contribution made by Christianity to the values of contemporary constitutionalism.[74]

If such a display is challenged on religious or conscience grounds by the person entitled to education or their parents,

> the headteacher, because of the principle of school autonomy, with due regard for protecting privacy and non-discrimination and considering the characteristics of the school community, seeks an agreement within a short timeframe, also by displaying additional religious symbols.[75]

If no arrangement can be reached, the headteacher

> adopts, after consultation with the district or school council, a solution that achieves a fair balance of the convictions of conscience of all the pupils in the classes involved and achieves the broadest possible consensus.[76]

However, on closer scrutiny, the envisaged solution is rather cumbersome and would place an additional burden on educational institutions. Educational institutions therefore become the arbiters in the balancing of conflicting constitutional rights,[77] though the basis for this is unclear. Nonetheless, this is a solution that has been at least partly accepted at the jurisprudential level.[78]

2.3.2 The **Lautsi II**

As is well known, the Italian Government brought an action under art. 43, ECHR,[79] and referred the case to the Court in the Grand Chamber for a new ruling.

73 Cf. art. 9, para. 2, Agreement between the Holy See and the Italian Republic amending the Lateran Concordat signed in 1984, which was ratified and implemented through law no. 121/1985 (*supra* para. 1.3.).

74 Draft law no. 1947/2009, art. 1, para. 1.

75 Draft law no. 1947/2009, art. 1, para. 2.

76 Draft law no. 1947/2009, art. 1, para. 3.

77 This appears in the French case discussed *infra* para. 3.5. concerning the symbols worn by students and the need for school directors to distinguish what may or may not be defined as religiously distinctive clothing.

78 SCC, United Civil Section, Judgment 9 September 2021, no. 24414, *infra* para. 4.1.

79 Pursuing art. 43, ECHR, "Referral to the Grand Chamber".

Several states, including those with Catholic and Orthodox traditions,[80] along with non-governmental organisations[81] and a collective action by thirty-three members of the European Parliament, are filling adhesive interventions to support the Italian Government.[82]

Additionally, numerous interventions are in place to reinforce the opposite viewpoint.[83]

The ECtHR, Grand Chamber, 18 March 2011, *Lautsi and others v. Italy* (appl. no. 30814/2006) first limited its judgment by stating that

> it is not required in this case to examine the question of the presence of crucifixes in places other than State schools. Nor is it for the Court to rule on the compatibility of the presence of crucifixes in State-school classrooms with the principle of secularism as enshrined in Italian law.[84]

80 Armenia, Bulgaria, Cyprus, the Russian Federation, Greece, Lithuania, Malta and the Republic of San Marino, Romania, and the Principality of Monaco. This last State shared "the viewpoint of the respondent Government according to which the crucifix was a 'passive symbol' that was found on the coats of arms and flags of many States and in the instant case reflected a national identity rooted in history". ECtHR, Grand Chamber, judgment 18 March 2011, *Lautsi and others v. Italy*, para. 48.

Regarding the Jewish American scholar invited to represent eight intervening States in the Oral Hearing of the appeal before the Grand Chamber, see J.H.H. Weiler, "State and Nation; Church, Mosque and Synagogue – On Religion Freedom and Religious Symbols in Public Spaces", in M.A. Glendon – H.F. Zacher (eds.), *Universal Rights in a World of Diversity. The Case of Religious Freedom*, The Pontifical Academy of Social Sciences, Vatican City, 2012, p. 578.

81 The *European Centre for Law and Justice*, *Zentralkomitee der deutschen katholiken*, *Semaines sociales de France* and *Associazioni cristiane lavoratori italiani*.

82 The interveners pointed out that the ECtHR "was not a constitutional court and had to respect the principle of subsidiarity and recognise a particularly broad margin of appreciation in favour of Contracting States not only regarding the relationship between the State and religion but also where they carried out their functions in the area of education and teaching". They added that "it was clear from the Court's case-law that a State which, for reasons deriving from its history or its tradition, showed a preference for a particular religion did not exceed that margin. Accordingly, in their opinion, the display of crucifixes in public buildings did not conflict with the Convention, and the presence of religious symbols in public space should not be seen as a form of indoctrination but the expression of cultural unity and identity". ECtHR, Grand Chamber, 18 March 2011, *Lautsi II*, para. 56.

83 The non-governmental organisation *Greek Helsinki Monitor*, *Associazione nazionale del libero Pensiero*, *Eurojuris* and *International Commission of Jurists, Interights and Human Rights Watch*.

For widely commented-upon judgments, see R. Pierik – W. van der Burg, "The Neutral State and the Mandatory Crucifix", and D. McGoldrick, "Religion in European Public Square and in European Public Life – Crucifixes in the Classroom?", resp., *Human Rights Law Review*, vol. 11, no. 3, 2011, p. 267 and p. 451; G. Puppinck, "The Case of *Lautsi v. Italy*: A Synthesis", *Brigham Young University Law Review*, no. 3, 2012, p. 873; M. Iglesias Vila – C. Ungureanu, "The Conundrum of Pluralism and the Doctrine of the Margin of Appreciation: The Crucifix 'Affair' and the Ambivalence of the ECtHR", in F. Requejo – C. Ungureanu (eds.), *Democracy, Law and Religious Pluralism in Europe. Secularism and Post-Secularism*, Routledge, Abingdon – New York, 2014, p. 179, and more generally J. Martínez Torrón, "Institutional Religious Symbols, State Neutrality and Protection of Minorities in Europe", *Law & Justice*, 2013, p. 21.

84 ECtHR, Grand Chamber, 18 March 2011, *Lautsi II*, para. 57.

After reasserting "that in the area of education and teaching article 2 of Protocol no. 1 is in principle the *lex specialis* in relation to article 9 of the Convention",[85] the Grand Chamber also stated that the first provision should be read in relation to the second one. In this regard,

> States have responsibility for ensuring, neutrally and impartially, the exercise of various religions, faiths and beliefs. Their role is to help maintain public order, religious harmony and tolerance in a democratic society, particularly between opposing groups. [. . .] That concerns both relations between believers and non-believers and relations between the adherents of various religions, faiths and beliefs.[86]

The Grand Chamber further observed that the crucifix is a religious symbol, as held by the domestic courts and the government, and excluded the relevance of whether another meaning beyond its religious symbolism can be attributed to the crucifix. Therefore, for the Grand Chamber, there is no evidence that

> the display of a religious symbol on classroom walls may have an influence on pupils and so it cannot reasonably be asserted that it does or does not have an effect on young persons whose convictions are still in the process of being formed.[87]

Regarding the Government's argument that

> the presence of crucifixes in State-school classrooms, being the result of Italy's historical development, a fact which gave it not only a religious connotation but also an identity-linked one, now corresponded to a tradition which [. . .] [the Government] considered it important to perpetuate.[88]

It is not for the Court to assess "whether to perpetuate a tradition falls in principle within the margin of appreciation of the respondent State". Rather, the Court must "take into account the fact that Europe is marked by a great diversity between the States of which it is composed, particularly in the sphere of cultural and historical development". This is a statement that the Court also made given the acknowledged divergence of views between the Council of

85 ECtHR, Grand Chamber, 18 March 2011, *Lautsi II*, para. 59.
86 ECtHR, Grand Chamber, 18 March 2011, *Lautsi II*, para. 60.
87 ECtHR, Grand Chamber, 18 March 2011, *Lautsi II*, para. 66.
88 ECtHR, Grand Chamber, 18 March 2011, *Lautsi II*, para. 67, where it is added that "beyond its religious meaning, the crucifix symbolised the principles and values which formed the foundation of democracy and western civilisation, and that its presence in classrooms was justifiable on that account".

State and the Supreme Court of Cassation and the fact that the Constitutional Court had not given a ruling.[89]

For the Court, in the absence of a "European consensus on the question of the presence of religious symbols in State schools",[90]

> the Contracting States enjoy a margin of appreciation in their efforts to reconcile exercise of the functions they assume in relation to education and teaching with respect for the right of parents to ensure such education and teaching in conformity with their own religious and philosophical convictions.[91]

For the Court, "the effects of the greater visibility which the presence of the crucifix gives to Christianity in schools needs to be further placed in perspective by consideration of the following points":

> [F]irstly, the presence of crucifixes is not associated with compulsory teaching about Christianity. [. . .] Secondly, according to the indications provided by the Government, Italy opens up the school environment in parallel to other religions. The Government indicated in this connection that it was not forbidden for pupils to wear Islamic headscarves or other symbols or apparel having a religious connotation; alternative arrangements were possible to help schooling fit in with non-majority religious practices; the beginning and end of Ramadan were "often celebrated" in schools; and optional religious education could be organised in schools for "all recognised religious creeds".[92]

Lastly, the Court noted that

> the first applicant retained in full her right as a parent to enlighten and advise her children, to exercise in their regard her natural functions as educator, and to guide them on a path in line with her own philosophical convictions.[93]

The ECtHR held by 15 votes to two that there was no violation of art. 2 of Protocol no. 1 and that no separate issue arose under art. 9 of the

89 ECtHR, Grand Chamber, 18 March 2011, *Lautsi II*, para. 68. See *amplius supra* para. 2.2. for Council of State, judgment 13 April 2006, no. 556, Constitutional Court, order 13 December 2004, no. 389 and *infra* para. 2.4. for SCC, United Civile Section, judgment 1 March 2000, no. 439.
90 ECtHR, Grand Chamber, 18 March 2011, *Lautsi II*, para. 70.
91 ECtHR, Grand Chamber, 18 March 2011, *Lautsi II*, para. 69.
92 ECtHR, Grand Chamber, 18 March 2011, *Lautsi II*, para. 74. To address any further concerns regarding the celebration of Ramadan, please refer to para. 4.3.
93 ECtHR, Grand Chamber, 18 March 2011, *Lautsi II*, para. 75.

Convention. Three concurrent[94] and one dissenting opinion[95] were added to the judgment.

More recently, the Ministry of Education, University and Research – Regional School Office of Emilia Romagna, issued a note related to the display of religious symbols in the classroom on 30 October 2013, no. 17143.[96] The episode stemmed from a teacher removing a crucifix from an elementary school in Bologna because of students' diverse religious affiliations. The Regional Office, in response to explicit requests from select school principals, issued a 67-page document meticulously outlining the legal and jurisprudential references regarding the issue, thereby establishing a clear framework.

Shortly thereafter, during the XVII Legislature, a draft law titled "Provisions concerning the display of the crucifix in schools and public administration offices" was also presented to the Chamber of Deputies on 28 July 2016, no. 4005 on the initiative of right-wing parliamentarians.[97]

Based on the assumption that the crucifix is an emblem of the universal values of Christian civilisation and culture and is recognised as an essential and constitutive element of Italy's historical and civic-cultural heritage, regardless of any specific religious denomination (art. 1), the proposal extended the obligation to display the cross or crucifix not only in schools of all levels but also in universities and academies and in all public administration buildings and local authorities (art. 3). A sanction was also envisaged in cases of the symbol's removal or non-compliance with the duty of posting by the relevant public entity charged with supervision (art. 4).

94 Cf. Concurring opinions of Judge Rozakis joined by judge Vajić; of judge Bonello and of judge Power.

Judge Bonello's concurring opinion states, significantly, "[A] court of human rights cannot allow itself to suffer from historical Alzheimer's. It has no right to disregard the cultural continuum of a nation's flow through time, nor to ignore what, over the centuries, has served to mould and define the profile of a people. No supranational court has any business substituting its own ethical mock-ups for those qualities that history has imprinted on the national identity. On a human rights court falls the function of protecting fundamental rights, but never ignoring that customs are not passing whims. They evolve over time, harden over history into cultural cement. They become defining, all-important badges of identity for nations, tribes, religions, individuals".

95 According to the dissenting opinion of Judge Malinverni, joined by Judge Kaladjieva, "[I]n view of the fact that there is still a mixed practice among European States on the issue, the only remaining guidance for the Court in achieving the correct balance between the rights involved comes from its prior case-law. The keywords deriving from the prior case-law are 'neutrality and impartiality'".

96 Cf. www.istruzioneer.gov.it/wp-content/uploads/2019/09/20131020_miur_usr-er_nota-17143_simboli-religiosi.pdf.

97 Available at www.camera.it/leg17/126?leg=17&idDocumento=4005. To explore further efforts at reform, refer to the para. 4.5.

2.4 Display of the crucifix in polling stations, courtrooms, and hospitals

Cases concerning the display of the crucifix in polling stations and courtrooms have spanned years and all levels of jurisdiction. The presence of symbols within hospitals presents a unique case because there are no specific regulations mandating their presence, which has resulted in fewer conflicts.

The first case concerns the office of scrutineers within polling stations. Public schools are usually designated as the locations for polling stations, where the aforementioned regulations regarding the display of crucifixes in schoolrooms are observed.[98]

Italian law provides for the cooperation of citizens in the exercise of certain public functions, as is the case with the execution of the electoral process (administrative or political) and referendums. These are persons normally appointed by drawing lots from among electors who have applied for enrolment on the list of persons eligible for the office. It is a compulsory office for the persons designated. This means that one can only renounce the office if there are serious and justified reasons; otherwise, an offence is committed.[99]

The case under examination pertains to the display of a crucifix in a polling station.[100] A man who was selected for the office of scrutineer notifies his municipality, the Municipality of Cuneo, and to the President of the Republic that he would carry out the duties of scrutineer only if the respect for freedom of conscience guaranteed to every citizen by the Constitution were made effective by the Ministry of the Interior removing symbols or images belonging to a single religious faith from polling stations, almost all of which were located in State institutions.

In the absence of a reply to his conditions, the scrutineer went to the polling station and recorded a statement. While recognising that the crucifix was not displayed in the polling station he was in charge of, he considered this circumstance to be entirely accidental and not motivated by a measure of the competent authority to remove the crucifix from display nationwide. As a result, he declared that he considered it his duty not to accept this situation, denouncing its unconstitutionality.

98 *Supra* para. 2.1. De Oto Antonello, “Presenza del crocifisso o di altre immagini religiose nei seggi elettorali: la difficile affermazione di una ‘laicità effettiva’. Osservazioni a Cass. pen. n. 439 del 2000”, *Quaderni di diritto e politica ecclesiastica*, no. 3, 2000, p. 837.

99 The office of president, scrutineer, and secretary is compulsory for the persons appointed (art. 40, para. 1, Consolidation Law on Elections, approved by d.P.R. 30 March 1957, no. 361). Art. 108 of the Consolidation Text stipulates that those who refuse to take office or are not present when the polling station is opened without a justified reason are subject to a fine of between €309 and €516. The same sanction is provided for members of the polling station office who leave before the end of the electoral operations without a justified reason.

100 In the present case, which occurred during the 1994 general election, the scrutineer was assigned to a polling station set up at the Santa Croce Hospital in Cuneo and not in a school.

The Magistrate's Court of Cuneo (*Pretura*), having jurisdiction, convicted the defendant of the crime of refusing to assume the office of scrutineer without justifiable reason in its judgment 4 April 1996.[101] This verdict was overturned by the Court of Appeal of Turin, judgment 11 February 1998,[102] which instead acquitted the defendant.

Following an application of the Public Prosecutor's Office, the case was brought before the Supreme Court of Cassation, Section III Criminal, which excluded the occurrence of an appropriate cause of justification in judgment, 11 October 1998, no. 10,[103] because in this specific case the service charged to the person was not itself of a religious nature. Consequently, the Court annulled the contested judgment and referred the case back to another section of the Court of Appeal of Turin for a new decision.

A new judicial phase thus opened. In judgment of 28 April 1999, the referring judge ruled in the same sense as the first ruling of the Magistrate's Court of Cuneo and sentenced the defendant.[104]

The never-ending story continued, and the measure was lodged again and brought back to the attention of the Supreme Court of Cassation. The Section IV Criminal, by judgment 1 March 2000, no. 439,[105] stated that the expression of freedom of conscience resulting in a conflict between adherence to the State's principles of *laicità* and the display of religious images on the premises is a justified ground for refusal to attend to the election office of an appointed member. In this way, the Supreme Court of Cassation also invoked the principle of impartiality of public administration from art. 97, para. 1, Const.[106]

The pronouncement stood in contrast to the guidance of the Council of State in opinion no. 63/1988 and inaugurated a strand of jurisprudence that sees the crucifix as an essentially religious symbol, thus diverging from the jurisprudence developed on the point by the High Administrative Court.[107]

101 Decision not available online. From the protagonist of this affair, see M. Montagnana, *Come scrocifiggere lo Stato. Processi, sentenze, polemiche sull'esposizione del simbolo cattolico nelle istituzioni statali italiane*, July 2005, 361 pp., available at www.uaar.it/uaar/campagne/scrocifiggiamo/montagnana/Marcello_Montagnana__Come_scrocifiggere_lo_Stato.pdf.

102 As far as is known, not accessible online.

103 Not available online. For the SCC's most recent pronouncements (starting from 2019), see the *SentencesWeb* portal at www.italgiure.giustizia.it/sncass/.

104 Court of Appeal of Turin, judgment 28 April 1999, also not accessible online.

105 The judgment of the SCC, which annulled the contested ruling without referral, can be accessed via the website www.uaar.it/uaar/campagne/scrocifiggiamo/07.html. For a comment, see N. Recchia, "Il caso Montagnana e l'affermazione del valore della laicità nell'evoluzione della giurisprudenza penale della Corte di cassazione", *Il Diritto ecclesiastico*, no. 4, 2001, p. 262.

106 Art. 97, para. 1, Const., "Public offices are organised according to the provisions of law, so as to ensure the efficiency and impartiality of administration".

107 Contrast also noted by the ECtHR, Grand Chamber, 18 March 2011, *Lautsi and others v. Italy*, para. 68, *supra* para. 2.3.

The interpretation of secularism by the Supreme Court of Cassation was excessively progressive as it effectively grants conscientious objection not through legislation but via a court ruling.[108]

Shortly afterwards, the TAR Lazio, Section I *ter*, judgment 22 May 2002, no. 4558[109] declared a new appeal lodged by the UAAR inadmissible. This appeal attempted to obtain the removal of crucifixes from polling stations before the beginning of voting operations.[110] Regarding the appeal's content, the Court – echoing the reasoning of the defending Ministry of the Interior – reiterated that

> according to the principles established by the Constitution regarding religious freedom, as interpreted by the Constitutional Court, there is neither an obligation nor a prohibition regarding the display of crucifixes in public offices in general.

In the context of polling stations, it is worth mentioning the judgment of the Court of Appeal of Perugia, 10 April 2006,[111] in a case where the appointed president of the polling station removed the crucifix placed in the room used as a polling station and did not replace it despite a request to do so from the Mayor of the Municipality. The Prefect subsequently requested to revoke the polling station president's nomination. However, the Court ruled against the revocation based on the argument that

> the suitability of the election premises to be an absolutely neutral space, thus devoid of symbols that may, in any way, even indirectly and/or unintentionally, create suggestions or influence the electorate.

The Court thus referred to the circumstance that the relevant provision (here the aforementioned Consolidated Law on the Election of the Chamber of Deputies) does not mention the presence of the crucifix among the characteristics that the "election venue" must have.[112] The Court of Appeal also pointed out that the same municipal order requiring the crucifix to be re-affixed was adopted based on r.d. no. 965/1924, which did not appear to be

108 Judgment written by Law and Religion scholar Nicola Colaianni.

109 Viewable at www.giustizia-amministrativa.it/web/guest/dcsnprr as the further rulings of administrative judges cited in the following where not otherwise detailed.

110 The UAAR, which had previously submitted a letter to the Ministry of the Interior on 15 December 2000, requested that appropriate measures be taken to prohibit the display of religious symbols in polling stations prior to the commencement of voting procedures. This letter was followed by a note from the Ministry stating that since the regulations adopted in the years 1924–1928 were still valid, there was no obligation for the public administration to remove the symbols.

This followed the submission of a new UAAR request on 7 February 2001 and a subsequent warning on 10 December 2001.

111 Available at www.uaar.it/uaar/campagne/scrocifiggiamo/52.pdf.

112 Art. 42, Consolidated Election Law.

relevant to the present case, as it relates only to educational establishments, i.e., schools, whereas, as noted above, it concerns polling stations, only incidentally, allocated in classrooms with, however, a completely different function.

In courtrooms, the display of the crucifix is even envisaged in a circular of the Ministry of Justice and Religious Affairs,[113] Division III, 29 May 1926, no. 2134/1867.[114] This circular prescribed the crucifix's presence above the judges' bench, "under our ancient tradition", so that "the venerated symbol may be a solemn admonition of truth and justice".

Once again, we are dealing with a prescription that dates back to the Fascist era – not coincidentally when the Minister in office was Alfredo Rocco, the father of the 1930 Criminal Code that is currently still in force. However, this prescription did not have a regulatory character since it is a mere circular and was binding only for the offices and civil servants to whom it is addressed.

As in the previous case, this dispute underwent several degrees of judgment and jurisdictions.[115] The judge L.T. of the Court of Camerino (MC) refused to hold a hearing because of the presence of the crucifix on 23 October 2003. The refusal was maintained, even though the chief of the Court office had granted permission for the judge to conduct hearings in his personal office or in a crucifix-free courtroom. The charge pertained to the refusal to comply with official acts pursuant to art. 328, para. 1, Criminal Code.[116]

Jurisdiction over the criminal proceedings was assigned to the Court of L'Aquila, which sentenced the defendant to seven months' imprisonment and with a ban from public office for one year by the judgment of 15 December 2005, no. 622.[117] This decision was confirmed by the Court of Appeal of L'Aquila on 23 May 2007.[118]

The Supreme Court of Cassation, Section VI Criminal then annulled without referral the judgment of condemnation in judgment 10 July 2009, no. 28482[119] "because the fact does not exist" since the judge had informed the

113 Jurisdiction later assigned to the Ministry of the Interior by r.d. 20 July 1932, no. 884, "Transfer of Attributions Relating to Religious Affairs to the Ministry of the Interior and Change of Name of the Ministry of Justice".

114 Available at www.uaar.it/uaar/campagne/scrocifiggiamo/03.html.

115 Regarding administrative justice, see TAR Marche, Section I, judgment 22 March 2006, no. 94 (www.uaar.it/uaar/campagne/scrocifiggiamo/51.pdf) declaring the action inadmissible for lack of jurisdiction.

116 Art. 328, Criminal Code, "The public official or the person in charge of a public service, who unduly refuses an act of his office which, for reasons of justice or public safety, or public order or hygiene and health, must be carried out without delay, shall be punished by imprisonment of from six months to two years".

117 Available at www.uaar.it/uaar/campagne/scrocifiggiamo/45.pdf.

118 Judgment unpublished.

119 Accessible at www.uaar.it/uaar/campagne/scrocifiggiamo/tosti/cassazione.pdf. Following the dismissal without referral of the SCC, judgment no. 28482/2009, the same Court

President of the Court of his abstention from the hearings and the President had promptly replaced him.

Thus, the criminal case had not been integrated, and Judge L.T.'s conduct could only be censured in disciplinary proceedings.

From a disciplinary point of view, however, the proceedings before the Superior Council of the Judiciary, led to the suspension of the judge from his office and the reduction of his wage (order 23 November 2006, no. 12).[120]

Given that "no administrative provision may restrict fundamental rights of freedom, outside the spaces that may be allowed by an ordinary law in complying with the Constitution", the Disciplinary Section of the CSM proposed the following in relation to Judge L.T.'s argument concerning the ineffectiveness of the administrative circular of 1926:

> the defendant's argument that the display of the crucifix in courtrooms, as a solemn "admonition of truth and justice", constitutes a use of a religious symbol as a way of pursuing State purposes and, therefore, appears to be in breach of the supreme principle of the secularism of the State. Also persuasive seems to be the assertion that the statement of a religious basis for the duties of truth and justice to which citizens are bound, may provoke in non-believers "disturbances, cases of conscience, conflicts of loyalty between the duties of the citizen and allegiance to his convictions" [. . .] and may therefore infringe the freedom of conscience and religion.[121]

While acknowledging the judge's prerogative to adhere to his own conscience, it is nevertheless noted that

> the exercise of this right cannot be performed in such a manner as to jeopardise the requirements of justice, the fulfilment of which is the purpose of undisputed functional duties – by implementing an obvious form of civil disobedience, which, however, by its very nature must incur the acceptance of the relevant sanction – cannot find recognition by the legal system, within which only the law could permit it.[122]

---

of Appeal of L'Aquila, judgment 15 September 2012, absolved L.T. from the criminal charge with revocation of the sentence inflicted (news available at https://blog.uaar.it/2012/07/06/aquila-corte-appello-assolve-giudice-luigi-tosti/).

120 Disciplinary action brought on 22 September 2005 by the General Prosecutor at the Supreme Court of Cassation for infringement of the duty of fairness, with a request for suspension of the judge's function. Request aimed in concrete terms at having the crucifix removed from all courtrooms or, as an alternative, to also display the *menorah* in courtrooms. This order is available at www.uaar.it/uaar/campagne/scrocifiggiamo/57.pdf.

121 CSM, Disciplinary Section, order no. 12/2006, para. 4.

122 CSM, Disciplinary Section, order no. 12/2006, para. 6.

Subsequently, the CSM, Disciplinary Section, ordered the expulsion of Judge L.T.[123] from the judiciary, holding that the subject of the proceedings was the repeated refusal to hold hearings despite the rules of the service and functional requirements for judicial functions, not the evaluation of the compatibility between the State's principle of secularism and the display of crucifixes in courtrooms.

Judge L.T. complained against this decision before the Supreme Court of Cassation, United Civil Sections. Judgment 14 March 2011, no. 5924,[124] rejected the claim, upholding the approach of the Superior Council of the Judiciary.

Regarding the alleged infringement of the State's principle of secularism (arts. 2, 3, 7, 8, 19, and 20, Const.), the United Civil Sections concluded that

> the presence of the crucifix in courtrooms, regardless of the lawfulness of the regulations providing for it, does not in itself, by the mere fact that it is generally observed, cause an infringement of Dr T.'s subjective right to religious freedom and opinion, which could be challenged only if he were required to exercise jurisdiction under its symbolic protection.[125]

Essentially, the absence of crucifixes in the courtroom where he conducted hearings ensured that there was no infringement of his religious freedom. Moreover, he could not have acted to defend the general interest of *laicità* of the State by protesting the crucifix in other courtrooms because an individual cannot represent diffuse or collective interests in opposition to the relevant institutions except in cases specifically provided for by law. Thus, the decision to withhold the hearing was without justification, and the disciplinary sanction was appropriate.[126]

As mentioned, the display of crucifixes in healthcare facilities differs because of the lack of rules concerning a requirement to display them. Nevertheless, many public hospitals display the crucifix. This practice is sometimes associated with the religious origin of a specific establishment, which may have been consecrated to a saint.[127]

123 CSM, Disciplinary Section, 25 May 2010, no. 88. The headnote of this order is accessible at www.csm.it/web/csm-internet/giurisprudenza-disciplinare/massimario.

124 Accessible at https://giurcost.org/casi_scelti/Cass.sent.5924-2011.htm.

125 SCC, United Civil Section, judgment no. 5924/2011, "*Motivi della decisione*", para. 5.

126 The now ex-magistrate also played a leading role in more recent times – in 2021 – for refusing to witness in the courtroom of Rimini, where the crucifix was displayed (N.A., "Ex Giudice 'Anti Crocifisso' rifiuta di deporre sotto croce", 29 September 2021, available at www.ladige.it/attualita/2021/09/29/ex-giudice-anti-crocifisso-rifiuta-di-deporre-sotto-croce-1.3008190). For examples of the presence of religious symbolism in foreign courts see *infra* para. 2.5.

127 Regarding the religious roots of healthcare, refer to L. Sabolla, *All'origine della cura. Pauper Christi. Assistenza e sanità tra Medioevo ed Età moderna*, Itaca, Castel Bolognese, RA, 2020 *passim* and L. Sabolla, *All'origine della cura. Homo viator. Dall'accoglienza dei primi pellegrini agli Ospedali Maggiori*, Itaca, Castel Bolognese (RA), 2023, *passim*.

However, there was a notable case involving Adel Smith, the same individual implicated in the crucifix incident at the school in Ofena (AQ).[128] After the case at the school but still in 2003, Smith was charged for throwing a crucifix out of a window at San Salvatore Hospital, where his mother was hospitalised. He was handed an eight-month prison sentence by the Court of L'Aquila for vilification of the Catholic religion in early January 2006.[129]

This affair overlaps with another episode dating back to 2001, when Adel Smith was hosted on Bruno Vespa's TV programme *Porta a Porta* on Rai 1, the first channel of the Italian Public Television. Smith declared himself against the presence of crucifixes in classrooms and other public buildings. Additionally, he described this symbol of Christianity as "the cadaver of a naked man affixed to a piece of wood used by the Romans to punish the worst criminals" and lamented its enforcement through outdated rules and regulatory status.[130] These declarations resulted in a charge of offense to a religious denomination by vilification of things,[131] though Smith was later acquitted by the Court of Rome on 5 July 2006.[132]

Another recent case in the healthcare context prompted submission of a query to the Regional Council of Friuli Venezia Giulia. The incident involved the two hospitals of Latisana and Palmanova and stemmed from the removal in the former of several crucifixes that were later found in a wastebasket and in the latter of a Virgin Mary statue. The episode was reported by in-patients and health workers.[133]

An earlier episode occurred at a hospital in Chivasso (Metropolitan City of Turin) where, following the conclusion of renovations, crucifixes were placed in every room[134] on the advice of the General Director of the Local Health Service TO4. The decision was motivated by the assumption that the crucifixes were not new but were merely replacing existing crucifixes that had been damaged by the renovations. This case provoked intense public debate.

128 *Supra*, para. 2.2.

129 Cf. N.A., "Getto crocifisso dalla finestra: (mesi a Smith)", 13 January 2006, available at www.ilgiornale.it/news/gett-crocifisso-finestra-8-mesi-smith.html.

130 N.A., "Crocifisso: Smith citato in giudizio per vilipendio", 31 October 2003, available at www.corriere.it/Primo_Piano/Cronache/2003/10_Ottobre/31/smith.shtml.

131 Art. 404, Criminal Code, as reformulated following the interventions of the Constitutional Court and the Legislator *ex* arts. 7–10 of law 24 February 2006, no. 85 concerning "Amendments to the Criminal Code Regarding Crimes of Opinion", together with the other provisions of Chapter, I, Title IV, Book II.

132 The defence statement is accessible at https://blog.uaar.it/2006/07/06/adel-smith-assolto/.

133 N.A., "Crocifissi rimossi dall'ospedale di Latisana e Palmanova, caso in Regione", 19 June 2024, available at www.friulioggi.it/primo-piano-5/crocifissi-rimossi-ospedale-latisana-palmanova-caso-regione-19-giugno-2024/.

134 News reported by E. Fiore, "'Crocifissi vanno in ogni stanza'. Ma all'ospedale di Chivasso scoppia la polemica", 6 June 2019, available at www.ilgiornale.it/news/cronache/crocefissi-ogni-stanza-all-ospedale-chivasso-scoppia-1706992.

Due to the increasing differences, including religious differences, in health-care users of both hospitals and health centres, there has been growing attention to the problem of accommodating this diversity. This discourse is predicated on the benefits of paying attention not only to the body but also to the spirit, which work in synergy for healing.[135] Studies have considered how to manage this problem[136] and have proposed initiatives such as multi-faith prayer rooms and rooms of silence for hospitals.[137]

2.5 The stance of the other national courts or institutions in similar cases

The presence of the crucifix or other religious symbols in schools or public institutions has been a subject of debate in various cases, including outside of Italy.[138]

State attitudes on this issue are diverse and reflect the approach of single legal systems towards religion and particularly public or institutional expression of religious symbols.[139]

Broadly speaking, the field of jurisprudence, and especially higher courts, is tasked with resolving the many contentious situations involving religious symbols in modern society. Religious symbols are a prevalent concern in various legal systems.[140] Indeed, the presence of similar issues in various national contexts has introduced the expression "judicial globalisation". This expression, first used in American legal doctrine,[141] describes the phenomenon by which

135 G. Boniolo – E. Martinelli (eds.), *La cura del paziente e la diversità spirituale. Per una medicina interculturale*, Mimesis, Milano – Udine, 2024, *passim*.

136 Azienda Sanitaria Locale Roma E. et al., "L'accoglienza delle differenze e specificità culturali e religiose nelle strutture sanitarie ospedaliere e territoriali della Regione Lazio. Raccomandazioni per gli operatori sanitari da parte delle comunità religiose", 14 December 2010, 42 pp., available at https://tavolointerreligioso.org/wp-content/uploads/2015/12/Opuscolo_Santo_Spirito-1.pdf.

See also, e.g. the 4 June 2012 protocol of intent between the San Camillo Forlanini Hospital in Rome and the representatives of seven non-Catholic religious denominations (Islamic Cultural Centre – Great Mosque, Evangelical Churches of Rome, Orthodox Church of Romania, Jewish Community of Rome, Italian Buddhist Institute Soka Gakkai, Italian Buddhist Union, Italian Hinduists). News available at https://tavolointerreligioso.org/progetti/.

137 Such is the case with the prayer rooms at the Santo Spirito and San Camillo Forlanini Hospitals in Rome and the room of silence at the San Giovanni Battista – Molinette Hospital in Turin.

138 On this issue, P. Stanisz – M. Zawiślak – M. Ordon (eds.), *Presence of the Cross in Public Spaces: Experiences of Selected European Countries*, Cambridge Scholar Publishing, Newcastle upon Tyne, 2016, *passim*, esp. R. Torfs, "The Presence of the Cross in Public Spaces from the Perspective of the European Court of Human Rights", p. 1, and G. Feliciani, "The Presence of the Cross in Public Spaces: Italy", p. 111.

139 *Supra* para. 2.1.

140 For a case law search, see the Council of Europe's Codices database (https://codices.coe.int/codices/documents/welcome), which facilitates comparative research, especially in the field of human rights.

141 Theory attributable to A.M. Slaughter, "Judicial Globalisation", *Virginia Journal of International Law*, vol. 40, no. 4, 2000, p. 1103 ff. This concept delineates an area of academic

courts and judges across different countries – especially the highest courts or supranational jurisdictions – increasingly reference, cite, and rely on the decisions of other jurisdictions. This process fosters a more interconnected global legal landscape and influences the development and harmonisation of legal standards worldwide, mainly in the field of human rights.

2.5.1 The European context

Regarding the European context, the issue of displaying the crucifix or other religious symbols in public institutions has arisen in various countries,[142] resulting in a body of legal precedents known to the European Court of Human Rights.[143]

In Switzerland, the Federal Supreme Court, First Public Law Chamber, judgment 26 September 1990,[144] ruled on the claim brought against the decision of the Municipality of Cadro (Canton of Ticino) to display crucifixes in all classrooms. While recognising the cultural and historical value of the crucifix (particularly considering that the cross figures on the federal flag),[145] the Court concluded that its display in elementary school classrooms violates equality of treatment, freedom of belief, and the neutrality of schools.[146] However, the Court noted that its judgment might have been different if it had been ruling on the presence of the crucifix in school premises employed for common use, such as the atrium, corridors, the refectory, or spaces intended for worship or classrooms hosting optional religious teaching. These principles

inquiry that gained prominence in the latter decades of the 20th century, exemplifying a growing fascination with comparative law and transnational jurisprudence. Additionally, please consult A.M. Slaughter, *A New World Order*, Princeton University Press, Princeton – Oxford, 2004, p. 65 ff. and R. Hirshl, *Towards Juristocracy. The Origin and Consequences of the New Constitutionalism*, Harvard University Press, Cambridge – London, 2004, pp. 100 and 169 ff.

142 For an overview, L.P. Vanoni, *Laicità e libertà di educazione. Il crocifisso nelle aule scolastiche in Italia e in Europa*, Giuffrè, Milano 2013, *passim*.

143 Cf. the yet evoked ECtHR, Grand Chamber, judgment 18 March 2011, *Lautsi and others v. Italy*, para. 28.

144 The judgment of the *Tribunale federale, I Corte di diritto pubblico*, can be viewed on the Court's portal at www.bger.ch/it/ under the heading "Main decisions DTF", DTF 116 I 252.

145 The Preamble of the Federal Constitution itself opens with the *invocatio Dei*. Although the Preamble does not have normative value, it nevertheless constitutes a reference to the Christian foundation of the State. The English text of the current Swiss Federal Constitution is available at www.fedlex.admin.ch/eli/cc/1999/404/en.

146 Parallels have been identified by scholars between the *Lautsi I* case and the 1990 Federal Supreme Court decision, as evidenced by S. Mancini, "La supervisione europea presa sul serio: la controversia sul crocifisso tra margine di apprezzamento e ruolo contro-maggioritario delle corti", *Giurisprudenza costituzionale*, 2009, p. 4065, f., and T. Zimmermann, "Le crucifix dans la salle de classe: l'arrêt *Comune di Cadro* revisité à la lumière de l'affaire *Lautsi*", *Praxis Juristische Aktuelle*, 2011, p. 1485.

were later confirmed by the Federal Court, Second Public Law Chamber in judgment 12 November 1997.[147]

The Federal Court, Second Public Law Chamber, judgment of 19 January 1995,[148] also intervened on the presence of crucifixes in public places. While not upholding the complaint on procedural grounds, it is interesting that in this proceeding, the background of the case was the display of crucifixes in courtrooms. The plaintiff-lawyer, who had previously criticised crucifixes,[149] repeated a request for the removal at his own divorce hearing.

More recently, the Council of State of the Republic and Canton of Ticino (the cantonal governing body)[150] with resolution 22 June 2011, no. 3540, rejected the claim of a teacher and confirmed the decisions of the Municipality of Cadro regarding the display of a crucifix in the hall of a municipal school. This resolution became the subject of inquiries.[151]

Spain has also been affected by controversies related to religious symbols in public institutions since the 1990s. The first noteworthy measure is the Constitutional Court, First Room, judgment 6 June 1991, no. 130,[152] regarding the removal of the image of the "Virgin of Wisdom" from the emblem of the University of Valencia, which was created in 1771.

The Constitutional Court deemed the Academic Senate's decision to change the university emblem by eliminating the religious image to be a legitimate exercise of the fundamental right of autonomy. Previous judgments had involved arguments that the presence of the religious reference was not contrary to the principle of the State's secularism based on the secularising nature of the symbol, regardless of its original religious meaning.[153]

147 The ruling of the Federal Court, First Public Law Chamber, related to the wearing of an Islamic headscarf by a (Lucia Dahlab) teacher which was later brought to the attention of the ECtHR can also be viewed on the Court's portal at www.bger.ch/it/, under the heading "DTF main decisions", DTF 123 I 296.

148 Accessible at www.bger.ch/it, under the heading "DTF main decisions", DTF 121 I 42. The decision was made without issuing a ruling on the merits.

149 The lawyer submitted a request on 22 October 1990 to the competent judicial authorities for the immediate removal in all cantonal courts of crucifixes affixed in rooms accessible to the public – i.e. courtrooms and waiting rooms – as well as of crucifixes displayed in offices not accessible to the public unless the officials working there unanimously agreed to their permanence.

150 *Amplius* at www4.ti.ch.

151 The answer of this institution, dated 18 January 2012, is accessible at https://m4.ti.ch/fileadmin/POTERI/GC/allegati/interrogazioni/risposte/pdf/r177.11.pdf. On the issue of minarets cf. *infra* para. 2.5.3.

152 *Tribunal Constitucional, Sala Primera* 6 June 1991, no. 130, available at https://hj.tribunalconstitucional.es/es-ES/Resolucion/Show/1769 through the constitutional case-law search engine (https://hj.tribunalconstitucional.es/es).

153 On the issue of the presence of symbols in the Spanish legal system, see M. Alenda Salinas – M. Pineda Marcos, *El símbolo religioso en el Estado laico español*, Tirant Lo Blanch, Valencia, 2016, *passim*.

In a later example, the Administrative Litigation Court of Valladolid, Section II, judgment 14 November 2008, no. 288,[154] pronounced on a resolution made by the School Board of the *Colegio Público Macías Picabea* in Valladolid. The school had kept religious symbols on display in compliance with parents' requests. A militant association for secular schools (*Asociación Cultural Escuela Laica*) challenged this decision.

The Administrative Court concluded in favour of the removal of the symbols because

> the presence of religious symbols in the classrooms and common areas of the public education centre where children who are in the midst of their personality development are educated undermines fundamental rights enshrined in articles 14 and 16.1 and 3[155]

of the Constitution (i.e. right to religious freedom and prohibition of discrimination). This ruling was then challenged and replaced by the Superior Court of Justice of Castile and Leon, Section III, judgment 14 December 2009, no. 3250.[156] In the judgment, which refers to the *Lautsi I* decision despite noting its incompatibility with the Spanish legal system, the Court of First Instance held that symbols should not be removed in the absence of conflict or when parents have expressly stated their desire for the symbols to be maintained.[157]

Polish jurisprudence has also contended with this topic since the early 1990s. The Constitutional Court ruled on 20 April 1993, no. U 12/32,[158] that an order issued by the Minister of Education on 14 April 1992 providing for the possibility of displaying crucifixes in public school classrooms was compatible with the freedom of conscience and religion and the principle of the separation of Church and State guaranteed by the Polish Constitution since this display was not compulsory.

However, the Polish press has recently reported on guidelines by the Warsaw City Council barring the hanging of crosses or crucifixes on walls and their display on desks in the city's public offices. Civil servants are still allowed to wear crosses or other religious symbols at the workplace. These new rules are part of a broader set of provisions designed to counter discrimination. Officials

154 This judgment of the *Juzgado de lo Contencioso Administrativo de Valladolid*, is available at www.poderjudicial.es.

155 Administrative Litigation Court of Valladolid, Section II, judgment no. 288/2008, "*Fundamentos de derecho*", para. 4.

156 This judgment of the *Tribunal Superior de Justicia de Castilla y León, Sala de lo contencioso-administrativo, Sección Tercera* is also accessible at www.poderjudicial.es.

157 For a comprehensive analysis, see R. Palomino, *La religión en el espacio público: Los símbolos religiosos antes el derecho*, Digital Reasons, Madrid, 2017, *passim*.

158 The judgment of the *Trybunał Konstytucyjny* is accessible at www.saos.org.pl/, the Polish jurisprudence portal.

have also been asked to use gender-neutral language, to address people with their preferred pronouns, and not to discriminate against same-sex couples.[159]

In Romania, case law has also addressed the matter of displaying religious symbols in schools. The High Court of Cassation and Justice's judgment 11 June 2008, no. 2393,[160] annulled the decision of the National Council on Countering Discrimination[161] 21 November 2006, no. 323, which recommended that the Ministry of Education regulate religious symbols in public schools and allow the display of such symbols only during religious instruction or in classrooms intended for religious instruction. Specifically, the Court established that the decision to hang such symbols (in this case religious icons) in educational institutions had to be made by the community of teachers, pupils, and pupils' parents.[162]

A German case, the decision of the First Senate, 16 May 1995, no. 1 BvR 1087/91 (the so-called *Kruzifix I*),[163] decided by the Federal Constitutional Court (the *BundesVerfassungsGericht* hereafter *BVerfG*) of Karlsruhe is particularly interesting.[164]

Although the Bavarian case is among the best known, the Federal Constitutional Court had already made a pronouncement on religious symbols in

159 This news was published on 16 May 2024 by the *Gazeta Wyborcza* newspaper and picked up by the international press. Cf. N.A., "Warsaw Bans Religious Symbols in City Hall and Require Staff to Respect Preferred Pronouns", 16 May 2024, available at https://notesfrompoland.com/2024/05/16/warsaw-bans-display-of-religious-symbols-in-city-hall/.

160 Available at www.scj.ro/736/Cautare-jurisprudenta. For further pronouncements of the *Înalta Curte de Casație și Justiție* see www.scj.ro.

161 *Consiliul Național pentruCombaterea Discriminării* (www.cncd.ro/).

162 On the national debate related to the removal of icons from public schools that sparked harsh reactions from the Romanian Orthodox Church, see G. Horváth – R. Bakó, "Religious Icons in Romanian Schools: Text and Context", *Journal for the Study of Religions and Ideologies*, vol. 8, no. 24, 2009, p. 189; M. Popa – L. Andreescu, "Religion and Education in Romania: Social Mobilization and the 'Shadow' of the European Court of Human Rights", *Politics and Religion*, no. 12, 2019, p. 79 and V. Cretu, "The Presence of Religious Symbols in Romanian Public Schools: Ethical Disputes and Legislative Interpretations", in V. Trif (ed.), *Analyzing Paradigms Used in Education and Educational Psychology*, IGI Global, Hershey, PE, 2020, p. 267.

163 Cf. www.bundesverfassungsgericht.de/DE/Homepage/homepage_node.html where relevant texts are available, in some cases also in English. For the German doctrine, see T. Lock, "Of Crucifixes and Headscarves: Religious Symbols in Germany", in M. Hunter-Henin (ed.), *Law, Religious Freedom and Education*, Ashgate, Farnham and Burlington, 2011, p. 347.

164 At www.bverfg.de/e/rs19950516_1bvr108791.html. First Senate consisting of judges Henschel, Seidl, Grimm, Söllner, Kühling, Seibert, Jaeger, Haas. Cf. The dissenting opinion of Judges Seidl, Söllner and Haas.

See also the reference to the German school prayer case: *BVerfG*, First Senate, decision 16 October 1979, 1BvR no. 647/70 and no. 7/74, instead available at https://original.religlaw.org/docs/German%20School%20Prayer%20Case.pdf. Regarding the expert opinions presented by the German Bishops' Conference, the Evangelical Lutheran Church in Bavaria, the Augsburg League for Spiritual Freedom, and the Free Religious Community of the State of Hesse, see *BVerfG*, First Senate, decision no. 1 BvR 1087/91, para. A, III, 2, 3 and 4.

institutions. Without expressing a judgment on the merits, the First Senate reiterated the following in judgment 17 July 1973, no. 1 BvR 308/69:[165]

> [A]s the Federal Constitutional Court has repeatedly emphasised, the fundamental right of freedom of belief and confession, which is guaranteed as inviolable, is closely related to human dignity as the highest value in the system of fundamental rights and must be interpreted extensively because of its status. [. . .] The right to freedom embodied in it, to remain unchallenged by state constraints in matters of ideology and religion, can justify minority protection even against relatively minor impairments, at least where – as in the area of state jurisdiction – the utilisation of this protection does not conflict with the rights of a majority of the population to exercise their freedom of belief.[166]

Returning to the well-known Bavarian case, the Court ruled that the display of a cross or crucifix in the classroom of a non-denominational State compulsory school infringes Art. 4.1 of the Basic Law.[167] Thus, para. 13(1), sentence 3, of the School Regulations for Elementary Schools in Bavaria (*Schulordnung für die Volksschulen in Bayern*) is incompatible with Art. 4.1. Basic Law and is null and void.[168]

According to the decision,

> the affixing of crosses in classrooms goes beyond the boundary thereby drawn to the religious and philosophical orientation of schools. [. . .] the cross cannot be divested of its specific reference to the beliefs of Christianity and reduced to a general token of the Western cultural tradition. It symbolizes the essential core of the conviction of the Christian faith, which has undoubtedly shaped the Western world in particular in many ways but is certainly not shared by all members of society and is indeed rejected by many in the exercise of their fundamental right under Art. 4(1) Basic Law.[169]

165 Accessible at https://openjur.de/u/270660.html. In this case, it was a Jewish lawyer who complained about the display of the crucifix in a lawsuit before the Düsseldorf Administrative Court.

166 *BVerfG*, First Senate, judgment 17 July 1973, no. 1 BVR 308/69, para 38.

167 Art. 4.1, German Basic Law – *GrundGesezt* (GG): "Freedom of Faith and of Conscience, and Freedom to Profess a Religious or Philosophical Creed, Shall Be Inviolable". English version available at www.bundesregierung.de/breg-en/chancellor/basic-law-470510.

168 Regarding schools, positive and negative religious freedom of students, and the right of parents to give their children the religious or ideological education they consider appropriate, see the two judgments of the *BVerfG*, First Senate, 17 December 1975, 1 BvR 63/68 and 1 BvR 428/69, resp. regarding the *Land* Baden Württemberg (https://openjur.de/u/187796.html) and Bavaria (https://openjur.de/u/209500.html).

169 *BVerfG*, First Senate, decision 16 May 1995, no. 1 BvR 1087/91, para. C, II, 3, (a).

Additionally,

> [I]t symbolizes the salvation of man from original sin brought about through Christ's sacrificial death, but at the same time also Christ's victory over Satan and death and his lordship over the world: suffering and triumph simultaneously.[170]

The decision provoked heartfelt popular protests, which shortly afterwards led to the amendment of the Bavarian Law on Education and Teaching (*Bay EUG*)[171] where art. 7, para. 4 was supplemented with the following: "[I]n view of the historical and cultural character of Bavaria, a cross is placed in every classroom" as "this expresses the will to realise the highest educational objectives of the Constitution based on Christian and Western values and preserving freedom of belief". The provision, which remains in effect,[172] outlines and offers a mechanism for resolving conflicts whereby

> if the attachment of the cross is objected to by the legal guardians for serious and obvious reasons of faith or ideology, the head teacher shall attempt to reach an amicable agreement. If an agreement cannot be reached, he or she shall, after informing the school authority, make an arrangement for the individual case that respects the freedom of belief of the objecting person and brings the religious and ideological convictions of all those affected in the class to a fair balance; the will of the majority shall also be taken into account, as far as possible.

A few years later, the Federal Constitutional Court once again addressed the issue with the so-called *Kruzifix II*.[173] The decision, which does not rule on the merits, rejects the three constitutional complaints lodged against a decision of the Bavarian Constitutional Court on 1 August 1997.[174] More

170 *BVerfG*, First Senate, decision 16 May 1995, no. 1 BvR 1087/91, para. C, II, 2, (b) which recalls the entry "Kreuz" in J. Höfer – K. Rahner (eds.), *Lexikon für Theologie und Kirche*, 2nd ed., Herder Verlag, Freiburg, 1961, vol. 6, col. 605 ff. and E. Fahlbusch et al. (eds.), *Evangelisches Kirchenlexikon*, 3rd ed., Vandenhoek & Ruprecht, Göttingen, 1989, vol. 2, col. 1462 ff.

171 The *Bayerisches Gesetz über das Erziehungs- und Unterrichtswesen* (*BayEUG*) outlines the framework for the entire Bavarian school system, including primary, secondary, and professional education. It has since undergone various amendments to address evolving educational needs and policies.

172 Cf. www.gesetze-bayern.de/Content/Document/BayEUG/true.

173 *BVerfG*, First Senate, decision 27 October 1997, no. 1 BvR 1604/97, no. 1 BvR 1615/97 and no. 1 BvR, 1659/97. Available in German at www.bundesverfassungsgericht.de/SharedDocs/Entscheidungen/DE/1997/10/rk19971027_1bvr160497.html.

174 The judgment of the *Bayerischen Verfassungsgerichtshofs* (BayVerfGH), 1 August 1997, nos. 6-VII-96, 17-VII-96, 1-VII-97 is accessible at www.bayern.verfassungsgerichtshof.de/media/images/bayverfgh/6-vii-96.pdf.

specifically, the Court rejected the complaints of legitimacy lodged against a reform of Bavarian education legislation that allowed the display of the crucifixes in primary school classrooms.

Additionally, the decision of the Administrative Federal Court, Sixth Senate, 21 April 1999, no. 6 C 18.98,[175] also concerned Bavarian legislation. The judgment started from the assumption that the regulation on Bavarian religious instruction, according to which a cross must be placed in all primary schools' classrooms "in view of the historical and cultural character of Bavaria" (art. 7, para. 3, *BayEUG*), is not contrary to the Federal Constitution or the principle of neutrality and negative freedom of religion, since the same regulation (art. 7, para. 3, *BayEUG*, sentences 3 e 4) provides a solution to any conflicts.[176] Provisions on the opposition to the display of crucifixes must be interpreted in compliance with the Federal Constitution. Such opposition must prevail only if it is based on serious and comprehensible grounds, an agreement cannot be reached, and there are no reasonable and non-discriminatory alternatives.[177]

The decision is noteworthy because it is consistent with the established doctrine that recognises the State's obligation to maintain ideological and religious impartiality, a duty that should not be confused with a complete separation of Church and State. This assertion is supported by the same Preamble of the Constitution, which commences with a reminder of the German people's responsibility to both God and humanity.[178]

The German Federal Constitutional Court has also made further rulings regarding religious symbols that are indirectly relevant to this issue.[179]

As elucidated in the following, German jurisprudence will still be summoned to adjudicate issues regarding the exhibition of crucifixes in public institutions.[180]

The final example is an Austrian' case, starting from the Constitutional Court's decision, 9 March 2011, no. G 287/09-25[181] (published just a few days before the so-called *Lautsi II* and therefore not considered by the *Grand*

175 In German at https://research.wolterskluwer-online.de/document/b496481e-fa71-4fb3-ae4f-c56a56801cc5.

176 *BverwG*, Sixth Senate, decision no. 6 C 18.98, para. II. 1.

177 *BverwG*, Sixth Senate, decision no. 6 C 18.98, para. II. 2.

178 *BverwG*, Sixth Senate, decision no. 6 C 18.98, para. II. 2, (aa).

179 Cf. *BVerfG*, First Senate, decision 16 April 1999, no. 1 BvR 622/99 and *BVerfG*, First Senate, 24 January 2001, no. 1 BvR 2623/95 and 1 BvR 622/99. The pronouncements originate from the authorisation refusal for the television broadcaster NTV to attend and record the hearing of the Federal Administrative Court, Sixth Senate on 21 April 1999 concerning the affixing of crucifixes in Bavarian schools. Both pronouncements are available in German at the *BVerfG* website.

180 *Infra* para. 4.5.

181 *VerfassungsGerichtsHof* (*VfGH*), decision 9 March 2011, no. G 287/09-25, available at www.vfgh.gv.at/downloads/VfGH_G_287-09_Noe_KindergartenG.pdf. For an analysis V. Trofaier-Leskovar Valerie, "The Crucifix in the Kindergarten", *Vienna Journal on International Constitutional Law*, vol. 5, no. 2, 2011, p. 246 ff.

Chamber), concerning art. 12, para. 2, of the Lower Austria Kindergarten Law 2006, no. 5060.[182] This is the provision requiring mandatory display of a cross in classrooms with a majority of Christian pupils.[183] The Court dismissed objections of unconstitutionality based on a violation of art. 2 of Protocol no. 1 and art. 9 of the ECHR.[184] Specifically, the Court contended that there is no basis in the law to suggest that placing the cross should sway preschool children in a specific religious direction.[185]

For the Court, the cross – aside from being a religious symbol of Christian churches – "has undoubtedly become a symbol of Western intellectual history".[186] However, this does not signify that the legislator intended to express a preference for a particular religion or even a religious belief within the constitutional context in which the contested rules are to be assessed in their totality.[187]

Indeed,

> in a system of state relationships such as the Austrian one, characterised by the principle of separation of church and state, an interpretation of the crucifix symbol as an expression of a state religion is excluded from the beginning.[188]

Thus,

> the legal obligation to display a cross in kindergarten classrooms cannot therefore be seen as a declaration by the State to express its preference for a particular religious belief.[189]

182 Bearing in mind also that, according to art. 3, para. 1, kindergarten may provide a fundamental contribution to the religious and ethical education of the children. For the text of the *NÖ Kindergartengesetz 2006*, see the Austrian Law Portal at www.ris.bka.gv.at/Dokumente/LgblNO/LRNI_2012061/LRNI_2012061.pdf.

183 Article 12 ("Equipments"), para. 2, "A cross must be placed in all kindergarten classrooms where the majority of children belong to the Christian religious faith". The rule continues to be enforced in the present day. In accordance with art. 29, "the kindergarten management must grant the legally recognised churches and religious societies the religion education of the children of their denomination [. . .] to a maximum total of one hour per week".

184 In Austria, according to the Federal Constitutional Law of 4 March 1964, available at www.ris.bka.gv.at/Dokumente/BgblPdf/1964_59_0/1964_59_0.pdf, the ECHR and its additional protocols have constitutional force and can be invoked directly before Austrian courts, including the Constitutional Court.

Nevertheless, freedom of belief and conscience was already recognised under art. 14, Fundamental Law on the General Rights of Citizens, 21 December 1867, being incorporated into the Federal Constitution (B-VG) through the reference in art. 149.

185 *VfGH*, decision no. G 287/09-25, para. 65.

186 *VfGH*, decision no. G 287/09-25, para. 66.

187 *VfGH*, decision no. G 287/09-25, para. 66.

188 *VfGH*, decision no. G 287/09-25, para. 69.

189 *VfGH*, decision no. G 287/09-25, para. 72.

Moreover, "the placement of crosses in kindergartens (as well as schools) cannot be seen as a means of indoctrination or proselytising".[190]

2.5.2 *Further foreign legal rulings concerning statues, crosses, and other religious symbols*

At this point, we consider cases of the display of religious symbols in public space in other legal orders where the principle of secularism is more decisively applied. This discussion is broken down according to the specificities of each system.

The presence of an explicit prohibition to affix any religious sign or symbol on public buildings or in any public space is a condition[191] of French law under art. 28 of the law on separation of Church and State. Despite this express prohibition, there have been numerous disputes, including recent cases decided by the French Council of State. In this regard, we consider the Council of State, III and VIII Chambers United, judgment of 25 October 2017, no. 396990. This judgment originated from a complaint by a local federation of free thought concerning a municipal council's placement of a statue depicting John Paul II in a square dedicated to him. In this decision,

> the Council of State makes a distinction between the statue – gift of a Russian sculptor – and its placement under another structure constituted by an arch, surmounted by a cross. Excluding the relevance of certain proposed arguments – such as the artwork character of the set of the structure or the theory that the cross would constitute the expression of a strong local Catholic tradition – the Council of Stale only orders the removal of the cross, which the character of a sign or religious emblem, prohibited by the 1905 Act, must be recognized.[192]

A more recent affair concerned a statue of the Virgin Mary placed at an intersection in the French town of La Flotte, overlooking the Atlantic Ocean. This statue was produced after the Second World War to fulfil a vow and initially positioned on a plot of land belonging to the Diocese.

Following roadworks, the city council decided in 1986 to place it on public property on Avenue on 8 May 1945, the date France celebrates the end of World War II. Damaged in a car accident on 17 May 2020, the municipality reinstalled a copy on 22 December of the same year. An association in defence of secularism (the *Fédération départementale de la libre pensée*) then lodged a complaint to the Administrative Court of Poitiers, Section II, invoking

190 *VfGH*, decision no. G 287/09-25, para. 75.
191 *Supra* para. 2.1, nt. 13.
192 M.C. Ivaldi, "The Meaning of 'Religion' in French Case Law", p. 133.

art. 28, *loi séparation*, to request its removal. In decision 3 March 2022, no. 2100952,[193] the Court ordered its removal.

This ruling was confirmed by the Administrative Court of Appel of Bordeaux, Chamber I, 2 January 2023, no. 22BX01113,[194] and by the Council of State, Chamber VIII, 18 October 2023, no. 472088,[195] which declared the application of the municipality of La Flotte as inadmissible. The statue was removed on 30 October 2023.

On 7 June 2024, the mayor – who frequently spoke of *cancel culture* – placed the restored original statue a few metres behind the original setting on private property, which had been purchased with the support of an association set up precisely for the aim of preserving the memorial.[196] In brief, to reconcile tradition with legal precepts that do not allow the affixing of symbols, the community intervened, devising contrivances, as happens in other cases overseas.

At least one similar dispute has also occurred in Italy. The conflict concerned the erection of a statue of the Virgin Mary in the atrium of the Municipality of Paternò (CT), a building where other religious images were already present. What was contested by an employee of the institution – a traffic policeman – was not only the physical presence of the Catholic symbols but also the repeated prayers held under the statue itself.[197] Both the repeated instances and the lawsuit against the Municipality will fail to yield the desired outcome by the applicant.[198]

In the United States, jurisprudence has also often had to decide issues concerning the placement of religious symbols in public spaces given the First Amendment's principle of separation.[199] This has occurred both in

193 Accessible at https://poitiers.tribunal-administratif.fr/Media/mediatheque-ta-poitiers/import/ta86-2100952-statue-vierge.

194 Available on the French legal portal at www.legifrance.gouv.fr.

195 Viewable on the *Ariane Web* at www.conseil-etat.fr/decisions-de-justice/jurisprudence/rechercher-une-decision-arianeweb as it is for the institution's other pronouncements as well. Regarding the opinions delivered by the CE in the exercise of its consultative competence, see *Consilia Web*, available at www.conseil-etat.fr/avis-consultatifs/rechercher-un-avis-consiliaweb.

196 Cf. Cf. F. Padoan, "Après plusieurs années de polémiques, la Vierge de la Flotte-en-Ré, sur l'île de Ré, a retrouvé sa place", 8 June 2024, available at https://france3-regions.francetvinfo.fr/nouvelle-aquitaine/charente-maritime/ile-de-re/apres-plusieurs-annees-de-polemique-la-vierge-de-la-flotte-en-re-sur-l-ile-de-re-a-retrouve-sa-place-2983535.html, where there is also a photo of the new location.

197 The entire affair, dating back to 2007, is reconstructed on the UAAR website under the voice "legal initiatives", available at www.uaar.it/uaar/iniziative-legali/#22.

198 Lastly, see SCC, United Civil Sections, order 7 July 2009, no. 17789, available at www.uaar.it/uaar/campagne/scrocifiggiamo/galvagno/cassazione.pdf, declaring the inadmissibility of the application on procedural grounds.

199 For the annotated text of the Constitution, see https://constitution.congress.gov/. For Italy, among the first to study US separatism, see F. Onida, *Uguaglianza e libertà religiosa nel separatismo statunitense*, Giuffrè, Milano, 1970, *passim*. For US, see M.P. Strasser, *Free*

relation to the display of crosses and the Ten Commandments[200] or other symbols.[201]

One case involving the cross, Supreme Court, judgment 29 June 1995, *Capitol Square Review and Advisory Board v. Pinette*.[202] is particularly significant due to its underlying political implications. The case originated from the prohibition by a state agency that manages an area near the Capitol in Columbus, Ohio to display a cross at the request of the Ku Klux Klan during the Christmas holidays. The First Amendment's freedom of speech clause is what is claimed to have been violated in this case.

The Court began by acknowledging that the square has historically been regarded as a public forum, and the requested religious display was purely private and therefore did not violate the Establishment Clause. Consequently, the act of denying installation constitutes a breach of the First Amendment.

However, the most significant case concerning this symbol in public space is the famous affair concerning the 27-metre white cross erected on Mount Soledad as a memorial to soldiers who died in the Korean War, which was originally placed in a public park located near San Diego, California.

The first legal action, initiated by an atheist veteran, occurred in 1989. A series of cases ensued, reaching a climax with the Ninth Circuit, judgment 4 January 2011, *Trunk v. City of San Diego*,[203] which pronounced the cross as a distinct and unconstitutional Christian symbol.

The Supreme Court, in the subsequent hearing of the lawsuit, decided to deny the review.[204] However, as in the French case with the Statue of the Virgin Mary in La Flotte, the order to remove the cross was obviated through the sale of the property to the Mount Soledad Memorial Association. This sale was allowed by the US Congress in 2014 and finalised in 2015.

Exercise of Religion and the United States Constitution. The Supreme Courts's Challenge, Routledge, Abingdon – New York, 2018, *passim*.

200 Regarding this subject, with a specific emphasis on the legal system in the United States, see M. Madera, "A Brief Introduction to the Religious Symbols Debate in Italy and the United States", in S. Ferrari – R. Cristofori (eds.), *Law and Religion in the 21st Century. Relations between States and Religious Communities*, Routledge, Abingdon – New York, 2010, p. 305; T.C. Berg, "Can State-Sponsored Religious Symbols Promote Religious Liberty", *Journal of Catholic Legal Studies*, vol. 52, no. 1&2, 2014, p. 23; F.M. Gedicks – P. Annicchino, "Cross, Crucifix, Culture: An Approach to the Constitutional Meaning of Confessional Symbols", *First Amendment Law Review*, vol. 13, no. 1, 2014, p. 71; M.L. Movsesian, "Crosses and Culture: State-Sponsored Religious Displays in the US and Europe", *Oxford Journal of Law and Religion*, vol. 1, no. 2, 2012, p. 338.

201 For an examination of the issue regarding the public display of cribs, see *infra* para. 4.2.

202 515 U.S. 733 (1995), available at www.law.cornell.edu/supct/html/94-780.ZO.html the Legal Information Institute of the Cornell Law School.

203 660 F.3d 1091 (9th Cir, 2011), available at www.justice.gov/sites/default/files/osg/briefs/2011/01/01/2011-1115.pet.aa.pdf.

204 Supreme Court, judgment 25 June 2012, *Mount Soledad Memorial Association v. Trunk*, 567 U.S. 944 (2012), available at https://caselaw.findlaw.com/court/us-supreme-court/11-998-nr1.html.

However, most of the relevant decisions involve other symbols besides the cross, especially representations of the Ten Commandments. The Supreme Court has addressed this issue since the 1980s, beginning with the judgment of 17 November 1980, *Stone v. Graham*.[205] In this case, it ruled that a Kentucky law requiring the display of the Ten Commandments in public schools was unconstitutional due to violating the Establishment Clause.

Nevertheless, the display of the Ten Commandments has received different assessments depending on the context of the display. In the 27 June 2005 Supreme Court decision in *Van Orden v. Perry*,[206] the Supreme Court declared the display of a Ten Commandments monument installed near a government building[207] constitutional because of its cultural and historical value.

A different approach was adopted when the Ten Commandments were displayed in courtrooms, per *McCreary County, Kentucky et al. v. American Civil Liberty Union of Kentucky et al.* of 27 June 2005.[208] In this case, the Court concluded that placing the Ten Commandments in this context had the effect of promoting a specific religious view due to the symbol's predominantly religious purpose.

With the judgment 25 February 2009, *Pleasant Grove City v. Summum*,[209] the Supreme Court once again ruled on the display of the Ten Commandments, this time regarding their erection in a public park. In this case, the dispute did not concern the request to remove the religious symbol but a demand by the Summum Church[210] to add another monument. This request was rejected by the city authority.

The Court unanimously concluded that Pleasant Grove City did not violate the First Amendment by granting local authorities' discretion in the selection of monuments or displays because permanent monuments are a form of government speech immune from First Amendment review.

In summary, these cases indicate that the Supreme Court first considers the context in which the symbol is displayed – institutional (as with schools or courtrooms) or in a public space (the grounds of the Texas Capitol or an urban park). Second, the Supreme Court attributes different values to the display depending on whether it has a recognisable religious intention (prohibited) or represents the value (historical and cultural) of the symbol or is the result of a choice of a form of governmental expression.

205 449 U.S. 39 (1980), available at https://caselaw.findlaw.com/court/us-supreme-court/449/39.html.

206 545 U.S. 677 (2005), available at www.law.cornell.edu/supct/html/03-1500.ZC2.html and https://caselaw.findlaw.com/court/us-supreme-court/545/677.html.

207 Located on grounds owned by the Texas State Capitol.

208 545 U.S. 344 (2005), accessible at www.law.cornell.edu/supct/html/03-1693.ZS.html.

209 555 U.S. 460 (2009), available at https://caselaw.findlaw.com/court/us-supreme-court/555/460.html.

210 The stone monument housed the "Seven Aphorisms of Summum" and was of comparable size to the Ten Commandments monument in Pleasant Grove City Park.

A last case worthy of mention concerns the reciting of the Pledge of Allegiance in public schools and specifically the phrase "Under God" inserted by the US Congress in 1954. A case was brought by the atheist father of a student and decided by the Supreme Court in judgment 14 June 2004 *Elk Grove Unified School District et al. v. Newdow et al.*[211] However, this was a purely procedural decision as the Court avoided ruling on the merits by dismissing the father's standing to bring the case. The Court cited that he did not have full legal guardianship of his daughter and that the child's mother had disagreed with Newdow's action.[212]

Remaining within the North American context, Supreme Court of Canada judgment 15 April 2015, *Mouvement laïque québécois v. Saguenay (City)*, no. 35496, deals with the setting of religious statues and crosses and especially the recitation of prayers.[213] The City Council of Saguenay housed a Sacred Heart statue fitted with a votive light and a crucifix on two different premises. An atheist citizen raised a complaint regarding the practice of starting every council meeting with the sign of the cross and the recital of a prayer. The Supreme Court unanimously concluded that the prayer breached the principle of religious neutrality of the State and resulted in discriminatory interference with the freedom of conscience and religion of the plaintiff.

South America has also witnessed several interesting cases. The Constitutional Court of Peru's judgment 22 March 2011, no. 06111–2009,[214] imposed the removal of symbols of the Catholic religion, such as the Bible or

211 542 U.S. 1 (2004), available at www.law.cornell.edu/supct/html/02-1624.ZS.html and https://caselaw.findlaw.com/court/us-supreme-court/542/1.html.

For the Italian doctrine, see A. Morelli, "Il giuramento di fedeltà alla bandiera: 'deismo cerimoniale' o violazione della *establishment clause*? Una complessa (e irrisolta) questione al vaglio della Corte Suprema statunitense", *Diritto pubblico comparato ed europeo*, no. 1, 2005, p. 281.

Regarding the exhibition of the manger in the public space in the USA, see *infra* para. 4.2.

212 For an example of legislation endorsing the Ten Commandments and the Pledge of Allegiance, see the North Dakota case represented by Senate Bill 2308 to amend the State's Century Code, presented on 5 January 2021, available at https://legiscan.com/ND/text/SB2308/2021 and passed on 19 April 2021, available at https://ndlegis.gov/cencode/t15-1c09.pdf. Under the approved legislation, the board of a school district may authorise "schools within the district to display the Ten Commandments with a display of other historical documents in the school and in a classroom" and "to allow students to recite the Pledge of Allegiance" (2 subsections added to 15.1-09-33). At the same time, there is immunity from liability "for damages resulting from a school's decision to display the Ten Commandments or to allow students to recite the Pledge of Allegiance" (section added to 15.1-09-33.5).

Even more recently, see the Louisiana law HB 71 passed on 19 June 2024, available at https://legiscan.com/LA/text/HB71/id/2978627. This law mandates the display of the Ten Commandments in all schools according to a specific text, determined by state legislation.

213 Viewable on the Supreme Court database at https://decisions.scc-csc.ca/scc-csc/scc-csc/en/item/15288/index.do.

214 The judgment of the *Tribunal Costitucional en sesión de Pleno Jurisdiccional* is accessible at https://tc.gob.pe/jurisprudencia/2011/06111-2009-AA.pdf. Concerning the neutrality of Italian courtrooms, see *supra* para. 2.4.

the crucifix, in all courtrooms and magistrates' offices nationwide because of infringement of the principle of equality without distinction of religion. It also barred proceedings or testimony before the judiciary from asking about the defendant's or plaintiff's religion.[215] In this ruling the Court considers the first request unfounded and the second well founded.[216]

Regarding the first hypothesis, the Court argued that

> the mere presence of a crucifix or a bible in an office or a courtroom does not oblige anyone to act against their convictions. Nor can it be argued that the presence of such symbols gives rise to an obligation (of adoration or veneration, for example) by the plaintiff, the fulfilment of which affects his conscience and could give rise to a conscientious objection.[217]

Similarly, there is no violation of

> the right not to be discriminated against on the grounds of religion, as the presence of such religious symbols in a public place does not determine an unjustified difference in the treatment of the applicant, but rather the presence of said symbols responds to the influence of the Catholic Church in the historical, cultural and moral formation of Peru that the Constitution recognises in its article 50, and this does not mean, as has already been shown, any impact on the applicant's religious freedom.[218]

Another noteworthy case is the Constitutional Court of Colombia's judgment 1 December 2023, no. T-530/23,[219] concerning the display of a statue of Our Lady of Mount Carmel on the first floor of a public building.[220] The

215 On the national law on religion, see Perù, Ministerio de Justicia y Derechos Humanos, *Derecho a la libertad religiosa en el Perù: normativa y jurisprudencia*, Sistema peruano de información juridica, Lima, 2019, p. 1 ff., also available online at https://spijweb.minjus.gob.pe.

216 Cf. *Tribunal Constitucional*, judgment no. 06111–2009, para. 63, in which the Court discussed the common (unregulated) practice of judicial authorities asking for one's religion. This practice was deemed invasive of religious freedom and information and irrelevant to the aim of the criminal trial or the administration of justice, except for the cases provided for in para. 66 or regarding crimes linked to terrorism of a religious nature.

217 *Tribunal Constitucional*, judgment no. 06111–2009, para. 45.

218 *Tribunal Constitucional*, judgment no. 06111–2009, para. 47. Pursuant to art. 50 of the Peruvian Constitution, "within an independent and autonomous system, the State recognizes the Catholic Church as an important element in the historical, cultural, and moral formation of Peru, and lends the church its cooperation. The State respects other denominations and may establish forms of collaboration with them", available at www.constituteproject.org/constitution/Peru_2021.

219 *Corte constitucional, Sala Quinta de Revisión*, judgment 1 December 2023, no. T-530/23, accessible at www.corteconstitucional.gov.co/Relatoria/2023/T-530-23.htm.

220 In this case, the Directorate of Transit and Transport of the City of Floridablanca. In Colombia, *Our Lady of Mount Carmel* is the patron saint of drivers.

Court addressed two complaints. The first related to the material presence of the statue inside the public building, while the second related to the celebration of religious rites and changes to the work schedule.

The Court retraces its constitutional history, highlighting how the 1991 Constitution abandoned the confessional approach to the Catholic religion followed in the fundamental charter of 1886. Analogous to what has happened in Italy, the Court outlined the model of the secular State characterised by the separation between State and Church:

> from a systematic understanding of the values, principles and rights embodied in the Constitution, which recognises the pluralistic nature of the welfare state under the rule of law (Articles 1 and 7 of the Constitution), excludes confessionism and enshrines freedom of religion and worship and the equal treatment of all denominations and churches (Article 19 of the Constitution).[221]

Nevertheless,

> the duty of neutrality does not imply a total isolation of religion from the interests of the State, but rather that the activities carried out by public authorities in religious matters have a (secular) aim or aim that does not disregard the separation between the Churches and the State, as well as religious pluralism and the equality of all faiths before the State and the law.[222]

Accordingly,

> the State is bound to respect the duty of neutrality, which means that its actions must have a secular purpose, and forbids its institutions, inter alia, to formally and explicitly identify themselves with a church or religion, to perform official acts of adherence, even symbolic, to a particular creed or to make decisions with a religious purpose.[223]

Regarding civil servants,

> on the one hand, they shall preserve the fullness of their freedom of religion and worship and, on the other hand, they shall perform their constitutional duties with prudence, respect and by abstaining from

221 *Corte constitucional*, judgment no T-530-23, paras. 77 and 78–79. The English version of the Colombian Constitution can be accessed at www.corteconstitucional.gov.co/english/Constitucio%CC%81n%20en%20Ingle%CC%81s.pdf.

222 *Corte constitucional*, judgment no. T-530-23, para. 80. For a list of previous proceedings rendered by the Court on secularism, see para. 82.

223 *Corte constitucional*, judgment no T-530-23, para. 83.

> associating any of their public functions or activities with a religion or belief, so that the exercise of these duties does not interfere with the neutrality that the State must maintain in religious matters and involve the public in the religious sphere.[224]

The Court concluded by demanding the removal of the statue and ordering the Directorate of Traffic and Transport to abstain from repeating actions in which it adopts institutional decisions with a religious purpose, identifies with or adheres to a specific religion, or promotes the practice of a particular religion. In the exercise of its official functions, it must respect the duty of neutrality in religious matters in the terms defined by constitutional case law.

2.5.3 *Notes on the theme of preserving the majority religious landscape*

Before closing this overview, we consider another issue concerning religious symbols that do not belong to the traditional religion of the majority. In this context, we refer to those architectonic elements of a symbolical nature that sometimes identify the places of worship of minority religious denominations.

In select European countries, efforts have been made to discourage the placement of symbols, such as minarets, that could potentially impact the established religious landscape. Conversely, in Italy, as we later observe,[225] the question has been posed in completely different terms, encompassing the existence of places of worship.

This issue arose in Switzerland and Austria in relation to minarets.

In Switzerland, there was a referendum aimed at prohibiting the construction of new minarets based on considerations that included concerns about the spread of political Islam and cultural integration. The referendum, which was held on 29 November 2009, resulted in a preponderance of votes in favour of introducing the prohibition.[226] This outcome piqued the interest of law scholars internationally.[227]

The ban, which did not extend to the construction of new mosques, was included in art. 72, para. 3 of the Swiss Constitution.[228]

224 *Corte constitucional*, judgment no T-530-23, para 95.

225 *Infra* para. 4.3.

226 Incorporated into the Constitution by federal decree 6 May 2010, available at www.fedlex.admin.ch/eli/oc/2010/293/it.

227 M. Stüssi, "Banning of Minarets: Adressing the Validity of a Controversial Swiss Popular Initiative", *Religion & Human Rights*, vol. 3, no. 2, 2008, p. 135 and V. Pacillo, "Stopp Minarett? The Controversy Over the Building of Minarets in Switzerland: Religious Freedom versus Collective Identity", in Silvio Ferrari – Sabrina Pastorelli (eds.), *Religion in Public Space. A European Perspective*, Routledge, Abingdon – New York, 2012, p. 337.

228 As a result of the amendment, the provision now reads: art. 72 ("Church and State") – "1. The regulation of the relationship between the church and the state is the responsibility of the Cantons. 2. The Confederation and the Cantons may within the scope of their powers

A further referendum – again concerning Islam – occurred just over a decade later. The vote took place on 7 March 2021 and sought a ban on face coverings in public spaces in the Federal Constitution. Following the narrowly positive results,[229] the Swiss Federal Constitution introduced the art. 10 heading "Ban on covering the face", which states:

1. No person may cover their face in public spaces or in places that are accessible to the public or where services are offered to anyone wishing to partake of them; the ban does not apply to places of worship.
2. No person may force another person to cover their face on the grounds of their sex.
3. The law shall provide for exceptions. These may only be justified on the grounds of health, safety, weather conditions or local custom.[230]

Austria experienced similar controversies regarding the construction of mosques with minarets around the same period, as seen in the well-known cases associated with the towns of Telfs in Tyrol and Bad Vöslau in Lower Austria.[231]

In 2008, the Austrian *Länder* of Carinthia[232] and Vorarlberg saw the introduction of building regulations which required special approval for any "unusual" buildings, effectively making it more difficult to construct mosques and minarets per the concept of *Heimat.* This is a difficult-to-translate term as it denotes a complex and multifaceted concept that transcends the simple idea of home or homeland. *Heimat* is intimately tied to the identity, history, and culture of an individual or community, and the religious factor also holds a special place within this dynamic.[233]

---

take measures to preserve public peace between the members of different religious communities. 3. The construction of minarets is prohibited".

229 According to official sources, the measure was approved with a majority of 51.2% to 48.8%.

230 Regarding the topic of the *burqa* and *niqab*, see *infra* paras. 3.2. and 3.5.

231 These construction plans were preceded by the building of the mosque in the capital Vienna in 1979.

232 In this *Land*, a mosque was nevertheless inaugurated in Klagenfurt in 2021, although without a minaret.

233 Cf. V. Pacillo, "'Die religiöse Heimat'. Il divieto di edificazione di minareti in Svizzera ed Austria", *Quaderni di diritto e politica ecclesiastica*, no. 1, 2010, p. 199.

3 Insights into the issue of religious symbols worn by believers

Summary: 3.1. The wearing of religious symbols by believers – 3.2. The *burqa* or *niqab* in the public space – 3.3. The covered head in courtrooms – 3.4. The case of the Sikh *kirpan* – 3.5. The French approach to the wearing of religious symbols – 3.5.1. *The duty of neutrality for public and private employees*

3.1 The wearing of religious symbols by believers

This issue has mainly emerged as a result of the migratory phenomena (including economic migrants, asylum seekers, and refugees) that have introduced individuals belonging to non-local cultural and religious traditions into Italy.

Generally, the wearing of religious symbols by individuals – even if they are public officials or are responsible for public services – does not give cause significant controversy in Italy.[1] In full observance of religious freedom, the current legal framework allows religious symbols to be worn, regardless of the symbol itself (cross, Star of David, hand of Fatima, etc.), the person wearing it (including public employees), and the place where it is worn (e.g. schools or other public places).

The Italian principle of *laicità* is not presumed to be violated through the use of religious symbols by public officials, who must perform the functions entrusted to them regardless of their convictions (i.e. in full compliance with the principle of impartiality of the public administration, pursuant art. 97, para. 2, Const.).[2] Public officials must exercise their functions independently of their religious convictions, except in cases of conscientious objection recognised by law.[3]

1 In general, see S. Pastorelli, "Religious Dress Code: The Italian Case", in S. Ferrari – S. Pastorelli (eds.), *Religion in Public Space. A European Perspective*, Routledge, Abingdon – New York, 2012, p. 2.

2 Art. 97, para. 2, Const.: "Public administrative offices shall be organised according to the provisions of law, so as to ensure the efficiency and impartiality of the administration".

3 As is the case with doctors and health personnel with respect to abortion practices or those relating to medically assisted procreation.

DOI: 10.4324/9780429242953-4

The principle of *laicità* within the Italian constitutional jurisprudence[4] demonstrates a tendency to support the religious phenomena of different faiths.

As a result, the act of wearing a cross or crucifix, whether by public officials or individuals responsible for public services or in private workplaces, has not caused any controversy. This differs significantly from other national contexts and the sphere of supranational legal jurisdiction.[5]

With regards to identity documents, there are various ministerial circulars that allow for the inclusion of veils and religious head coverings as long as they do not hinder identification.[6] This is the case with the national identity card[7] and driving licences.[8] Nonetheless, some cases have made headlines and have led to institutional or jurisprudential interventions.

The wearing of the hijab is not forbidden in Italy. However, local authorities (especially in Northern Italy) have sometimes used their powers to penalise, for example, the use of the *burqa* and *niqab*, based on supposed reasons of protecting public order. Yet this assessment does not pertain to local authorities since the matter of rights and freedoms remains within the competence of the national legislator under art. 117, para. 2, (m), Const.

In other cases, good administrative practices have offered solutions to specific situations, as in the case of the Sikh ritual knife.[9]

3.2 The *burka* or *niqab* in the public space

Italy has not adopted a general ban on the full veil, although in some parts of the country local authorities have attempted to introduce it or have *de facto* introduced it.[10] The *niqab* is a veil covering a woman's full body, including the face, leaving only the eyes uncovered. The *burqa* is a women's garment

4 *Supra* para. 1.4.

5 We refer especially to the jurisprudence of the European Court of Human Rights and the extensive rulings of the Court of Justice of the European Union on religious symbols worn by believers in the workplace. *Amplius infra* subpara. 3.5.1.

6 This is, however, a possibility that has always been recognised for Catholic nuns.

7 As exemplified by the Ministry of the Interior in its circular 15 March 1995, no. 4, "Issuance of identity cards to citizens professing religious cults other than the Catholic one – use of headgear" (www.immigrazione.biz/circolare.php?id=871) with respect to the turban or veil, which are authorised on condition that facial features are clearly visible. For an extension of this possibility to residence permits, see from the Ministry of the Interior's subsequent circular 24 July 2000, no. 300, "Measures to Prevent the Use in Public of Garments Capable of Disguising the Features of the Persons Wearing Them", available at www.immigrazione.biz/circolare.php?id=870.

8 In this regard, see the recent circular of the Ministry of Infrastructure and Transport, 20 October 2016, no. 23176, "Photographs to Be Affixed to the Driving Licence", available at www.immigrazione.biz/circolare.php?id=1031.

9 *Infra* para. 3.4.

10 On this topic, see A. Ferrari Alessandro, "A Besieged Right: Religious Freedom and the Italian War on the Burqa and the Niqab", in A. Ferrari – S. Pastorelli (eds.), *The burqa Affair Across Europe Between Public and Private Space*, Routledge, Abingdon – New York, 2013, p. 37 ff.

that completely conceals the body, including the head, with a fabric grid over the eye area that allows the woman to see. The wearing of these garments is expressly forbidden by law in certain countries, such as France.[11]

Current Italian legislation prohibits the use of helmets, clothing, or other accessories that make it difficult, without legitimate reason, to be identified in public places within the meaning of art. 5, law 22 May 1975, no. 152, "Provisions for the protection of public order". Art. 5 also totally prohibits the aforementioned garments at events taking place in public places or that are open to the public, with the exception of sports events.

However, several mayors in Northern Italy imposed a ban on any headwear or clothing that makes identification difficult without a legitimate reason, though these measures were subsequently annulled by the competent prefects.[12] For example, the ordinance issued by the Mayor of Azzano Decimo on 27 July 2004[13] was annulled by the Prefect and challenged before the TAR Friuli Venezia Giulia, decree 16 October 2006, no. 645,[14] and then referred to the Council of State.

The Council of State, Section VI, judgment 19 June 2008, no. 3076, considered religious or cultural character a justified reason for wearing the *niqab*, *burqa*, or other types of Islamic veil that cover the face. However, the Council of State reiterated that the ban on wearing clothing that prevents identification is absolute in the case of events that take place in a public place or are open to the public.[15]

In this regard, paragraph 26 of the Charter of Values, Citizenship and Integration (adopted by the Ministry of the Interior on 23 April 2007)[16] provides that

> in Italy, there are no restrictions on people's attire, as long as it is chosen freely and is not detrimental to their dignity. It is not acceptable to cover the face because this impedes the person's recognition and hinders establishing relations with others.

However, this provision is contained in a document that has the value of a simple general directive for the Interior Administration, and it has no binding force.

11 *Infra* para. 3.5. Cf. R. Vázquez Gómez, "Religious Freedom and the Burqa Ban in Italy", *Canopy Forum*, November 2022, p. 1, available at https://canopyforum.org/2022/11/21/religious-freedom-and-the-burqa-ban-in-italy/.

12 Cf. G. Cavaggion, "Gli enti locali e le limitazioni del diritto alla libertà religiosa: il divieto di indossare il velo integrale", *Stato, Chiese e pluralismo confessionale*, Rivista telematica (wwwstatoechiese.it), no. 28, 2018, p. 1 ff., in order to examine the implementation of prohibition measures by other municipalities.

13 This information received extensive coverage in the media, including national outlets.

14 Accessible at www.eius.it/giurisprudenza/2006/116.

15 Council of State, Section VI, judgment 19 June 2008, no. 3076, para. 6.

16 *Amplius infra* para. 4.3.

As far as ordinary case law is concerned, a notable virtuous example can be mentioned. It is noteworthy to mention the solution employed by a court in Northern Italy. In this particular instance, a woman was granted permission to wear a *burqa* during her court appearance due to having undergone identification screening as requested by the authorities.[17]

Proposals concerning the banning of the *niqab* and *burqa* in public spaces have been submitted to Parliament in the past legislatures.[18] However, these drafts were never subjected to a vote, indicating a perception that the issue has already been adequately addressed by art. 5 of law no. 152/1975 or the impracticality of achieving consensus in finding solutions.

Regional legislators, on the other hand, have taken a different stance. Recently, the Lombardia Region[19] approved a ban on helmets, clothing, and other accessories that make identification difficult, including the *burqa* and *niqab*, in hospitals and local government offices. This ban followed recent terrorist attacks in Europe, specifically those that occurred in Paris on 13 November 2015.[20]

This is the first time that an Italian region has banned Islamic clothing on the basis of an interpretation of art. 5 of law no. 152/1975. This contradicts what was established by the Council of State in decision no. 3076/2008 and posits that religious traditions or customs cannot constitute justified grounds for a derogation from this prohibition.

For the Lombardia Region, the rationale of the measure is based on the need to strengthen security measures:

> religious traditions and customs [. . .] cannot constitute justified grounds for exception under article 5 of law no. 152/1975 with respect to security requirements within the regional structures.

17 Court of Cremona, 27 September 2008, *amplius infra* para. 3.4.

18 Cf. for example, bill no. 1543, filed in the Senate on 8 May 2007, "Modification to Law 22 May 1975, no. 152 on the Protection of Public Order", available at www.senato.it/leg/15/BGT/Schede/Ddliter/28234.htm; bill no. 2343, filed in the Senate on 23 September 2010, "Modification to Article 5 of Law 22 May 1975, no. 152, Concerning the Prohibition of Wearing the Garments Called *niqab* and *burqa*", available at www.senato.it/leg/16/BGT/Schede/Ddliter/35829.htm; draft law no. 3205, submitted to the Chamber of Deputies on 11 February 2010, "Modification of Article 5 of Law 22 May 1975, no. 152, Concerning the Protection of Public Order and the Wearing of Garments Worn for Religious or Ethno-Cultural Reasons", available at https://leg16.camera.it/126?idDocumento=3205; draft law no. 1571, submitted to the Chamber of Deputies on 11 September 2013, "Amendments to Article 5 of Law 22 May 1975, no. 152, Concerning the Prohibition of the Use of Clothing or other Objects that Prevent Identification in Public Places or Places Open to the Public, as Well as the Introduction of Articles 612 *ter* of the Criminal Code and 24 *bis* of Law 5 February 1992, no. 91, Concerning the Crime of Coercion to Conceal the Face", available at www.camera.it/leg17/126?tab=2&leg=17&idDocumento=1571&sede=&tipo=.

19 Lombardia, Regional Council, deliberation 10 December 2015, no. X/4553.

20 *Supra* para. 2.5.

Hearing a civil case against discrimination brought by associations for the protection of the rights of foreigners, the Court of Milan, Section I, dismissed the claim in the order of 20 April 2017.[21] While recognising per European case law that the ban on the full headscarf cannot be generalised, the order reiterates that the same case law allows that reasons such as those pertaining to public security may permit the rights set out in arts. 8 and 9 of the European Convention to be restricted in accordance with conditions fulfilled by the disputed provisions.[22]

Since the Constitution exclusively grants the State Legislator[23] the authority to regulate public security, the decision made by Lombardia a decade ago is perplexing.

The Lombardia's example was followed by the Veneto Region[24] and, more recently, the Friuli Venezia Giulia Region.[25]

Other religious garments have also given rise to controversy in recent years, such as the wearing of the *burkini*, a special swimming suit made with a technical fabric designed for observant Muslim women that covers the entire body except for the face, hands, and feet.

There have been several statements, mainly by mayors of seaside municipalities in the Northeast, in favour of banning the wearing of the *burkini* on public beaches in their respective territories.[26] Nevertheless, there have been no recorded instances regarding inquiries for entry to public swimming

21 Available at www.rivistalabor.it/wp-content/uploads/2017/05/Trib.-Milano-20-aprile-2017.pdf.

22 Decision confirmed in second instance by the Court of Appeal of Milan, 28 October 2019, no. 4330/19. Notice available at www.lombardianotizie.online/divieto-di-burqa-nei-luoghi-pubblici-ok-dalla-corte-dappello-di-milano.

23 Art. 117, para. 2 (h), Const.

24 Cf. the regional regulation of 4 July 2017, no. 2, "on the modalities of access and permanence in the institutional premises of the Veneto Region, of the entities of the regional health service, of the instrumental entities and of the bodies subject to control and supervision by the Region". The usage of ethnic-religious garments, specifically the *burqa* or the *niqab*, which are frequently utilised to conceal the face, is prohibited under art. 2 (regulation can be found at https://bur.regione.veneto.it/BurvServices/pubblica/DettaglioRegolamento.aspx?id=349241).

25 Motion no. 19/2019, "Adoption of appropriate measures to strengthen the control and identification system for access to the premises of entities and companies that are part of the regional system", voted by a large majority (www.consiglio.regione.fvg.it/pagineinterne/Portale/comunicatiStampaDettaglio.aspx?ID=622240).

26 For the cases of Monfalcone (AN) and Trieste in the summer of 2023 reported in the national press see F. Galici, "'Chi viene in Italia deve rispettare le nostre regole'. Scatta la stretta sul burkini in spiaggia", 16 August 2023, available at www.ilgiornale.it/news/nazionale/stretta-sul-burkini-ecco-sar-nuova-legge-2197334.html. English news reported by S. Mattozzi, "Muslim Women Harassed at Northern Italian Beach for Wearing Modest Clothing", 14 August 2023, available at www.euronews.com/culture/2023/08/14/muslim-women-harassed-at-northern-italian-beach-for-wearing-modest-clothing.

facilities, except for an incident mentioned in the local news pertaining to a swimming pool situated in San Donà di Piave (Venice Metropolitan City) in summer 2023.[27]

However, the *burqini* has been repeatedly brought before administrative courts in the transalpine region.[28]

3.3 The covered head in courtrooms

The issue of believers wearing religious symbols in courts has only sporadically emerged in Italy in recent decades.[29] Nevertheless, there are positive rules in procedural law that directly[30] or indirectly regulate the matter or that can be used for this purpose.[31]

At least two cases have given rise to rulings in this regard. The first concerns the aforementioned wearing of a *burqa* in a courtroom by the wife of a defendant.[32] The woman was referred to court pursuant to art. 5, law no. 152/1975. The woman's acquittal was based on the fact that there were no significant obstacles in recognising her in the relevant case following her willingness to temporarily remove the *burqa* for identification.

27 The pool management made the decision to not impose any restrictions on these two women wearing *burkinis*. The mayor of the municipality made efforts to downplay the controversy, likening it to the common practice of using wetsuits for diving. Cf. N.A., "In piscina nuotano col 'burkini': scoppia il caso", 18 August 2023, available at www.polesine24.it/cronaca/2023/08/18/news/in-piscina-nuotano-col-burkini-scoppia-il-caso-226296/ (*infra* para. 3.5, for an analysis of the French context).

28 *Infra* para. 3.5.

29 For a comparative approach, see A. Madera, "Il porto di simboli religiosi nel contesto giudiziario", *Stato, Chiese e prluralismo confessionale*, Rivista telematica (www.statoechiese.it), no. 4, 2020, p. 39, and X. Delgrange – D. Koussens, "Quelles laïcités en salle d'audience? A propos de quelques arrêts canadiens et européens sur le port de symboles religieux dans les prétoires", *Revue trimestrielle des droits de l"homme*, no. 2, 2019, p. 447.

30 Article 129, Code of Civil Procedure, which provides that persons attending or intervening in the hearing must be bareheaded.

31 Article 470, Code of Criminal Procedure, gives the President or the Attorney General the power to regulate the criminal hearing to ensure the dignity and respect of the jurisdiction. This provision could be used if the persons indicated agree to an interpretation that does not comply with the constitutional dictate.

The former Code of Criminal Procedure of 1930, art. 142, explicitly provided for the obligation to swear an oath with a bare head. The agreement signed on 27 February 1987 between the State and the Union of Communities (then still called "Israelitic") implemented by law 8 March 1989, no. 101, provided that "Jews who so request are permitted to take the oath provided for by the laws of the State with their heads covered" (art. 6). This oath was expunged from civil and criminal trials following several interventions by the Constitutional Court and by the enactment of the new Code of Criminal Procedure in 1989.

32 Court of Cremona, judgment 27 November 2008, available at www.jstor.org/stable/23204871?seq=2.

In the second case, a Muslim defendant's refusal of the judge's invitation to remove his headscarf and the defendant's subsequent refusal to participate in the hearing may have deteriorated his right to defence.[33]

Approximately a decade ago, the Superior Council of the Judiciary (CSM), an important organ of the Italian legal system with an autonomous function of governing the ordinary judiciary, expressed its opinion.[34] In a deliberation on 22 February 2012, the CSM ruled on the issue of the refusal of an interpreter to remove his Islamic headscarf during a criminal trial in 2011. For the CSM, total respect must be ensured for any conduct that, without disturbing the smooth running of the public office, constitutes a legitimate exercise of the right to profess a religion, supplementing the prescriptions concerning clothing and other external signs.

More recently, there was a case in which a young trainee lawyer was unjustly forbidden to enter the courtroom of the TAR Emilia Romagna because her head was covered by a simple Islamic veil.[35]

This is an issue the European Court of Human Rights has ruled on in relation to a case concerning the refusal of a member of the Wahhabi community who was a witness during a trial to remove his headgear,[36] as well as the expulsion of a woman who was a civil party in a criminal trial, justified on the basis of her refusal to remove her veil during the hearing.[37]

3.4 The case of the Sikh *kirpan*

Returning to the use of religious symbols by believers in Italy,[38] the matter of the ceremonial dagger used by the Sikhs, a group recently established mainly in

33 Court of Milan, order 26 February 2009, by which the plea of violation of the right of defence raised by the defendant's lawyer was not upheld. For an analysis of both cases, see G.L. Gatta, "Islam, abbigliamento religioso, diritto e processo penale: brevi note a margine di due casi giurisprudenziali", *Stato, Chiese e pluralismo confessionale*, rivista telematica (www.statoechiese.it), June 2009, p. 1.

34 Cf. www.csm.it. This institution was previously referred to in connection with a judge's refusal to hold a hearing in a courtroom with a crucifix (*supra* para. 2.4.).

35 For a critical commentary, see M. Croce, "Sulla laicità dello Stato nelle aule giudiziarie: il caso della praticante velata", 1 February 2018, p. 1, available at www.forumcostituzionale.it/wordpress/wp-content/uploads/2018/02/croce.pdf.

36 ECtHR, Fourth Section, 5 December 2017, *Hamidovic v. Bosnia and Herzegovina* (appl. no. 57792/15). In this case, the Court concluded that the applicant's sanction for contempt of court imposed by the domestic courts was not necessary in a democratic society. The domestic authorities had thus exceeded the "wide margin of appreciation" granted to them, in violation of the fundamental right recognised by art. 9 of the Convention.

37 ECtHR, Second Section, 18 September 2018, *Lachiri v. Belgium* (appl. no. 2313/09). In the present case, the Strasbourg Court held that the expulsion of the applicant from the courtroom due to her refusal to remove her hijab during the hearing was unlawful. The measure was not necessary for the protection of public order, and the applicant had not displayed any disrespectful or threatening behaviour towards the court or others present at the trial.

38 For a famous foreign case, see Supreme Court of Canada, 2 March 2006, *Multani v. School Board Marguerite-Bourgeoys*, no. 30322, available at https://decisions.scc-csc.ca/scc-csc/scc-csc/en/item/15/index.do?q=.

Northern Italian regions, has also emerged.[39] The issue of the ***kirpan*** was raised in relation to art. 4, para. 2, law 18 April 1975, no. 110, "laying down additional rules for the control of weapons, ammunition and explosives", as an unauthorised pointed object liable to cause injury if used outside the home and nearby areas.

According to the available information, the first judicial interventions in relation to the ***kirpan*** include the Criminal Court of Vicenza, decree 23 January 2009, and the Criminal Court of Cremona, judgment 19 February 2009.[40] In the first case, the proceedings were closed as the ***kirpan*** was deemed insufficiently sharp to constitute a weapon. In the second case, the judges entered into the merits of case by qualifying the ***kirpan*** as a distinctive sign of adherence to a religion. Hence, the ***kirpan*** was deemed an expression of religious freedom guaranteed by the Constitution and therefore was a "justified reason" to exclude the existence of an offence.[41]

The Council of State adopted a different stance in exercising its consultative role regarding the recognition of a non-Catholic religious organisation, particularly a Sikh association. In accordance with the legislation from 1929 to 1930, it will issue a negative opinion based on the wearing of the kirpan.[42]

At the level of jurisprudence, the most noteworthy interventions are those of the Supreme Court of Cassation since 2016.

In an initial pronouncement, the Supreme Court of Cassation, Criminal Section I, judgment 14 June 2016, no. 24739, excluded the lawfulness of carrying a dagger because

> the freedom of worship or faith always finds an insurmountable limit – see art. 8, para 2, Const. which excludes that the statutes of religious denominations other than Catholic may conflict with the Italian legal system – in the peaceful coexistence and in compliance with the rules protecting public security.[43]

39 The five Ks represent characteristic elements of the personality for Sikhs. They are uncut long hair (***kesh***), a small wooden comb (***kanga***), an iron bracelet (***kara***), a specific type of undergarment (***kachera***), and the sacred dagger (***kirpan***). In addition to the five Ks, another identifying element is the sacred turban. The ***kirpan*** is considered a symbol of respect and moral integrity, and it may only be used to protect the weak and needy and, in extreme cases, for self-defence.

40 For a commentary and reconstruction, as well as reproductions of the texts of the two decisions, see S. Carmignani Caridi, "Ostentazione di simboli religiosi e porto di armi od oggetti atti ad offendere. Il problema dil ***kirpan*** dei fedeli Sikh", *Il Diritto ecclesiastico*, no. 3–4, 2009, p. 739.

41 The part of the decision under "*Motivi della decisione*" is particularly significant. Here, the Court refers to common sense and examples of ordinary life and states that "if the offence is not to be regarded as occurring where the carrying of a large kitchen knife outside the home is motivated by the plausible need to cut bread for a family going on a picnic, it is hard to see why the offence should not also be regarded as not having been perpetrated where the carrying concerns a ***kirpan*** (i.e., a small knife with a notoriously shorter blade)".

42 Cf. Council of State, Section I, opinion, 23 June 2010, no. 4768 on the recognition of the legal personality required by the Sikhism Association Region Italy (not available online).

43 SCC, Criminal Section I, judgment no. 24739/2016, available at https://corsoculti.it/wp-content/uploads/2017/05/cass.-pen-24739-2016.pdf, "*Considerato in diritto*", para. 2 as well as "*Ritenuto in fatto*", para. 2 where the Court recalls the statement of the Council of State.

In the second ruling, the Supreme Court of Cassation, Criminal Section I, judgment 16 June 2016, no. 25263, reiterated the previous approach, specifying that "the expression of religious practices must necessarily conform to the fundamental values of the Italian legal system, with which they cannot conflict".[44]

Critically, the Supreme Court of Cassation, Criminal Section I, affirmed the stance conveyed in its two 2016 statements in judgment 15 May 2017, no. 24084. For the Court, religious convictions do not constitute justification for carrying the *kirpan*, and freedom of religion, through established case law, "finds limits established by legislation for the protection of other needs, including those of peaceful coexistence and security, as summarised in the formula of public order".[45] On the basis of the constitutional principles on religion, to be censured is the part of the ruling in which the Court defines as the essential

> obligation for the immigrant to conform his values to those of the Western world, in which he has freely chosen to fit in, and to verify in advance the compatibility of his behaviour [. . .] and thus the lawfulness of it in relation to the legal system that governs it.[46]

In other words, for the Supreme Court of Cassation,

> the multi-ethnic society is a necessity, but it cannot lead to the formation of cultural archipelagos that are configured according to the ethnic groups that make it up, precluding the uniqueness of the cultural and legal fabric of our country, which identifies public security as a good to be protected and, to this end, places the ban on the carrying of weapons and offensive objects.[47]

The orientation of the Supreme Court of Cassation was also confirmed later.[48]

44 SCC, Criminal Section I, judgment no. 25163/2016, available at https://corsoculti.it/wp-content/uploads/2017/05/CASS-pen.-25163-2016.pdf, "*Considerato in diritto*", para. 2. Case originated with the carrying of the *kirpan* in a public office (post office). For a commentary on both decisions, see A. Licastro, "Il motivo religioso non giustifica il porto del kirpan: una discutibile sentenza della Cassazione su immigrazione e 'valori del mondo occidentale'", *Stato, Chiese e pluralismo confessionale*, Rivista telematica (www.statoechiese.it), no. 1, 2017, p. 1.

45 SCC, Criminal Section I, judgment no. 24084/2017, www.astrid-online.it/static/upload/sent/sentenza-15-maggio-2017-cassazione-integrale.pdf, "*Considerato in diritto*", para. 2.3.

46 SCC, Criminal Section I, judgment no. 24084/2017, www.astrid-online.it/static/upload/sent/sentenza-15-maggio-2017-cassazione-integrale.pdf, "*Considerato in diritto*", para. 2.3.

47 SCC, Criminal Section I, judgment no. 24084/2017, www.astrid-online.it/static/upload/sent/sentenza-15-maggio-2017-cassazione-integrale.pdf, "*Considerato in diritto*", para. 2.3. For a commentary, see A. Negri, "Sikh condannato per porto del kirpan: una discutibile sentenza della Cassazione su immigrazione e 'valori del mondo occidentale'", *Diritto penale contemporaneo*, no. 7–8, 2017, p. 246, which we refer to for comparative references.

48 SCC, Criminal Section VII, order 18 April 2019, no. 16917. Available on the public SCC *Sentenze Web* database, where post-2019 decisions are viewable (www.italgiure.giustizia.it/sncass/).

In any case, it is worth noting the repeated attempts that the Italian Legislator has made to regulate the issue, starting with the bill filed in the Senate on 6 May 2015, during the XVIII Legislature.[49] The bill, which was not approved, aimed to authorise the wearing of the ***kirpan*** on the condition that it is manufactured in such a way that it does not cause injuries and is impossible to sharpen. This bill reflected an initiative introduced on an experimental basis by the Prefecture of Cremona, which recommended the production of a ***kirpan*** similar to the traditional one but without the sharpened blade that would make it a potentially deadly weapon.[50]

Another significant is the Council of State, Section I, opinion 29 October 2021, no. 1685,[51] which supports recognising the legal personality, by the meaning of art. 2, law no. 1159/1929, and art. 10, r.d. no. 289/1930, of the "Sikh Gurdwara Parbandhak Committee Italy" as a non-Catholic religious entity. A large portion of the document is devoted to the ***kirpan*** and also provides an account of the consultation held with the Ministry of the Interior and the Sikh Association, resulting in the formulation of a new statute on 15 May 2020. The Council of State highlights the adoption of a form of ***kirpan***[52] that has a different and smaller piercing capacity than a kitchen knife.[53]

Additionally, the Council of State opinion recalls the last ministerial report's[54] emphasis that the negative judgments rendered earlier had been made in relation to

> a different legal situation, concerning another association, marked by profound differences with respect to the applicant association "Sikh Gurdwara Parbandhak Committee Italy", whose doctrinal principles and religious practice do not present the difficulties of harmonisation with the principles of the Italian legal system encountered in the other case, as evidenced by art. 6B of the statute.[55]

Lastly, legislative proposal no. 179, tabled in the Chamber of Deputies, on 13 October 2022, had a similar tenor to the previous one in 2015.[56]

Despite the difficulties outlined earlier, the Sikh population seems to have integrated in Italy without any particular difficulties. They possess adequate

49 Bill no.1910/2015, "Provisions on the wearing of kirpans by citizens or foreigners of the Sikh denomination legally residing in the territory of the Republic", available at www.senato.it/leg/17/BGT/Testi/Ddlpres/00967593.html.

50 Bill no. 1910/2015, "*Relazione introduttiva*", para. 5.

51 Council of State, Section I, opinion 29 October 2021, no. 1685, available on the mentioned database at www.giustizia-amministrativa.it/web/guest/dcsnprr.

52 Statutes, 15 May 2020, art. 6b.

53 Accepting the ministerial conclusions based on the observations of the "Banco Nazionale di prova per le armi da fuoco e le munizioni commerciali" i.e. the National Proof House for Commercial Firearms and Ammunition.

54 Report of 20 July 2021, not available online.

55 Council of State, Section I, opinion no. 1685/2021, para. 3.

56 Available at www.camera.it/leg19/126?leg=19&idDocumento=179.

places of worship[57] and publicly practise their religious festivals, such as the many Vaisakhi parades that take place in spring, especially in Lombardia, Emilia Romagna, and Veneto, where the most numerous Sikh communities reside. They also represent a workforce without which many agribusiness industries could not function.[58]

3.5 The French approach to the wearing of religious symbols

The French case is emblematic and allows comparison with a system that adopts a form of secularism that is completely different from the Italian one, starting with the reference framework outlined by the aforementioned law of separation[59] and constitutional *laïcité*.[60] These represent a unique and exclusive model of secularism specific to the French context. Within this particular context, the term "*laïcité*" holds a distinctly French connotation of rigid division between religion and government, commonly translated as "secularism".[61] The original French form is retained here to preserve its specific meaning.

57 The Sikh community owns the largest temple in Continental Europe (the Gurdwara Shri Kalgidhar Sahib). The building, inaugurated in 2011, is located in the municipality of Pessina, near Cremona.

58 D. Mitzman, "The Sikhs Who Saved Parmesan", 25 June 2015, available at www.bbc.com/news/magazine-33149580.

59 The law, in recognition of freedom of conscience and the free exercise of religion and the related restrictions in the interests of public order (art. 1), states, "The Republic does not recognise, pay or subsidise any religion" (art. 2, para. 1). Pursuant to the aforementioned art. 28, "It is prohibited, in the future, to erect or affix any religious sign or emblem on public monuments or in any public location whatsoever, with the exception of buildings used for worship, burial grounds in cemeteries, funerary monuments, as well as museums or exhibitions". Norms available on the mentioned French law portal at www.legifrance.gouv.fr.

60 Art. 1, Const. 1956, which states in the first part of para.1 that "France shall be an indivisible, secular, democratic and social Republic. It shall ensure the equality of all citizens before the law, without distinction of origin, race or religion. It shall respect all beliefs". For an in-depth analysis of the reconstruction of French secularism, refer to the following monographic studies, see G. Calvès, *La laïcité*, La Découverte, Paris, 2022, 113 pp.;

P. Weil, *De la laïcité en France*, Grasset, Paris, 2022, 144 pp.; R. Schwarz, *Un siècle de laïcité*, Berger-Levrault, Paris, 2007, 204 pp.; J. Baubérot, *Laïcité 1905–2005, entre passion et raison*, Le Seuil, Paris, 2004, 288 pp.; J.P. Costa – G. Bedouelle, *Les laïcité à la française*, PUF, Paris, 1998, 266 pp. and M. Barbier, *La laïcité*, L'Harmattan, Paris, 1995, 320 pp. However, it should be emphasised that French doctrine recognises that there is no uniformity in the reconstruction of the evolution of *laïcité* and the contents it has assumed over time. For all, see J. Baubérot, *Les 7 laïcités françaises*, Éditions de la Maison des sciences de l'homme, Paris, 2015, *passim*.

61 For a significant exception to the principles of separation and secularism in metropolitan France, see the three eastern departments (*Haut Rhin*, *Bas Rhin* and *Moselle*) where, by virtue of their control by Germany from 1870–1918, the law of 9 December 1905 does not apply and the Napoleonic Concordat of 1801 and a system of recognised cults are still in force. For a comprehensive reconstruction of the French legal system with regard to religion, see F. Messner – P.H. Prélot – J.M. Woehrling, *Traité de droit français des religions*, Lexis Nexis, Paris, II ed., 2013, *passim*.

Particularly since the early 2000s, there has been a continuous implementation of various regulations and interventions that affect and restrict the sphere of religious freedom. Schools[62] have been especially targeted as these are considered essential in the teaching of the values of the French Republic to young people and to preserve them from all forms of communitarianism or separatism, to use the term adopted by President Macron in speeches from 18 February[63] and 2 October 2020.[64]

The famed law of 15 March 2004, no. 2004–228 governs the wearing of conspicuous religious symbols or clothing expressing a religious affiliation in state schools.[65] This law operates within the framework of legislation that already provides for the observance of the strict principle of neutrality for civil servants and those in charge of a public service.[66] According to the law, it is strictly prohibited for students in state schools to display signs or wear clothing that conspicuously indicates their religious affiliation.

This matter resulted in numerous legal disputes that have subsequently been brought before the ECtHR.[67]

Nevertheless, the no. 2004–208 law is not the only one to regulate the presence of religious symbols worn by believers. These measures have a broad

62 Starting in the late 1980s. Reference is made to an episode that occurred in 1989 at the *Collège* Gabriel Havez in Creil concerning the wearing of the *hijab* by three Muslim students. Receiving wide coverage in the French national press, this case gave rise to a series of ministerial circulars, interventions by administrative jurisprudence, and the establishment of study commissions aimed at prefiguring a discipline on this subject.

63 E. Macron, "Protéger les libertés en luttant contre le séparatisme islamiste", *Mulhouse*, 18 February 2020, available at www.elysee.fr/front/pdf/elysee-module-15216-fr.pdf. All the speeches, texts, and videos are available on the official website of the Presidency of the Republic, which can be found at www.elysee.fr.

64 E. Macron, "La Rèpublique en acte: discours sur le thème de la lutte contre le séparatisme", *Les Mureaux*, 2 October 2020, also available in English at www.elysee.fr/front/pdf/elysee-module-16114-en.pdf

65 *Loi encadrant, en application du principe de laïcité, le port de signes ou de tenues manifestant une appartenance religieuse dans les écoles, collèges et lycées publics.* Law enforced by Ministerial Circular 18 May 2004 (NOR MENG0401138C). For an analysis, see M.C. Ivaldi, "Verso una nuova definizione della laicità? La recente normativa a proposito dei segni religiosi nella scuola in Francia", *Il Diritto ecclesiastico*, no. 4, 2004, p. 1.

66 *Amplius infra* same para.

67 Cf. the decisions of inadmissibility decisions against France ECtHR, Fifth Section, 30 June 2009 *Aktas* (appl. no. 43563/08), *Bayrak* (appl. no. 14308/08), *Gamaleddyn* (appl. no.18527/08), *Ghazal* (appl. no. 29134/08), *J. Singh* (appl. no. 25463/08), and *R. Singh* (appl. no. 27561/08).
When the law was not yet in force, the ECtHR, Fifth Section, in the coeval rulings 4 December 2008 pronounced unanimously the absence of a breach of art. 9 ECHR, founded on the constitutionally acknowledged principle of *laïcité* within the French legal framework and established prior case law by the Council of State. Cf., *Dogru* (appl. no. 27058/05) and *Kervanci* (appl. no. 31645/04).
Regarding precedents on the subject of the veil not in relation to France, please refer to ECtHR Second Section, 15 February 2001, *Dahlab v. Switzerland* (appl. no. 42393/98) and the two rulings *Leyla Sahin v. Turkey* (appl. no. 44774/98) resp. ECtHR, Second Section, 24 June 2004 and ECtHR, Grand Chamber, 10 November 2005.

impact, but they specifically target Islam. We refer to the law banning concealment of the face in the public space from 11 October 2010, no. 2010–1192.[68]

This law preceded an analysis by the Council of State titled "Study on the legal possibilities of banning the full veil".[69] The analysis contemplates two distinct hypotheses: the case relating to the conduct of a person who violates the prohibition of concealment of the face;[70] and the crime of forced concealment of the face, which penalises conduct involving threats, violence, coercion, and abuse of authority or power to impose the concealment of the face of one or more persons by reason of their sex.[71]

In the broader European context, the Parliamentary Assembly of the Council of Europe unanimously adopted resolution 23 June 2010, no. 1783 "Islam, Islamism and Islamophobia in Europe"[72] against a general ban on the wearing of the *burqa* or *niqab* that would have the effect of denying women who freely wished to do so the right to cover their faces.[73] This resolution emerged shortly before the passing of law no. 2010–1192. The ban could have produced the opposite effect of making Muslim women suffer additional exclusion "if they were to leave educational institutions, stay away from public places and abandon work outside their communities, in order not to break with their family tradition".[74] In the simultaneous recom-

68 *Loi interdisant la dissimulation du visage dans l'espace public.* For the application see also the two circulars dated 2 March 2011 (NOR PRMC1106214C) and 11 March 2011 (NOR IOCD1109134C) issued by the Prime Minister and the Minister of the Interior, respectively.
According to art. 1, it is not allowed to wear clothing that conceals the face in public places. Art. 2, para. 1, very broadly defines the public space as that comprising public streets as well as places open to the public or dedicated to a public service. For an analysis, see A. Fornerod, "The Burqa Affair in France", in A. Ferrari – S. Pastorelli (eds.), *The burqa Affair Across Europe Between Public and Private Space*, Routledge, Abingdon – New York, 2013, p. 57.
For a study concerning the prohibition of wearing religious symbols during the SARS-CoV-2 pandemic, see M. Ricca, "Don"t Uncover that Face! Covid-19 Masks and the Niqab: Ironic Transfigurations on the ECtHR's Intercultural Blindness", *International Journal of Semiotics of Law*, vol. 35, no. 3, 2022, pp. 119–1143 (original paper 2020).

69 The document titled "*Étude relative aux possibilités juridiques d'interdiction du port du voile intégral*" was adopted by the Plenary General Assembly of the State Council on 25 March 2010, available at www.conseil-etat.fr/publications-colloques/etudes/etude-relative-aux-possibilites-juridiques-d-interdiction-du-port-du-voile-integral.
It is worth noting that the draft text was referred prior to approval, pursuant to art. 61, para. 2, Const., to consideration by the *Conseil constitutionnel* (www.conseil-constitutionnel.fr). In decision 7 October 2010, no. 2010–613, the *Conseil constitutionnel* expressed the draft's conformity with the Constitution, albeit with interpretive reservations.

70 The prescribed fine for offences of a second-class nature is to be imposed in this case. Furthermore, one may be required to complete the training period mentioned in art. 131–35-1, para. 1, Criminal Code.

71 Rule inserted in art. 225-4-10, Criminal Code, in the chapter devoted to the "Offences against human dignity".

72 Available at https://pace.coe.int/en/files/17880.

73 COE, Resolution no. 1743 (2010), para. no. 16.

74 COE, Resolution no. 1743 (2010), para. no. 17.

mendation no. 1927, the Parliamentary Assembly reiterated its position by asking the Committee of Ministers to urge member states not to implement an absolute ban, recalling the limits on circumscribing individuals' religious freedom under art. 9, ECHR.[75]

This law was also given particular attention in the case law of the Convention in relation to the judgment of the Grand Chamber, 11 July 2014, *S.A.S. v. France* (appl. no. 43835/11), which established how the relevant prescriptions do not violate the Convention. The broad and precise reasoning starts with the well-known margin of appreciation recognised for national states, of which the *Lautsi II* judgment is an exemplification. While recognising that the French perspective is not widely shared in Europe, the ECtHR considers the potential limitations imposed by the law to be reasonable in relation to the pursued aim of safeguarding the principles of "*vivre ensemble*" (living together) as an essential aspect of protecting the rights and freedoms of others.

Moreover, the aforementioned French presidential speeches in 2020 set the stage for a further hardening of the principle of secularism as a *laïcité de combat*, which took the form of the enactment of the law 24 August 2021, no. 2021–1109, reinforcing respect for the principles of the Republic.[76]

Briefly, this law aims to strengthen respect for the principle of secularism and the neutrality of public service. It also provides for the formal establishment of the "*Journée de la laïcité*",[77] as well as a series of legislative changes affecting education, sport, the control of religious associations, the fight against online hate crimes, and criminal law. Measures are largely aimed at combating radical Islam and separatism according to the *éxposé des motifs* of Government bill no. 3649, filed in the National Assembly on 9 December 2020 and presented on behalf of the Prime Minister Jean Castex by the Minister of the Interior Gérald Darmanin and the Minister in Charge of Citizenship Marlène Schiappa.[78]

The new legislation was drafted against the background of an increasing demographic of Muslims in France, a legacy of France's colonial past and of the great migratory movements affecting the country. These shifts in population have come with related problems of integration and have stoked fears of

75 COE, Recommendation 1927 (2010), para. 3.13. The document can be accessed at https://pace.coe.int/en/files/17881/html.

76 The law "*confortant le respect des principes de la République*", the so-called *loi séparatisme* consists of 103 articles, divided into four titles: I *Garantir le respect des principes de la République et des exigences minimale de la vie en société*; II *Garantir le libre exercices du culte*; III *Dispositions diverses* and IV *Dispositions relatives à l'Outre-Mer*.

As an illustration of the copious doctrine on this point, see the *dossier* edited by V. Fortier – G. Gonzalez, *La loi confortant le respect des principes de la République*, published in no. 13, 2022 of the *Revue du droit des religions*, dedicated to the law, available on *Open Édition* at https://journals.openedition.org/rdr/pdf/1725, p. 1.

77 Set on 9 December each year, the anniversary of the enactment of the *loi séparation* of 1905.

78 Available at www.assemblee-nationale.fr/dyn/15/textes/l15b3649_projet-loi#D_non_amendable.

fundamentalism and the consequent spread of terrorist attacks, which have occurred several times since the second half of 2015,[79] including recently.[80]

A final step regarding schools is the recent intervention of the Minister for Education, Youth, and Sport through the service note of 31 August 2023 "*Respect des valeurs de la République*" (Respect for the values of the Republic).[81] This intervention relates to issues that have arisen following the increasing presence of the *abaya* or the *qamis*,[82] which are considered unequivocally linked to one's professed faith and are therefore prohibited by law no. 2004–228. This ban has been in place since the 2023–2024 school year and was immediately the subject of complaints.[83]

At the international level, it must be emphasised how the extensive interpretation of law no. 2004–228 has captured the attention of the world press, especially in Arabic-speaking countries. An example of attention at the institutional level is the United States Commission on International Religious Freedom (USCIRF)[84] press release from 8 September 2023, which highlights how France "continues to wield a specific interpretation of secularism to target and intimidate religious groups, particularly Muslims".[85] According to the USCIRF, unlike law no. 2004–228, which abstractly prohibits the wearing

79 We refer, among others, to the Islamic terrorist incidents that marked the two-year period from 2015 to 2016. In 2015, besides minor but bloody, episodes, major events in Paris occurred from 7 to 9 January, i.e. the attacks on the Charlie Hebdo publication headquarters and the Hypercacher kosher shop, and from 13 to 14 November, where of three attacks the massacre at the Bataclan Theatre alone claimed 90 victims. In 2016, we recall the tragic attack in Nice on 14 July, when a terrorist drove a truck into a crowd on the *Promenade des Anglais* following the celebrations of a French national holiday, causing 86 deaths. Additionally, there was an attack near Rouen on the church of Saint-Étienne-du Rouvray on 26 July in which the elderly priest Jacques Hamel was executed.

80 We refer here to the two incidents involving two teachers less than three years apart. The first, which occurred on 16 October 2020, concerns the murder of the teacher Samuel Paty. Paty had shown his class cartoons on Islam previously published by the satirical periodical Charlie Hebdo and was killed in a Paris suburb. The second attack was likely connected to the climate created following the Hamas attacks on Israel on 7 October 2023. On 13 October, literature teacher Dominique Bernard was killed, and three other people wounded by a former pupil of Gambetta-Carnot Lycée in Arras. The attacker was an immigrant aged just 20 who shouted "*Allah Akbar*" during the crime.

81 At www.education.gouv.fr/bo/2023/Hebdo32/MENG2323654N.

82 Generally, these are dresses (the *abaya* for women and the *qamis* for men) that cover the entire body and are normally worn in Arab countries.

83 The interlocutory appeals were ultimately not allowed. Council of State, "*Juges des référés*", order 7 September 2023, no. 487891 (*référé liberté ex* art. L. 521–2, Code of Administrative Justice), and Council of State, "*Juges des référés*", order 25 September 2023, no. 487896 (*réréré suspension ex* art. L. 521–1, Code of Administrative Justice).

84 An independent, bipartisan US federal agency established by the International Religious Freedom Act of 1998 (www.uscirf.gov) to monitor compliance with the right to freedom of religion or belief abroad.

85 Available *online* at www. uscirf.gov/news-room/releases-statements/uscirf-concerned-frances-expanding-interpretation-ban-religious.

of religious clothing or symbols, such as *kippahs*, large crosses, and *hijabs*, the new French interpretation implies a new prescription directed only at a specific religion (Islam) in blatant violation of art. 18 of the International Covenant on Civil and Political Rights (1966) and art. 18 of the Universal Declaration of Human Rights (1948).

Other controversies in France concern the wearing of the aforementioned *burkini*.[86] The situations that have given rise to legal disputes have produced different solutions depending on whether the *burkini* is worn in swimming pools or on public beaches. In the first case, an emergency procedure was introduced by law no. 2021–1109 (*loi séparatisme*) in the General Code of Local Authorities.[87] This law allows the competent authority of the administrative justice system, on the initiative of the prefect, to pronounce the suspension of the effects of a measure of a local authority[88] when the contested act is liable "to seriously undermine the principles of secularism and neutrality of public services".

One of the first uses of this instrument occurred in the sporting sphere regarding a resolution of the Grenoble Municipal Council of 16 May 2022 adopting new municipal swimming pool regulations, a derogation from the rules of hygiene and safety that implicitly allows the wearing of the *burkini*.[89] This measure was suspended by the Administrative Court[90] with an order that was confirmed by the Council of State.[91]

Incidentally, the jurisprudence of the Council of State concerning the wearing of the *burkini* on public beaches is different sign in terms of the merits of the proceedings.[92] Most recently, the decision of 17 July 2023, no. 475636,[93] reiterates that for a ban on outfits ostensibly displaying a religious affiliation in public space to be lawful, it must be justified by a current and proven risk to public order, a circumstance not demonstrated by the Municipality.[94] The

86 Cf. *supra* para. 3.2., with regard to the smaller disputes that occurred in Italy.

87 Art. 5, law no. 2021–1109.

88 Municipalities, departments, or regions.

89 For a review, see. Nicolas, "Le principe de laïcité (ré)conforté: le référé-laïcité, le juge administratif et le burkini", *Revue des droits de l'homme, Actualité Droits-Libertés*, Octobre 2022, p. 1, available at http://journals.openedition.org/revdh/15934.

90 Administrative Court of Grenoble, "*Juges des référés*", order 25 May 2022, no. 2203163. The order, which appears to be unavailable on www.legifrance.gouv.fr, can be accessed at https://blog.landot-avocats.net/wp-content/uploads/2022/05/TA-Grenoble-ord.-25-mai-2022-n%C2%B02203163.pdf.

91 Council of State, "*Juges des référés*" (*formation collégiale*), order 21 June 2022, no. 464648.

92 For precedents, see Council of State, order 26 August 2016, no. 402742 concerning the Municipality of Villeneuve-Loubet and Council of State, III and VIII Chambers United, decision 11 December 2020, no. 426483 the Municipality of Châlon-sur-Saône.

93 Council of State, X Chamber, decision 17 July 2023, no. 475636.

94 It concerns the Municipality of Mandelieu-la-Napoule, which had essentially banned access to beaches and bathing for people wearing a burkini from 15 June to 31 August 2023. This measure was challenged by the *Ligues des Droits de l'Homme l'Homme* (www.ldh-france.org/) before the Administrative Court of Nice, which did not grant its request for suspension under art. L. 522–3, Code of Administrative Justice. This censure was upheld by the Council of State.

premise of the argumentative process lies in the distinction between the rules applicable to public space versus those applicable to public services (as was the case with the swimming pools of the Municipality of Grenoble), which are instead governed by the principles of neutrality and good organisation. If the recurrence of such an event occurs in a public space, it is necessary that

> a measure restricting a freedom guaranteed by law must be appropriate, necessary and proportionate in the light of the circumstances of time and place and justified by the proven risk of undermining public order.[95]

This circumstance did not occur in the present case.

3.5.1 The duty of neutrality for public and private employees

The distinction between the public space and the space in which a public service is provided introduces another facet, namely, the duty of neutrality among public employees. This issue does not arise in the Italian case insofar as there are no limits set for these in terms of the expression of their religious affiliation. While it is true that France is also a paradigmatic case in this respect, it is equally true that this is an issue that has affected European supranational courts. Similarly, there are also interesting normative and jurisprudential examples from overseas.

As noted,[96] the first corollary of French principles of separation and secularism derives from the obligation for civil servants not to manifest their religious convictions during the performance of their duties; this ensures that the State remains neutral with respect to all religions and beliefs. This principle is fundamental to guarantee impartiality and inclusiveness in public service.

The documentation on this point is significant.[97] This principle has sometimes led to disputes that have come to the attention of the ECtHR. For example, the judgment of the Fifth Section, *Ebrahimian v. France*, 26 November 2015 (appl. no. 64846/11), ruled that there was no violation of art. 9 ECHR in the non-renewal of a social worker's contract with a public hospital after she refused to remove her headscarf. The assumption was based on French constitutional recognition of the principle of *laïcité* and the related national jurisprudence on the neutrality of public services.

95 Council of State, decision no. 475636/2023, para. 6.

96 *Supra* para. 3.5.

97 Regarding *laïcité* and neutrality in public service, see the webpage www.fonction-publique.gouv.fr/etre-agent-public/mes-droits-et-obligations/laicite-et-neutralite-de-la-fonction-publique where is also available the "*Charte de la laïcité dans les services publics*". Regarding the obligation of neutrality, please refer to the detailed information provided, particularly in arts. L. 121-2 and L. 121-4, General Code of the Public Service.

Observance of the principle of neutrality was first extended to public service delegates and later found application in the private sphere as well, as demonstrated by the celebrated *Baby Loup* case and the many rulings related to it.[98] This case confirmed the possibility for private employers to impose religious neutrality policies, while at the same time it emphasises the need to balance individual religious freedom with the requirements of neutrality and social cohesion in specific work contexts. The case in question led to the inclusion of a provision in the Employment Code authorising private companies to expressly sanction the obligation of neutrality in their internal regulations.[99]

Moreover, the ECtHR has presented several rulings on religious symbols in both public and private employment contexts, such as the *Eweida* and *Chaplin* judgments,[100] *Dahlab*,[101] and *Lachiri*.[102] These judgments demonstrate how the Court seeks to balance protection of religious freedom with other public and private interests, thereby maintaining a broad and contextual vision of specific situations.

In recent years, there have also been several interventions by the Court of Justice in Luxembourg, some concerning the public sector and others the private sector.[103] Preliminary rulings in relation to the prohibition of discrimination under the Directive 2000/78/EC, have established a general framework for equal treatment in employment and occupation.

Most recently, the CJEU, Grand Chamber judgment 28 November 2023 in case C-148/22 ruled that public administrations in European Union member states can prohibit employees from wearing visible religious symbols at work.[104] The case was brought by a Muslim employee of the Municipality of Ans (Belgium) who was barred from wearing a headscarf at work due to a regulation prohibiting visible religious symbols for all employees. The Court determined that such a regulation does not constitute indirect discrimination if it aims to ensure the principle of neutrality and is applied systematically to all employees. The judgment upheld the principle that public administrations can enforce regulations to maintain a neutral environment by prohibiting visible religious symbols, provided the rules are applied equally to all employees and aim to achieve a legitimate objective.

98 Most recently, see the decision of the Court of Cassation, Plenary Assembly, 24 June 2014, no. 13–28369, which upheld the legitimacy of Fatima Afif's dismissal, finding that the neutrality policy of the Baby Loup Nursery, which prohibited the use of visible religious symbols, was justified and proportionate in relation to the need to ensure a neutral environment that respected different religious and philosophical beliefs.

99 Cf. art. L. 1321, Employment Code, introduced by art. 2, law 8 August 2016, no. 2016–1088 relating to work, modernising social dialogue, and securing professional pathways.

100 *Supra* para. 2.3.

101 *Supra* subpara. 2.5.1.

102 *Supra* para. 3.3.

103 Case law accessible at https://curia.europa.eu/.

104 Cf./2024/696, available at https://eur-lex.europa.eu/eli/C/2024/696/oj.

Other previous rulings have concerned private employment. For example, *Achbita v. G4S Secure Solutions* (C-157/15), decided on 14 March 2017,[105] concerned the dismissal of an employee for wearing an Islamic headscarf in the workplace in violation of a company policy of neutrality. In this case, the Court ruled that a company policy prohibiting the use of visible religious symbols does not constitute direct discrimination if it is applied generally and is undifferentiated. However, it may constitute indirect discrimination if it is not justified by a legitimate objective, such as neutrality, and if it is not proportionate.

Bougnaoui v. Micropole SA (C-188/15), decided on the same date,[106] also concerned the dismissal of an employee, in this case a software engineer, who wore an Islamic headscarf following complaints from a client. In this instance, the CJEU ruled that a client's request cannot justify a derogation from the principle of non-discrimination, and the employers had to prove that the neutrality policy was applied consistently and systematically.

Similar legislation regarding civil servants can also be found on the other side of the Atlantic in Canadian State of Quebec.

The "Act to foster adherence to State religious neutrality and, in particular, to provide a framework for requests for accommodations on religious grounds in certain bodies", 1 July 2017, CQLR c R-26.2.01,[107] establishes the principle of State religious neutrality and provides specific rules for the requests of religious accommodation in certain contexts. Additionally, the "Act respecting the laicity of the State", 18 June 2019, CQLR c L-0.3,[108] specifies in the preamble that "the Québec nation has its own characteristics, one of which is its civil law tradition, distinct social values and a specific history that have led it to develop a particular attachment to State laicity",[109] referring to the area's French heritage.[110]

In the articles, the law specifies that State laicity requires parliamentary, government, and judicial institutions to comply with the prohibition on wearing religious symbols and with the duty of religious neutrality.[111]

This is a controversial law that was immediately subject to complaints. Recently, the Quebec Court of Appeal, judgment 29 February 2024, upheld the validity of this act, known as Bill 21. This long decision represented a

105 Again, the CJEU, Grand Chamber, intervened at the request of a Belgian Court for a preliminary ruling.

106 The CJEU, Grand Chamber was responding this time to a request for a preliminary ruling by the French Court of Cassation, Civil, Social Chamber, decision 9 April 2015, no. 13-19955.

107 Accessible at www.canlii.org/en/qc/laws/stat/cqlr-c-r-26.2.01/latest/cqlr-c-r-26.2.01.html. Cf. art. 1 "The State of Québec is a lay State".

108 Available at www.canlii.org and also at www.legis.quebec.gouv.qc.ca.

109 Preamble, para. 1, Act respecting the laicity of the State.

110 A reference that can also be inferred from the choice of using the term "laicity" – largely unheard of in the English-speaking context – instead of secularism.

111 Arts. 3–4, Act respecting the laicity of the State.

significant victory for proponents of the law.[112] The ruling maintains that the law, which prohibits public employees in positions of authority from wearing visible religious symbols, does not violate constitutional rights and can be fully enforced. It also concretely overturns the lower court ruling,[113] exempting English-language schools from the application of Bill 21, arguing that minority language education rights do not justify an exemption from the law. At the same time, the judgment partially confirmed the part of the ruling stating that the law's ban on head coverings for members of the provincial parliament violates the Charter of Rights and Freedoms.[114]

As an additional example from United States, there is an interesting case concerning the recitation of public prayer by a public worker. A football coach from a public high school would pray at half-court after games; the school asked him to stop this practice to avoid potential lawsuits based on the Establishment Clause of the First Amendment. After he refused, the School District decided not to renew his contract. The Supreme Court decision on 27 June 2022, *Kennedy v. Bremerton School District*,[115] ruled in a 6–3 decision that the School District's action constituted a violation of Kennedy's constitutional rights to free speech and the free exercise of religion. The decision emphasised that the government may not suppress an individual's personal and private religious expression simply to comply with the Establishment Clause.[116]

France, too, has encountered challenges with the harbouring of religious symbols in the context of sport.[117] In particular, an appeal was brought by certain associations against art. 1 of the statutes of the *Féderation Française de Football* prohibiting "the wearing of any sign or dress ostensibly expressing a political, philosophical, religious or trade union affiliation".[118]

The Council of State, II and VII Chambers United, decision 29 June 2023, nos. 458088, 459547 e 463408,[119] rejected the grievance. The Council of

112 At https://courdappelduquebec.ca/fileadmin/Fichiers client/Actualites/500-09-029537-214_Arret_EN_2024-02-29_VF.pdf.

113 Quebec Superior Court, Civil Chamber, District of Montreal, judgment 20 April 2021, *Hak c. Procureur général du Québec*, available at www.canlii.org/fr/qc/qccs/doc/2021/2021qccs1466/2021qccs1466.html.

114 Charter unanimously adopted by the National Assembly, on 27 June 1975, and still in force.

115 597 U.S. 507 (2022). Decision available at www.supremecourt.gov/opinions/21pdf/597us2r62_d92h.pdf.

116 For a commentary, see T. Pagotto, "Il motto statunitense 'In God We Trust' alla luce della storia e della tradizione del Primo ementamento", *Stato, Chiese e pluralismo confessionale*, Rivista telematica (www.statoechiese.it), no. 19, 2022, p. 118, where she speaks of the (definitive) abandonment of the Lemon test in favour of the hermeneutic criterion oriented towards "history and tradition".

117 On the many interactions between sport and religion, see M.C. Ivaldi, "Discrimination and Religious Propaganda in Football Law", *State, Churches and Confessional Pluralism*, Rivista telematica (www.statoechiese.it), 2 February 2015, p. 1 ff.

118 The latest statutes and regulations of the FFF are available online at at www.fff.fr/11-les-reglements/index.html.

119 Also viewable at www.legifrance.gouv.fr/ceta/id/CETATEXT000047772138.

State, in its actions, demonstrated a disregard for the differing opinion of the public prosecutor.[120] Similarly, the Council of State fails to adequately examine the inherent implications of the interactions between the French domestic football regulations and the universally applicable *Laws of the Game* governing football. These *Laws of the Game* have permitted the wearing of the veil since 2014.[121]

The debate that accompanied the proceedings led to the presentation of a draft law aimed at explicitly ensuring, once and for all, the prohibition of the wearing of the veil and other symbols in any discipline pertaining to French national sports federations, given that players are delegates of a public service and therefore required to observe the principle of neutrality.[122] Sports federations, as delegates of a public service, are also required to issue provisions to this effect "for the time of the events and competitions in which they take part in this function".[123]

Concerning the ban on wearing signs or outfits ostensibly manifesting religious affiliation during match times and at venues, the decision states that the FFF "can legitimately, by virtue of the regulatory power delegated to it for the proper running of the competitions for which it is responsible, enact such a prohibition, which is appropriate and proportionate to the circumstances".[124]

For the French Council of State, it followed *de plano* and apodictically that all other allegations brought to its attention by the applicants – namely, those relating to the disregard by censured rule of the rights set out in arts. 9–10, ECHR and 10–11, Charter of Fundamental Rights of the European Union, specifically freedom of thought, conscience, religion, and expression, together with the denial of discrimination (at least indirect discrimination) within the meaning of art. 14 ECHR and art. 1, law 27 May 2008, no. 2008–496[125] – were outweighed.

This ban also formally applies to the 2024 Summer Olympics, except for the Olympic Village where the athletes will stay.[126]

120 Available at www.legifrance.gouv.fr/jorf/id/JORFTEXT000047704524.

121 Law 4 "Players'equipment. The version of *Laws of the Games* valid for the 2024–2025 season are available at www.theifab.com/downloads/laws-of-the-game-2024-25?l=en.

122 Cf. draft law no. 1585, registered at the Presidency of the Assemblée Nationale on 20 July 2023, "*visant à interdire le port de signes religieu et politiques ostensibles dans les compétitions et les événements sportifs*" (i.e. prohibiting the wearing of conspicuous religious and political symbols at sporting competitions and events), available at www.assemblee-nationale.fr/dyn/16/textes/l16b1585_proposition-loi.

123 Draft law no. 1585/2023, paras. 11–12.

124 Draft law no. 1585/2023, para. 14.

125 "*Loi portant diverses dispositions d'adaptation au droit communautaire dans le domaine de la lutte contre les discriminations*" (Law adopting various provisions adapting to community law in the field of anti-discrimination).

126 Most recently, C. Licoys, "Paris 2024: les athlètes ont-ils le droit de porter des signes religieux au JO?", 14 Juin 2024, available at www.la-croix.com/sport/paris-2024-les-athletes-ont-ils-le-droit-de-porter-des-signes-religieux-aux-jo-20240613.

4 Additional recent cases concerning religious symbols and other "symbolic" issues in Italy

Summary: 4.1. A recent significant affair judged by the Supreme Court of Cassation concerning the display of crucifixes in classrooms – 4.2. Further "symbolic" issues within the legal framework on religion in Italy – *4.2.1. Advertising and religion* – 4.3 The long-standing issue of Muslim places of worship – *4.3.1. The jurisprudence of the Constitutional Court on the rights to places of worship* – *4.3.2. The two most recent cases involving existing places of worship* – *4.3.3. The issue pertaining to art. 71, para 1, Third Sector Code* – 4.4. The ongoing lack of a general law on religious freedom and the wide margin of State decision-making in the negotiation of *intese* – *4.4.1. The denial of an* intesa *to the Union of Atheists Agnostics Rationalists* – 4.5. The latest questions concerning the crucifix

4.1 A recent significant affair judged by the Supreme Court of Cassation concerning the display of crucifixes in classrooms

As noted, since the *Lautsi II* pronouncement, there have been no particularly significant episodes concerning religion symbols in public institution from the point of view of law.[1] However, one significant question did arise before delivery of the ECtHR's judgment in *Lautsi I*.

In a professional institute in Terni in 2008, the students of a specific class voted to keep the crucifix on their classroom wall during instructional sessions. This was followed by a circular from the school headmaster inviting all teachers to respect the students' wishes. Additionally, a service order has issued to the teachers to ensure the permanent display of the symbol inside the classroom.

Despite being advised against doing so, one humanities teacher persisted in removing the crucifix at the start of their lessons and reattaching it at the end. The teacher claimed to be exercising their freedom of teaching and conscience in religious matters,[2] and cited the principle of neutrality in state schools.

1 See *supra* para. 2.3.

2 Freedom guaranteed by art. 33, para. 1, Const., according to which "[t]he arts and sciences are free, as shall be their teaching".

DOI: 10.4324/9780429242953-5

This repeated behaviour[3] led to disciplinary proceedings against the teacher by the provincial school board, culminating in the teacher's suspension from teaching for 30 days without pay.[4] The teacher filed a lawsuit against the sanction. After several years, the case was elevated to the Supreme Court of Cassation.

The teacher lodged appeals against both the service order issued by the school headmaster and the disciplinary sanction imposed on them. In the first case, the teacher's appeal was based on the discriminatory nature of the measure toward teachers who do not recognise the crucifix; in the second case, the sanction penalised the teacher's legitimate power of self-defence – which took the form of the removal of the symbol for the duration of their lessons – in relation to the fundamental rights of freedom of teaching and freedom of conscience in religious matters. The main measures of this case are discussed briefly in the following.[5]

The Court of Terni, Labour Section, judgment 29 March 2013, no. 122,[6] rejected the teacher's claims. In fact, the case *de quo* is not a question of ruling on the issue of the legitimacy of displaying crucifixes in classrooms, which, moreover, would fall within the administrative jurisdiction,[7] but rather on matters of civil relevance, as is the case with the antidiscrimination action pursuant to art. 4, d.lgs. 9 July 2003, no. 216.[8]

In order to exclude discriminatory conduct, the Court, referring to the ECtHR, Grand Chamber judgment 18 March 2011, *Lautsi and others v.* Italy (appl. no. 30814/06), determined that the presence of the crucifix during school hours

> is not capable, as such, [of] restrict[ing] the freedom of religion, expression or teaching of a professor of literary subjects, that is to say, of a person with an age, experience, maturity and education far beyond that of a boy.

3 In a new class council meeting (3 November 2008) it was emphasised that the display of the crucifix had not given rise to any problems, including among the few Muslims present.

4 As of 16 February 2009. The measure was justified due to the teacher's persistent engagement in behaviour that contradicted the wishes of the majority of the students. Additionally, the act of placing and removing the crucifix, which was associated with the teacher's entrance into the classroom, lacked educational value as it failed to consider the unique sensitivity of the individuals in the developmental stage under the teacher's care.

5 For an initial measure rejecting some of the grievances brought by Prof. F.C., see Court of Terni, order 22 June 2009, available at www.uaar.it/uaar/campagne/scrocifiggiamo/coppoli/ordinanza.pdf.

6 The measure's text can be accessed at the following link: https://win.gildavenezia.it/normativa/archivio_norme/2015/crocifisso_all7.pdf.

7 As pointed out by the SCC itself, United Civil Sections, order 10 July 2006, no. 15614, pertaining to the case raised by Adel Smith (*supra* para. 2.4).

8 Laying down rules for the "Implementation of Directive 2000/78/EC for equal treatment in employment and occupation".

Similarly, the teacher – who does not adhere to the religious symbol – is not prevented from exercising "towards his pupils his functions as a teacher and educator, in line with his philosophical convictions".

In other words, according to the Court, if the presence of the crucifix cannot be considered an undue influence on pupils, *a fortiori*, it cannot be shown to restrict the freedom of religion, expression, and teaching of a humanities teacher. Consequently, the existence of the religious symbol does not impede the teacher from fulfilling their role as an educator and instructing their students in alignment with their personal moral or philosophical beliefs. Likewise, the existence of discrimination within the meaning of d.lgs. no. 216/2003 is also excluded.

The teacher submitted an appeal challenging the unfavourable decision. Nonetheless, the Court of Appeal of Perugia,[9] Labour Section, judgment 9 December 2014, no. 165, rejected his grievances, stating that

> the display of the crucifix did not restrict freedom of education and that the applicant is not entitled to complain of the alleged breach of the principle of good practice and impartiality of the Public Administration and of the principle of the *laicità* of the State, because those principles do not give rise to the subjective rights of individuals, but to diffuse interests, the protection of which is entrusted to the exponential bodies of the community as a whole and only in cases expressly provided for by law to associations or collective bodies which are the spokesmen of those interests.

Additionally, the Court of Appeal ruled that the regulatory provisions regarding the placement of crucifixes in primary- and lower-secondary schools do not apply to higher-secondary schools. At the same time, the Court considered that an absolute ban on such a display could be deduced from the consideration presented, nor could the indications given by the school head in the directive addressed to all teachers that merely prescribed the presence of the crucifix in accordance with the assembly resolution of only a specific class be considered illegitimate.

This case produced an ongoing legal dispute as the teacher appealed to the Supreme Court of Cassation, Labour Section. Pursuant to the interlocutory order dated 18 September 2020, no. 19618, the Labour Section forwarded the acts to the First President for potential assignment of the dispute definition to the United Civil Sections given the case's exceptional nature regarding the equilibrium between safeguarded freedoms and rights.[10]

9 Not available online.

10 First President, who ordered under art. 374, para. 1, Code of Criminal Procedure, the assignment of the appeal to the United Civil Section, which, at the public hearing on 6 July 2021 treated it in council chambers since no request for oral argument was received from

The Supreme Court of Cassation, United Civil Sections, decided the claim with judgment 9 September 2021, no. 24414.[11] The ruling upheld one of the grounds of appeal (the third one) and dismissed the case by referring to the Court of Appeal of Perugia, Labour Section, with a different composition.[12]

This is a hypothesis that occurs when the Supreme Court, after setting aside (annulling) a judgment of a lower court (court or court of appeal), does not decide directly on the merits of the case but refers the matter to another judge of the merits to re-examine the case in light of the indications given. In re-examining the case, the referring court is bound by the principles of law set out in the judgment of annulment.

It is a very long and elaborate measure.[13]

First, the United Civil Sections did not agree with the interpretation of the Court of Appeal of Perugia and the Labour Section of the Supreme Court of Cassation insofar as they considered art. 118, r.d. no. 965/1924, inapplicable to higher-secondary schools.[14]

That said, for the United Sections, "the display of the crucifix is no longer a due act, since it is not constitutionally permitted to impose its presence".[15] The central point of the argument was that

> the regulatory provision can no longer be read as implying an obligation to display the crucifix in schools, but must be interpreted as meaning that the classroom may accommodate its presence when the school

---

the interested parties. The order is accessible online at https://sentenze.laleggepertutti.it/sentenza/cassazione-civile-n-19618-del-18-09-2020.

11 Available on the aforementioned public SCC "*Sentenze Web*" database, where post-2019 decisions are viewable and at www.rivistalabor.it/wp-content/uploads/2021/09/Cass.-sez.-un.-9-settembre-2021-n.-24414.pdf.

More precisely, it upheld the third plea in law of the appeal, as stated in the grounds; it declared the first, second, and fourth grounds unfounded; the fifth, sixth, and seventh pleas in law absorbed; and the eighth one inadmissible, referring the case back to the Court of Appeal of Perugia in another composition. For a commentary, see N. Colaianni, "Dal 'crocifisso di Stato' al 'crocifisso di classe'", *Stato, Chiese e pluralismo confessionale*, Rivista telematica (www.statoechiese.it), no. 17, 2021, p. 18 and A. Licastro, "Crocifisso 'per scelta'. Dall'obbligatorietà alla facoltatività dell'esposizione del crocifisso nelle aule scolastiche", *Stato, Chiese e pluralismo confessionale*, Rivista telematica (www.statoechiese.it), no. 21, 2021, p. 17.

12 SCC, United Civil Sections, judgment no. 24414/2021, "*Motivi della decisione*", para. 11.2.

Cf. Court of Appeal of Perugia, judgment 29 April 2022, ordering the annulment of the sanction originally imposed, which received a favourable comment from the President of UAAR, available at https://blog.uaar.it/2022/04/29/corte-appello-perugia-chiude-definitivamente-vicenda-coppoli/.

13 On this topic, see F. Alicino, "*Ceci n'est pas une pipe*: The Crucifix in Italian Schools in the Light of Recent Jurisprudence", *Canopy Forum*, 30 November 2021, p. 1, available at https://canopyforum.org/2021/11/30/ceci-nest-pas-une-pipe-the-crucifix-in-italian-schools-in-the-light-of-recent-jurisprudence/.

14 They arrived at this conclusion based on the assumption that, during the enactment of r.d. no. 925/1924, the term "secondary education" encompassed both high schools and technical colleges.

15 SCC, United Civil Sections, judgment no. 24414/2021, "*Motivi della decisione*", para. 12.

> community concerned independently assesses and decides to display it, while respecting and safeguarding the convictions of all, placing alongside the crucifix, if so requested, the other symbols of religious faiths present within the same school community and seeking a reasonable accommodation that favours the coexistence of pluralities.[16]

In other words,

> [t]he regulatory provision on school furnishings is capable of expressing a meaning that conforms to the new constitutional context and to the legislation that constitutes the development and implementation of constitutional principles, on the basis of an evolutive interpretation that transforms the obligation to display the crucifix into an option, entrusting to individual school communities the decision on the presence of religious symbols in their classrooms. Where there was authoritative imposition of the presence of the crucifix, it is now to be understood as optional placement, reported to a request coming from below, from the students. Where the regulatory provision was characterised by exclusivity (only that symbol), there is now room for an extensive interpretation in the direction of the plurality of symbols, inspired by a concrete universalism, empirically based and democratically responsive to the changing ethnic and therefore also religious composition of the population.[17]

In my opinion, this seems to be an evolutionary interpretation that in any case goes far beyond the original meaning of the rule. A state of obligation corresponds with a state of non-obligation and certainly not a capacity (*facoltà*), which also includes the display of other symbols. This is a choice that is not up to a judge, not even a judge deputed to the function of nomofllachy. From this perspective, it would have seemed more respectful, including of the principle of the division of powers, to adhere to the interpretation of the possible disapplication of regulations contrary to the Constitution.[18]

However, the United Civil Sections went even further, opting for

> a "mild" solution (the white wall of the classroom is born white, it may remain so, but it may also not remain bare and accommodate the presence of the crucifix to satisfy a need of the students) that is articulated in choices to be made on a case-by-case basis, in the light of concrete needs, in single school institutes, with the participation of all those involved using the method of seeking the broadest consensus.[19]

16 SCC, United Civil Sections, judgment no. 24414/2021, "*Motivi della decisione*", para. 12.1.
17 SCC, United Civil Sections, judgment no. 24414/2021, "*Motivi della decisione*", para. 12.1.
18 E. Maritinelli, "Una sentenza sul crocifisso: verso un nuovo modello di laicità?", *La Nuova Giurisprudenza Civile Commentata*, no. 1, 2022, p. 121.
19 SCC, United Civil Sections, judgment no. 24414/2021, "*Motivi della decisione*", para. 12.1.

Nonetheless, for the United Civil Sections the absence of the display obligation does not translate into a ban on the presence of crucifixes in classrooms[20] because

> Italian *laicità* is not "neutralising": it does not deny the peculiarities and identities of every creed and does not pursue an objective of the gradual irrelevance of religious feeling, which is destined to remain in the intimacy of the individual's conscience.[21]

Specifically, for the United Civil Sections, embracing and expressing the concept of *laicità* as delineated by the Constitutional Court,

> the *laicità* of the Constitution is based on an inclusive and open concept of neutrality and not-excluding secularisation: as such, it recognises the religious dimension present in society and is nourished by the coexistence of different faiths and convictions. The principle of *laicità* neither denies nor misunderstands the contribution that religious values can make to the growth of society; rather, it aims at ensuring and enhancing the pluralism of personal choices in religious matters as well as guaranteeing the equal social dignity and equality of citizens. Ours is a *laicità* open to the different identities that emerge in a society where different faiths, religions and cultures have to coexist welcoming of differences, it does not demand the sacrifice of its own historical, cultural and religious identity by those who confront each other and share the same public space, but respects people's faces and needs. And it is a *laicità* that translates, on the level of individual consciences, into the recognition for all of the equal value of individual ethical convictions in the construction and safeguarding of a public sphere in which to dialogically compare the various positions present in pluralist society.[22]

Despite the consistency in the definition of the principle of *laicità*, as elucidated by the United Civil Sections, I find the suggested approaches for resolving the issue of religious symbols in schools to be lacking in consensus.

For the United Civile Sections,

> the public school does not and cannot have its own creed to propose, has no faiths to defend, nor agnosticism to favour. The school environment is removed from the principle of transcendent authority. In the Italian school open to all, the Constitution constitutes the punctuation that unites the plane of memory with that of the future, personal

20 SCC, United Civil Sections, judgment no. 24414/2021, "*Motivi della decisione*", para. 13.
21 SCC, United Civil Sections, judgment no. 24414/2021, "*Motivi della decisione*", para. 13.1.
22 SCC, United Civil Sections, judgment no. 24414/2021, "*Motivi della decisione*", para. 13.1.

> and social identity with cultural pluralism, the institutions and rules of democracy with the horizontality of solidarity expressed in and through social groups. The state school is an open place that fosters inclusion and promotes the encounter of different religions and philosophical convictions, and where students can acquire knowledge about their respective thoughts and traditions.[23]

This is an ideal approach that, in my opinion, is fully compatible with the constitutional set-up. However, as shown in the following paragraphs, it is still far from being achieved.

Another interesting aspect of the ruling addresses the display of crucifixes in classrooms as an inclusive environment open to the presence of other symbols.[24]

In this view,

> [t]he symbol of Christianity, which is also an expression of the cultural roots of our society, inserted in a context open to the presence of symbols of other religions or other cultures belonging to members of the school community and therefore to the plural richness of the contributions offered, contributes to delineating a shared public space, characterised by a multiplicity of dialoguing reasons and inspired by a welcoming neutrality of identities. Other symbols, born as religious and external to the traditional identity of the country, are also likely to become, in the public school open to all, cultural symbols of integration.[25]

That said, for the United Civil Sections the presence or absence of the crucifix falls "within the autonomy of individual school institutions".[26]

From an operational point of view, the Court believes that reasonable accommodation is the way to go. This approach is

> understood as the search, together, for a mild, intermediate solution, capable of satisfying the different positions to the extent practically possible, in which all concede something by taking, each, a step in the direction of the other.[27]

23 SCC, United Civil Sections, judgment no. 24414/2021, "*Motivi della decisione*", para. 13.2.
24 SCC, United Civil Sections, judgment no. 24414/2021, "*Motivi della decisione*", para. 13.3.
25 SCC, United Civil Sections, judgment no. 24414/2021, "*Motivi della decisione*", para. 13.3.
26 SCC, United Civil Sections, judgment no. 24414/2021, "*Motivi della decisione*", para. 14. The Court, following the approach of *Lautsi II*, emphasises the value of the crucifix as a passive symbol that "does not imply on the part of the potential recipient of the message any act, not even implicit, of adherence to it", nor does it represent an act of propaganda or proselytisation. Rather, it "is an act of witness, of profession of religious faith on the part of the members of that community of life in formation that is a school classroom" (para. 14.4.).
27 SCC, United Civil Sections, judgment no. 24414/2021, "*Motivi della decisione*", para. 19.

Given that in the case of conflicts between rights it is not possible to simply invoke majority rule without correction,[28] reasonable accommodation would not have occurred in the present case.[29]

More specifically, the Court upheld the applicant's grievances insofar as it found a violation and misapplication of arts. 2, 3, 7, 8, 19, and 20, Const., and of the supreme principle of *laicità* of the State. Following this principle, the affixing of the crucifix is not compulsory, pursuant to an interpretation of art. 118, r.d. no. 965/1924, in accordance with the Constitution.

In other words,

> the school community may decide to display the crucifix in the classroom with an assessment that is the result of respect for the convictions of all members of the same community, seeking a "reasonable accommodation" between any differing positions.[30]

Consequently, the school headmaster's circular reminding all the teachers in the class of their duty to respect and protect the wishes of the students – expressed by a majority in an assembly – to see the crucifix displayed in their classrooms failed to seek a reasonable accommodation with the position expressed by the dissenting teacher. Hence, the circular must be considered unlawful. The illegitimacy of this action invalidates the disciplinary sanction inflicted on the teacher, even though there is no evidence of discrimination on religious grounds against them.[31]

4.2 Further "symbolic" issues within the legal framework on religion

Apart from the issue of religious symbols being displayed by institutions or believers, Italy also faces other concerns that, due to the way they are addressed – or, more accurately, not addressed – acquire "symbolic" significance. Symbolic matters are being talked about due to their indication of situations lacking regulation and potential constitutional implications.

28 SCC, United Civil Sections, judgment no. 24414/2021, "*Motivi della decisione*", para. 21.

29 SCC, United Civil Sections, judgment no. 24414/2021, "*Motivi della decisione*", para. 22. Moreover, for the Court, the path of reasonable accommodation in religious matters can also be deduced from examples in foreign case law. Cf. "*Motivi della decisione*", para. 24, where it refers to the German precedent of 1995 on the crucifix and to the Canadian precedent of 2006 on the *kirpan*.

30 SCC, United Civil Sections, judgment no. 24414/2021, "*Motivi della decisione*", para. 30.

31 SCC, United Civil Sections, judgment no. 24414/2021, "*Motivi della decisione*", para. 30. On 15 June 2024, the UAAR awarded the teacher F.C. with the *Soile Lautsi 2024* prize for his commitment to the *laicità* of the school (N.A., "Gli atei premiano Franco Coppoli, l'insegnante che tolse il crocefisso in un'aula pubblica", 20 June 2024, available at https://terninrete.it/notizie-di-terni-gli-atei-premiano-franco-coppoli-linsegnante-che-tolse-il-crocefisso-in-unaula-scolastica-pubblica/).

In this section, other conflicts of *sensu lato* symbolic value concerning the school are discussed. Specifically, the focus is on recurring practices of installing nativity scenes in buildings or requests for liturgical celebrations and blessings to coincide with major Catholic holidays. In this case, references are also made to foreign jurisprudence, where similar cases can often be found not only in schools but within public institutions more broadly.

At the same time, there are increasing requests for observance of Ramadan. A brief analysis follows of several disputes concerning the symbolic use of religion in commercial advertising.

In the educational sphere, nativity scenes in public schools have often been an occasion for controversy between those who argue the inappropriateness of their presence due to the principle of *laicità* and those who, on the contrary, claim their perfect constitutional compatibility as a practice that can be traced back to the cultural heritage of the majority of the Italian population.[32]

However, before giving an account of the most recent institutional initiatives in Italy, it is appropriate to mention the jurisprudence of other countries, especially that of France, the United States, and Mexico, where there have been several similar cases.

In fact, the Council of State – the institution at the apex of French administrative jurisprudence – albeit sustaining the prohibition "to erect or affix any religious sign or emblem on public monuments or in any public place whatsoever" – has left possibilities open on the subject of the installation of mangers. Let us consider two cases[33] judged by the Council of State *Assemblée*, decision 9 November 2016, no. 395122 and no. 395223, regarding the Christmas nativity scenes.[34]

As outlined in the doctrine,

> starting from the assumption that the crib can assume a plurality of meanings, the CE rules that the display of Nativity scenes by a public authority in a public space is lawful, only if it has a cultural, artistic or festive purpose, but not if it expresses a public recognition or a preference for a religion.[35]

32 For an acknowledgement of the historical and cultural value of the nativity scene from an economic point of view, see TAR Campania, Section III, 25 October 2023, no. 5817, which upholds the legitimacy of the resolution of the Municipality of Naples that provided for specific regulations for San Gregorio Armeno Street, in which the opening of any new activity other than for the production and sale of nativity scene artworks is strictly forbidden.

33 Concerning the *Fédération départementale des libres penseurs de Seine-et-Marne* and the Mayor of the Municipality of Melun and the *Fédération de la libre pensée de Vendée* and the President of the General Council of Vendée, respectively.

34 This judgment is available in English at www.conseil-etat.fr/en/judgments, together with a selection of significant cases.

35 M.C. Ivaldi, "The Meaning of 'Religion' in French Case-Law", p. 132.

In essence, the Council of State distinguishes between two cases based on the display location. First, nativity scenes cannot be displayed inside public buildings unless specific circumstances support their cultural, artistic, or festive purpose. Second, these scenes can be lawfully displayed on other public properties for year-end celebrations given their festive nature, unless they constitute an act of proselytisation or the expression of a religious opinion. In other words, the permissibility of displaying a nativity scene depends on the location and the intended purpose of the display.[36]

The Supreme Court of the United States has also been called upon to rule on the presence of nativity scenes in public spaces, starting with the ruling, 5 March 1984, *Lynch v. Donnelly*,[37] which by a 5–4 vote held that public display of the nativity scene did not violate the Constitution. This case dealt with a Christmas display sponsored by the City of Rhode Island in which the manger was featured along with other symbols such as the Christmas tree, gingerbread houses, and Santa Claus.

Considering the overarching secular backdrop and the widespread recognition of the cultural and historical importance of Christmas, the Court affirmed that there was no violation of the First Amendment.

In the Supreme Court, judgment 3 July 1989, *County of Allegheny et al v. ACLU Greater Pittsburgh Chapter et al.*,[38] the Court judged two different types of symbolic displays. One related specifically to a nativity scene with the inscription "*Gloria in Excelsis Deo*", placed in the lobby of a courthouse; the other concerned the display of the *menorah* (the seven-armed Jewish candelabrum) next to a large Christmas tree placed outside City-County Building. The Court ruled 5–4 for the violation of the Establishment Clause for the first display, reasoning that the display of the nativity scene constitutes a sign of public support of Christianity capable of conveying a religious message. In the second, the Court ruled out that the overall presence of several symbols, both religious and secular, constitutes sponsorship of religion.

In closing this brief review, it is worth highlighting a recent Mexican case. This case is noteworthy due to the constitutional formalisation of the principle of secularism within the Mexican system.[39] The principle of separation between Church and State is made explicit, prohibiting any kind of religious intervention in political affairs and vice versa.[40] Mexican higher courts have

36 M.C. Ivaldi, "The Meaning of 'Religion' in French Case-Law", p. 132.

37 465, U.S. 668 (1984), available at https://caselaw.findlaw.com/court/us-supreme-court/465/668.html. For a brief examination of other cases, see *supra* para. 2.5.

38 492 U.S. 573 (1989), available at https://caselaw.findlaw.com/court/us-supreme-court/492/573.html.

39 Art. 40, *Constitución Política de los Estados Unidos Mexicanos*, available at www.diputados.gob.mx/LeyesBiblio/pdf/CPEUM.pdf. For an historical reconstruction, see P. Valvo (ed.), *La libertà religiosa in Mexico. Dalla Rivoluzione alle sfide dell'attuale*, Studium, Roma, 2020, *passim*.

40 Art. 130, Const. Regarding this topic, R.C. Fonseca Luján, "Marco constitucional de la laicidad en México", *Revista de la Facultad de Derecho de México*, vol. LXXIV, no. 288, 2024, p. 379.

thus likewise been called upon to pronounce on the subject of religious symbols, particularly with regard to the display of nativity scenes in public institutions.

Supreme Court of Justice of the Nation, First Chamber, judgment 9 November 2022, no. 216/2022,[41] concerned an amparo proceeding[42] against the display of a Christmas manger in the Municipality of Chocholá, Yucatán. The Supreme Court of Justice referred to foreign legislation, in particular that of Spain, France, and the United States, on the basis of the assumption that "although they are different legal systems, it is possible to identify in them elements that are relevant to our law".[43] Building from this, the Court reconstructed its own constitutional framework on secularism and religious neutrality in recognition of religious freedom and the principle of equality and non-discrimination.[44]

After elaborating on this reconstruction, the Court concluded by ordering the Municipality of Chocholà to refrain from putting up signs in public spaces that allude to specific religious beliefs and from using public resources for that purpose in the exercise of its legal and constitutional powers.

Returning to Italy, the December 2023 holiday period saw renewed discussions on this topic. In the same period, a bill was presented in the Senate dedicated to "Respect for and protection of Italian religious traditions".[45] The short text, consisting of only four articles, is essentially based on the duty of the Republic to value, preserve, and protect "Christian religious festivities and traditions as the most authentic and profound expression of the identity of the Italian people".[46]

Moreover, the introductory report stated that

> the present bill intervenes on respect for Christian religious traditions and the symbols that distinguish them. In particular, with regard to Christmas and Easter, the reference is to the setting up of the nativity scene and the performance of the related ceremonies, plays, and celebratory representations".

41 *Suprema Corte de Justicia de la Nación*, *Primera Sala*, judgment 9 November 2022, no. 216/2022, available at www.scjn.gob.mx/sites/default/files/listas/documento_dos/2022-10/AR-216-2022-20102022.pdf.

42 Raised by the Kanan Human Rights Association (www.kanandh.org).

43 *Suprema Corte de Justicia de la Nación*, judgment, no. 216/2022, para. 126 ff. where specific references to the jurisprudence of these countries can also be found, especially to that of the United States.

44 *Suprema Corte de Justicia de la Nación*, Judgment, no. 216/2022, para. 183 ff.

45 XIX Legislature, bill no. 962, "Respect for and protection of Italian religious traditions", communicated on 11 December 2023 to the Senate Presidency, on the initiative of Senator Lavinia Mennuni, and a number of senators belonging to the centre-right government majority. This bill is available at www.senato.it/service/PDF/PDFServer/DF/429731.pdf. To follow the path of this bill, see www.senato.it/leg/19/BGT/Schede/Ddliter/57792.htm.

46 Art. 1, bill no. 962/2023.

In practical terms, it assigns to public education institutions the

> the prohibition of preventing initiatives, promoted by parents, students or the competent school bodies, aimed at supporting the activities related to the traditional celebrations linked to the Christmas and Easter festivities, such as the setting up of the nativity scene, plays and other events linked to them, in order to recall their deep meaning of humanity and the relationship that binds them to the Italian national identity.[47]

Non-compliance with the mentioned provisions entails the commencement of disciplinary proceedings, provided for by law, for public administration employees.[48]

The introductory report as well as the subsequent articles fail to clarify whether "ceremonies" and "recitations and other events" associated with the aforementioned festivities can encompass liturgical celebrations and the bestowal of blessings, despite their usual occurrence outside of school hours. This is also a recurring issue in Italian media.

However, there is an authoritative case law precedent in this regard, namely, Council of State, Section VI, judgment of 27 March 2017, no. 1388.[49] This judgment ruled in favour of the legitimacy of school premises for blessings – in this case Easter blessings – requested by local parish priests, provided that they are given on the basis of voluntary participation and during extracurricular hours.[50]

The Council of State specified that

> the participation in any religious manifestation or rite (whether at school or elsewhere) can only be optional and free, as it cannot but enjoy, just because it is such, less room for freedom and less respect than those accorded to manifestations of other kinds, as well as being tolerant towards those who express different feelings and faiths, or those who do not express or manifest any faith at all.[51]

Naturally, there is always an abundance of controversy within schools. Most recently, there has been a case in which the headmaster of the Raffaele Sanzio Comprehensive Institute – for schools located in the province of Pesaro Urbino – prohibited Easter celebrations by virtue of the principle of scholastic

47 Art. 2, bill no. 962/2023. See also the subsequent art. 3, according to which "the Minister of Education and Merit shall take the necessary measures for the implementation of the provisions of article 2".

48 Art. 4, bill no. 962/2023.

49 Viewable as usual at www.giustizia-amministrativa.it/web/guest/dcsnprr.

50 For a comment, see T. Di Iorio, "Luci e ombre della benedizione nella scuola tra libertà religiosa e laicità dello Stato", *Stato, Chiese e pluralismo confessionale*, Rivista telematica (www.statoechiese.it), no. 24, 2017, p. 1 ff.

51 Council of State, Section VI, no. 1388/2017, "*Diritto*", para. 3.

laicità. The episode was highlighted in the press, which in some cases emphasised the more conciliatory attitude held by some schools towards the practice of Ramadan.[52]

Indeed, Ramadan celebrations in 2024 captured public interest regarding a number of issues in the school environment.[53]

Concerns were raised regarding children under the age of ten who chose to fast during the day despite no obligation to do so.[54] In instances where parents expressed the requirement for their children to observe fasting, schools endeavoured to identify solutions that reconciled the various interests involved, occasionally even considering permitting students to leave the premises during meal breaks. Nevertheless, honouring families' requests typically did not allow for the provision of reserved rooms and dedicated staff for these minors. As a result, they were required to stay in the school canteen premises alongside other students.

The incident that received the most extensive coverage in national news involved the State Comprehensive Institute Iqbal Masih[55] in Pioltello, situated in the province of Milan.

The school administration decided to utilise one of the suspension days for teaching activities, which is allowed under the principle of school autonomy. This specific day was chosen to coincide with the conclusion of Ramadan in consideration of the significant population of Muslim students. The Minister of Education, Giuseppe Valditara,[56] expressed disapproval of this decision and stressed the necessity for a strict inclusion policy that adheres to a limit of 30% foreign students per class.[57]

The actions taken by this school did not and could not result in changing the officially acknowledged schedule of national public holidays;[58] rather, the choice aimed solely at accommodating the religious practices of a considerable

52 Cf. F. Boezi, "Sì al Ramadan, no al parroco. Il preside vieta la benedizione", 30 March 2024, available at www.ilgiornale.it/news/politica/s-ramadan-no-parroco-preside-vieta-benedizione-2303151.html.

On similar issue, N.A., "Italian School Closes to 'Celebrate' Ramadan, While Another Prevents Easter Blessing", 21 March 2024, available at https://catholicherald.co.uk/italian-school-closes-to-celebrate-ramadan-while-another-prevents-easter-blessing/.

53 On the long-standing issue of Islamic places of worship, see *infra* para. 4.3.

54 V. Fronzoni, "Ramadhan: digiuno dei minori a scuola, esigenze religiose e libertà educativa", April 2024, available at www.rivistadirittoereligioni.com, p. 1.

55 This is a tribute to the valiant 12-year-old Christian boy who fearlessly represented the cause of exploited children in a carpet factory and tragically met his demise on 16 April 1995, in Lahore, Pakistan, as he made his way home after Easter Mass.

56 Regarding this news, see N.A., "Pioltello, i docenti: 'Indignati e offesi'. Valditara: 'Non è violazione dell'autonomia scolastica'", 22 March 2024, available at www.rainews.it.

57 On this topic, see S. Coppetti, "Chiusura per Ramadan. Il provveditore avverte: 'Delibera da revocare'. Il ministro minacciato", 21 March 2024, available at www.ilgiornale.it/news/politica/chiusura-ramadan-provveditore-avverte-delibera-revocare-2299314.html.

58 It should be recalled that in the Italian legal system public holidays are established by law. Cf. law 27 May 1949, no. 260, "Provisions on public holidays" and subsequent amendments. Art. 2 lists these holidays.

number of students, as has already happened in the past. Furthermore, the school received high praise from the President of the Italian Republic, Sergio Mattarella.[59]

4.2.1 Advertising and religion

Tensions have also emerged in the context of utilising symbols within the realm of figurative arts, encompassing painting, literature, theatre, cinema, and similar forms of expression.

In this context, we refer more generally to all those symbolic representations related to religion, whether they are expressed in mere objects or in the depiction of persons, facts, or episodes connected to the religious sphere.

In Italy, particularly in previous times, these symbolic representations have been the target of censorship[60] or legal actions related to religious disrespect.[61] Within the juridical discussion concerning the adequacy and boundaries of safeguarding religious sensibilities in the artistic realm, a compromise was reached that prioritised the freedom to express artistic ideas over the protection of religious sentiment.

Italy has also experienced considerable controversy surrounding satirical depictions of religion.[62] However, in terms of consequences, the cases pertaining to France are the most relevant. First and foremost, are the well-known cartoons lampooning Islam published in September 2005 by the weekly magazine *Charlie Hebdo*, which replicated cartoons already released by the Danish newspaper *Jyllands-Posten*. This publication was followed by the previously described attack on the magazine's editorial office on 7 January 2015, resulting in the loss of 12 lives. Additionally, the showing of the cartoons in question led to the tragic murder of teacher Samuel Paty on 16 October 2020.[63] In light of these incidents, French President Emmanuel Macron has taken a stance in support of the freedom of blasphemy, asserting its place within the broader framework of freedom of expression as stipulated by the law.[64]

59 Cf. N.A., "Mattarella risponde alla scuola di Pioltello: 'Apprezzo il vostro lavoro'", 26 March 2024, available at www.ansa.it/sito/notizie/cronaca/2024/03/26/mattarella-scrive-a-pioltello-apprezzo-i-vostro-lavoro_53c6bc62-7544-4618-b590-4a0ef0431314.html.

60 On this subject, D. Loprieno, "Libertà dell'arte vs. Libertà religiosa: il caso della censura cinematografica", in *Stato, Chiese e pluralismo confessionale*, Rivista telematica (www.statoechiese.it), gennaio, 2009, p. 1 ff.

61 M.C. Ivaldi, *La tutela penale in materia religiosa nella giurisprudenza*, esp. p. 80 ff. and 95 ff. For a recent case in the United Kingdom, see the film *The Lady of Heaven*, released in June 2022 and condemned by the Muslim Council of Britain as divisive. The film was later withdrawn by the production company (Cineworld).

62 For an example, see the decisions of the Court of Appeal of Florence, 18 October 1993 and the Court of Rome, 20 January 1998, analysed by M.C. Ivaldi, *La tutela penale in materia religiosa nella giurisprudenza*, risp. p. 219 and 272.

63 Cf. *supra* para. 3.5.

64 We refer here to the aforementioned speech delivered on 2 October 2020 in Les Mureaux (*supra* para 3.5.) as well as to the presidential speech of 21 October 2020, delivered

As time has passed, other conflict profiles have developed concerning the specific manifestation of thought conveyed through advertising messages. The attention on advertising messages has been a subject of ongoing public debate both in Italy and internationally.[65] Advertising has not been exempt from attention regarding protection of religious sensitivity.[66] Potential conflicts were initially resolved mainly by resorting to the criminal regulations on defamation mentioned earlier.[67] Subsequently, conflicts were increasingly resolved by consulting the Institute of Advertising Self-Discipline (*Istituto di Autodisciplina Pubblicitaria*; IAP) and its bodies (i.e. Jury[68] and Control Committee).[69]

during the national tribute ceremony to Samuel Paty held at the Sorbonne (www.elysee.fr/front/pdf/elysee-module-16345-fr.pdf). For an analysis of President Macron's previously expressed positions on this topic, see N. Colaianni, "Il presidente Macron e la libertà di blasfemia", 29 September 2020, pp. 1–14, available at www.questionegiustizia.it/articolo/il-presidente-macron-e-la-liberta-di-blasfemia.

65 This topic was also recently attested to by the ECtHR, Fourth Section, judgment 30 January 2018, *Sekmadienis Ltd. v. Lithuania*, appl. no. 69317/14, in relation to an advertisement for clothing, the protagonists of which featuring Jesus and Mary. The Court ruled in favour of the violation of freedom of expression provided for in art. 10, para. 2, ECHR. First, the ECtHR considered that the "freedom of expression constitutes one of the essential foundations of a democratic society and one of the basic conditions for its progress and for each individual's self-fulfilment. Subject to paragraph 2 of article 10, it is applicable not only to 'information' or 'ideas' that are favourably received or regarded as inoffensive or as a matter of indifference, but also to those that offend, shock or disturb. Such are the demands of pluralism, tolerance and broadmindedness without which there is no 'democratic society'" (para. 70). Second, the ECtHR observed that "the domestic authorities failed to strike a fair balance between, on the one hand, the protection of public morals and the rights of religious people, and, on the other hand, the applicant company's right to freedom of expression" (para. 83).

66 On the subject of religious symbolism used in advertising from a sociological point of view, see C. Nardella, *La migrazione dei simboli. Pubblicità e religione*, Guerrini Scientifica, Milano, 2015, *passim*. This research analyses a 50-year period of Italian advertising, identifying the most used religious symbols as well as the tensions caused by their use. Regarding the approach from a marketing perspective, see M. Kalliny et al., "Capitalising on Faith: A Cross-Cultural Examination of Consumer Responses to the Use of Religious Symbols in Advertising", *Journal of Global Marketing*, vol. 33, no. 3, 2020, p. 158.

67 As was the case with an advertisement inspired by Da Vinci's *Last Supper* in which Christ, instead of passing the chalice of wine, invites people to drink *Jaffa Royal* beer. The episode provoked lively reactions, including from the local Islamic Community, which expressed itself in a letter of complaint dated 9 May 1984. The letter accused the advertisement in question of being offensive to Islam, according to which the prophet Jesus is to be counted "among the greatest envoys of God". The matter was decided by the Court of Turin, judgment of 4 January 1986. Cf. M.C. Ivaldi, *La tutela penale in materia religiosa nella giurisprudenza*, p. 152.

68 The body that judges commercial communications at the request of the Control Committee or companies. If a message contravenes the rules, the Institute orders its termination. The decision is always published on the Institute's website (www.iap.it/conoscere-iap/organizzazione/).

69 Self-disciplinary body responsible for the protection of citizen-consumers that acts both *ex officio* and on the recommendation of the public (format available at www.iap.it/le-attivita/per-i-cittadini/segnalare-pubblicita-ingannevole/).

The Committee may submit any messages to the Jury that it deems to be non-compliant with the Code; it may act as a moral suasion, inviting advertisers to change any communications that are unfair; it may issue cease-and-desist injunctions in cases of manifest non-compliance

In these cases, the Institute applies the Advertising Self-Regulatory Code, the latest version of which has been in force since 1 June 2023.[70] Art. 10 of the Code, under the heading "Moral, civil and religious convictions and dignity of the person", states that "commercial communication must not offend moral, civil and religious convictions", "must respect the dignity of the person, in all its forms and expressions", and "must avoid all forms of discrimination".[71]

The IAP Control Committee recently scrutinised a religiously motivated advertisement. The clip takes place in a church where a priest is conducting the Eucharist for nuns, while an older Sister observes the scene from the sacristy. The clip was released in three different versions determined by the transmission channel (public television, commercial television, and social media). Through a crescendo of increasingly explicit references, the last version comes to identify the chip in question with the consecrated Host, concluding in all cases with the slogan "Amica chips, the daily divine". The Italian Television Viewers Association (AIART),[72] a clearly Catholic-inspired organisation, reported the advertisement to the Advertising Self-Discipline Institute. The IAP's Control Committee injunction 9 April 2024, no. 7/24,[73] judged the advertisement in question to be disrespectful to Christian religious beliefs and blocked its dissemination in all versions and on all communication channels.[74]

In the measure, which explicitly recalled several precedents, it is specified that the advertising campaign is in violation of art. 10 as "it takes the form of direct mockery and consequent debasement of the sacrament of the Eucharist, which for believers assumes a fundamental importance and centrality". In other words,

---

with the Code. Similarly, upon request, it may examine in advance commercial communications that have not yet been disseminated.

70 *Codice di autodisciplina della comunicazione commerciale.* Its 75th Edition is available at www.iap.it/codice-e-altre-fonti/il-codice/. The first edition of the Code dates back to 12 May 1966. An integral part of the Code is the Digital Chart Regulations on the Recognisability of Marketing Communication distributed over the Internet (www.iap.it/wp-content/uploads/2020/06/Digital-Chart-Regulations.pdf).

71 The text of the measures is available at the institution's address, where there is also an archive (https://archivio.iap.it/). For an accurate reconstruction of the measures taken to protect religious sensibilities, see M. Toscano, "Immagini e simboli religiosi nella comunicazione commerciale: profili giuridici", in V. Montieri (ed.), *La manipolazione del sacro. L'immagine religiosa nel mondo della comunicazione*, Mimesis, Milano – Udine, 2021, p. 343 as well as A. Arcopinto, "L'utilizzo delle religioni nel marketing d'impresa. Profili di tutela giuridica", *CALUMET – intercultural law and humanities review*, Rivista telematica (www.calumet-review.it), 15 April 2019, p. 1.

72 *Associazione italiana telespettatori. Amplius* in www.aiart.org/.

73 In www.iap.it/decisioni/amica-chips/.

74 For AIART's positive reaction to the injunction, see the press release of 9 April 2024 (www.aiart.org/category/comunicati-stampa/) reconfirming the Association's commitment to respectful publicity language and to building a civilisation "that needs to grow with respect for cultural and religious identities".

> the parallelism that the advertising message establishes between the chips, described as "*the daily divine*", and the host [. . .] takes the form of a mockery of the profound meaning of the sacrament of the Eucharist, making it more than reasonable for the believer and others to feel disproportionately offended.

It is also worth noting another recently concluded incident involving the UAAR and atheistic propaganda. This case arose with the Municipality of Verona's 2013 prohibition of ten posters, put up by the UAAR, that depicted the word "God" with the letter "D" crossed out by a diagonal "X". These posters featured the message that "10 million Italians live well without D. And when they encounter discrimination, the UAAR stands by their side".[75]

The issue can be approached from two opposing points of view: that of the content of the posters, which can be assumed to be potentially shocking to the religious sensibilities of believers, and that of the right to propaganda, including non-religious propaganda, covered by art. 19, Const.

The long and troubled trial process was only recently concluded with the Court of Appeal of Rome, Second Section, judgment 9 February 2023, no. 1923,[76] which ruled definitively on the referral, ordered by the Supreme Court of Cassation, First Civil Section, judgment 17 April 2020, no. 7893.[77]

The Court of Appeal of Rome[78] ruled in favour of the discriminatory character of the refusal by the Municipality of Verona to display atheistic propaganda

75 At www.uaar.it/uaar/campagne/senzad. For information on the other campaigns supported by the UAAR, please visit www.uaar.it/uaar/campagne.

The 2009 campaign in question involved posting on public buses "The bad news is that God does not exist. The good news is that you don't need him" (www.uaar.it/uaar/campagne/bus).

It recalls the idea of atheist buses proposed by the British Humanist Association from 2017 Humanist UK (https://humanists.uk/), which was then taken up by other countries around the world, including Italy. On this issue, S. Baldassarre, "Campagne pubblicitarie ateiste: un'applicazione asimmetrica del principio di laicità", in A. Cardone – M. Croce (eds.), *30 anni di laicità dello Stato: fu vera gloria?* Nessun Dogma, Roma, 2021, pp. 367–382.

76 Initiated with civil anti-discrimination action (arts. 43 and 44, d.lgs. 25 July 1998, no. 286), according to the simplified modalities of art. 28, d.lgs. 1 September 2011, no. 150). Action conceived within the framework of the immigration regulations and rules on the condition of foreigners can be brought if "the conduct of a private individual or the public administration results in discrimination on racial, ethnic, linguistic, national, geographical origin or religious grounds". These actions focused on putting an end to discriminatory practices and rectifying their impact.

77 SCC, judgment no. 7893/2020, "*Ragioni della decisione*", para. 2.2., which traces the jurisprudence used by the Constitutional Court to reconcile the so-called negative freedom of religion with art. 19, Const. SCC, which then elaborates on the principles of law that bind the referring court in its decision (SCC, judgment no. 7893/2020, "*Ragioni della decisione*"`, para. 3).

For an analysis, see N. Colaianni, "Propaganda ateistica: laicità e divieto di discriminazione", 10 Juin 2020, p. 1 ff, available at www.questionegiustizia.it/articolo/propaganda-ateistica-laicita-e-divieto-di-discriminazione_10-06-2020.php.

78 UAAR press release available at https://blog.uaar.it/2023/02/22/una-sentenza-riscatta-i-diritti-di-atei-e-agnostici-e-condanna-il-comune-di-verona-viviamo-bene-senza-d/. For an

posters, maintaining that the censured content deserves the protection of arts. 19 and 21, Const., and does not involve any form of aggression against or debasement of the religious beliefs of others. The Municipality was obligated to compensate for non-pecuniary harm, bear the full costs of the trial, and promptly display the censured posters.

In a study also aiming to verify the application of the supreme principle of *laicità*, as articulated by the Constitutional Court – in its interaction with individual religious freedom (art. 19, Const.) and with the equal freedom recognised to religious denominations (art. 8, para. 1, Const.) – there are additional matters that necessitate attention.

In particular, certain crucial matters arise in what is commonly referred to as the "ecclesiastical politics" (a somewhat outdated terminology that nevertheless remains effective within the Italian context) of the State. With this expression, we refer to the assortment of legislative, administrative, and judicial powers concerning matters of law and religion. This also considers the innovations produced by the 2001 constitutional reform,[79] which amended Title V of the Italian Constitution, redesigning the relations between the State and the other territorial institutions and increasing the powers of the latter.[80]

Within the institutional setup, there are two situations that are especially jarring. One concerns the issue of Muslim places of worship; the other, the absence of a comprehensive legal framework concerning religious freedom to supersede the existing legislation governing recognised the so-called "admitted cults", which remains applicable to religious denominations lacking an *intesa* per art. 8, para. 3, Const.

Additionally, it is important to note that these matters are closely interconnected in determining the legal framework surrounding organised Islam in Italy.

4.3 The long-standing issue of Muslim places of worship

Islam represents a significant challenge in terms of fulfilling the constitutional framework of religious freedom and implementing the legal setting

overview, see M. Croce, "Una storica condanna antidiscriminatoria a tutela della propaganda dei non credenti (Corte d'appello di Roma, II sez., 9 febbraio 2023, n. 1923)", *Quaderni di diritto e politica ecclesiastica*, no. 3, 2023, p. 919 ff.

79 Constitutional law, 18 October 2001, no. 3.

80 On the subject of religious relevance, see art. 117, para. 2, (c), Const., which reserves exclusive legislation on "relations between the Republic and religious denominations" to the State. This provision must be read in relation to the provisions of the subsequent letter (m), which reserves the task of determining "the basic level of benefits relating to civil and social entitlements to be guaranteed throughout the national territory" to the State. In any case, these and the other prerogatives must be exercised "in compliance with the Constitution and with the constraints deriving from EU legislation and international obligations" (art. 117, para. 1, Const.). For an analysis, see P. Consorti, "Nuovi rapporti tra la Repubblica e le confessioni religiose? Sui riflessi ecclesiasticistici della riforma del Titolo V, parte seconda della Costituzione", *Quaderni di diritto e politica ecclesiastica*, no. 1, 2003, p. 13 ff.

for religious denominations. Italian doctrine has recently devoted significant attention to the investigation and detailed analysis of this subject, including in the English language.[81]

The topic commonly known as the "Islamic question" is encompassed within a comprehensive framework that surpasses religious diversity and is intricately connected to security dynamics in numerous European and global nations.[82] The presence of these and other concerns has led to the formulation of crucial queries regarding the designation of suitable individuals to collectively advocate for the interests of Islam. It is imperative that these individuals are endorsed by the various factions of the Islamic world but also deemed "acceptable" by national institutions.[83]

Taking this perspective into account and an emphasis on the issue of places of worship, we limit our discussion to the scenario in which initiatives from different Muslim denominations in Italy, along with institutional initiatives, are situated.

In the past, during the commencement of the so called *intese* season, specific Islamic denominations would prepare texts for discussions with the relevant authorities.[84] Therefore, it is possible to remember the unilaterally proposed draft of *intese* from the 1990s, which underwent no examination.[85]

Nevertheless, there has been no shortage of state initiatives, beginning with the establishment of the Council for Italian Islam (*Consulta per l'islam italiano*) through a decree issued on 10 September 2005[86] by the Minister of

81 F. Alicino, *Constitutional Democracy and Islam*, *passim*.

82 S. Ferrari, "Individual Religious Freedom and National Security in Europe After September 11", *Brigham Young University Law Review*, no. 2, 2004, p. 357 and the various essays in L. Papadopoulou (ed.), *Islam and Human Rights in the European Union*, *passim*.
Regarding the uniqueness of the French case and the many terrorist incidents that have plagued that country, see *supra* para. 3.5.

83 Cf. S. Ferrari, "Islam and the European System of Church-State Relations: A (False) Problem?", *Derecho y Religion*, pt. I, 2006, p. 87.

84 *Amplius infra* para. 4.4. It should be recalled that the conclusion of *intese* is the charge of the Presidency of the Council of Ministers. This responsibility was confirmed by art. 2, para. 3, law 23 August 1988, no. 400, which submits both the acts concerning the relations between the State and the Catholic Church provided for in art. 7, Const., and those provided for in art. 8, Const., to the deliberation of the Council of Ministers, without prejudice to the other competences of the Ministry of the Interior regarding religious denominations.

85 Among the more structured ones are: the Union of Islamic Communities and Organisations in Italy (*Unione delle Comunità Islamiche Italiane* – UCOII), the Association of Italian Muslims (*Associazione dei Musulmani Italiani* – AMI) and the Italian Islamic Religious Community (*Comunità Religiosa Islamica* – COREIS), respectively formulated in 1992, 1994 and 1996. For an assessment from the perspective of Islamic law see A. Cilardo, *Il diritto islamico e il sistema giuridico italiano. Le bozze di intesa tra la Repubblica Italiana e le associazioni islamiche italiane*, Edizioni Scientifiche Italiane, Napoli, 2002, p. 211 ff.

86 Available on the historical website of the Ministry of the Interior at www1.interno.gov.it/mininterno/site/en/sections/old_services/legislation/religions/legislation_691.html.

the Interior. Its main responsibilities included conducting research, carrying out in-depth studies, and presenting proposals,

> with a view to fostering institutional dialogue with Italy's Muslim communities, improving knowledge of integration issues in order to identify the most appropriate solutions for the harmonious integration of these communities into national society, in accordance with the Constitution and the laws of the Republic.

The Council's most interesting outcome lies in the preparation of the "Charter of values of citizenship and integration".[87] However, this document primarily holds symbolic value rather than practical utility as it mirrors the constitutional principles governing religious affairs along with their jurisprudential and doctrinal interpretations.[88]

Paras. 20–26, dedicated to "secularism and religious freedom", are particularly noteworthy. Two prescriptions concerning symbols emerge here.

First, para. 25 states that

> on the basis of its religious and cultural tradition, Italy respects the symbols and the signs of all religions. No one can say to be offended by the signs and symbols of a religion different from his/her own. As established by international Charters, it is convenient to educate the youth to respect the other's religious beliefs, without finding in them elements of division.

Subsequently, para. 26 specifies that

> in Italy, there are no restrictions on people's attire, as long as it is chosen freely and it is not detrimental to his/her dignity. It is not accepted to cover the face because this impedes the person's recognition and hinders establishing relations with the others.

Shortly thereafter, on 13 February 2008, the "Declaration of intent for the federation of Italian Islam" was issued.[89] This document was endorsed by the groups that had already committed to the "Charter of value of citizenship and integration" and was formulated in alignment with its provisions, with the purpose of facilitating potential *intese*.

87 Cf. Ministry of the Interior, decree 23 April 2007, "Carta dei valori della cittadinanza e integrazione". This Charter is available also in English at www.libertaciviliimmigrazione.dlci.interno.gov.it/sites/default/files/allegati/0919_charter_of_values_of_citizenship_and_integration_inglese.pdf.

88 The Scientific Committee entrusted with the preparation of the text consisted of esteemed academics, including professors Roberta Aluffi Beck Peccoz and Carlo Cardia.

89 *Dichiarazione di intenti per la federazione dell'islam italiano*, available on the website of the Ministry of the Interior at www1.interno.gov.it/mininterno/export/sites/default/it/assets/files/15/0679_DICHIARAZIONE_DI_INTENTI.pdf.

A reform of the Council led to the establishment of the Committee for Italian Islam by the Minister of the Interior through decree 2 February 2010.[90] The Committee was tasked with providing specific guidelines on integration and the exercise of civil rights to foster harmonious coexistence within Italian society. There are three noteworthy opinions that were established during this advisory institution's operation: "*Burqa* and *niqab*",[91] "Islamic places of worship",[92] and "Imams and education".[93]

Representatives from Islamic organisations on the Committee joined the "Permanent National Conference on 'Religions, Culture, and Integration'", which was established on 19 March 2012 under the guidance of Minister for Integration and International Cooperation Andrea Riccardi, who was also the founder of the Community of Sant'Egidio. It was an experience of transition, perhaps also considering the short-lived nature of the government that had envisioned it.[94]

After the activation of a consultation table in 2015, the State's institutional initiative was revived under the name "Council for Relations with Italian Islam", and its inaugural meeting was held on 19 January 2016.[95] On 1 February 2017, the Institution drew up the "National Pact for an Italian Islam, expression of an open, integrated community and adherent to the values and principles of the State order".[96]

This document begins by emphasising the paramount importance of the State's *laicità* as a "guarantee of freedom of religion in a regime of confessional and cultural pluralism".

90 *Comitato per l'islam italiano*. The accompanying news can be accessed at www1.interno.gov.it/mininterno/export/sites/default/en/sections/sala_stampa/notizie/Comitato_Islam_italiano/0776_2010_02_11_Islam.

91 *Comitato per l'islam italiano*, opinion 7 October 2010, available at www1.interno.gov.it/mininterno/export/sites/default/en/assets/files/19/00036_Comitato_Islam_-_relazione_Burqa_07_10.pdf.

92 *Comitato per l'islam italiano*, opinion 27 January 2011 available at www1.interno.gov.it/mininterno/export/sites/default/en/assets/files/20/0457_Luoghi_di_culto_islamici_-_Parere_del_Comitato_per_lxIslam_Italiano.pdf.

93 *Comitato per l'islam italiano*, opinion 31 May 2011, available at www1.interno.gov.it/mininterno/export/sites/default/en/assets/files/21/0664_Comitato_per_Islam._parere_del_31_maggio_on_imam_e_formazione.pdf.

94 The Monti Government, serving as the VXI Executive of the Italian Republic, held office from 16 November to 28 April 2013.

95 *Consiglio per le relazioni con l'Islam italiano*. News available at www.interno.gov.it/it/stampa-e-comunicazione/comunicati-stampa/comunicati-stampa-raccolta-anni-precedenti/alfano-prima-riunione-consiglio-relazioni-lislam-italiano.

96 For a comment, see A. Fabbri, "Il Patto nazionale per un islam italiano come condizione preliminare per la stipula di intese con l'islam, le fasi costitutive", *Rivista di diritto pubblico, comparato, europeo*, Rivista telematica (www.federalismi.it), no. 10, 2017, p. 1 ff.

The *Patto nazionale per un Islam italiano, espressione di una comunità aperta, integrata e aderente ai valori e principi dell'ordinamento statale* is accessable at www.interno.gov.it/sites/default/files/patto_nazionale_per_un_islam_italiano_1.2.2017.pdf.

The Council for Relations with Islam received further boost with decree 10 November 2020 by Minister of the Interior Luciana Lamorgese. Lamorgese appointed its new members,[97] including many Italian experts in Law and Religion. However, the Council's last known meeting was on 13 July 2023.[98]

4.3.1 The jurisprudence of the Constitutional Court on the right to place of worship

It is important to note that the Constitutional Court has frequently intervened regarding the matter of places of worship. Such interventions have not been exclusive to cases related to Islamic prayer places, such as in the instance of sentence 27 April 1993, no. 195.[99] This ruling is significant because, in addition to strictly linking the presence of a place of worship to the exercise of religious freedom, it attempts to define the very concept of religious confession,[100] stating that

> it cannot be sufficient for the applicant to self-qualify with the religious denominations. *Nulla quaestio* when there is an *intesa* with the State. In the absence of this, the nature of a confession may also result from previous public recognition, from statutes that clearly express its characteristics, or in any case from common consideration.[101]

With this ruling concerning Jehovah's Witnesses, the Constitutional Court declared the unconstitutionality of Abruzzo regional law 6 March 1988, no. 29, on "Urban planning regulations for religious services".[102] This law subordinated the favourable measures provided for the building of places of worship to the condition that the religious denominations requesting them have

97 News available at www.interno.gov.it/it/notizie/nuovo-impulso-consiglio-relazioni-lislam-italiano-decreto-ministro-lamorgese.

98 News accessible at www.interno.gov.it/it/notizie/riunito-viminale-consiglio-relazioni-lislam-italiano.

99 Incidental proceedings for constitutionality brought by the TAR Abruzzo, order 19 February 1992, in the ruling proposed by the Christian Congregation of Jehovah's Witnesses against the Municipality of L'Aquila.

100 This concept was much debated by the doctrine and jurisprudence of the time, especially in relation to so-called new religious movements such as the Church of Scientology. For the doctrine, see F. Onida, "Nuove problematiche religiose per gli ordinamenti laici contemporanei: Scientology e il concetto giuridico di religione", *Quaderni di diritto e politica ecclesiastica*, no. 1, 1998, p. 279; G. D'Angelo Giuseppe, "Nuovi movimenti religiosi tra (pretesa) uniformità di qualificazione e (reale) diversificazione dei relativi profili disciplinari: la Chiesa di Scientology nella più significativa giurisprudenza", *Il Diritto ecclesiastico*, no. 1, 2003, p. 710 and G. Carobene, "Problems on the Legal Status of the Church of Scientology", *Stato, Chiese e pluralismo confessionale*, Rivista telematica (www.statoechiese.it), no. 21, 2014, p. 1.

101 Constitutional Court, judgment no. 195/1993, "*Considerato in diritto*", para. 5.

102 Measure still available on the institutional regional website at www2.consiglio.regione.abruzzo.it/leggi_tv/testi_vigenti/Cronologico/1988.asp#29.

regulated their relations with the State by means of *intese*, pursuant to art. 8, para. 3, Const.

This serves as the first intervention related to places of worship, but the majority of subsequent interventions took place in the 2000s. The regional legislation that has garnered the most attention pertains to Lombardia.

The Constitutional Court ruling of 16 July 2002, no. 346, decided on the question[103] of the constitutional legitimacy of art. 1, Lombardia regional law, 9 May 1992, no. 20, "Norms for the construction of places of worship and facilities intended for religious services". Similar to Abruzzo regional law 6 March 1988, no. 29, art. 1 of Lombardia regional law, 9 May 1992, no. 20, reserved the benefits provided for the construction of facilities of common interest intended for religious services to the Catholic Church and religious denominations with an *intesa*.

The Court's judgment upheld the complaints, determining that the article

> violated also the equality of individuals in the effective enjoyment of freedom of worship, of which the equal freedom of denominations to organise themselves and operate represents the necessary projection at community level, and on which the possibility of the various denominations to access economic benefits such as those provided for by the law under review exerts an obvious, albeit indirect influence.[104]

The Region subsequently enacted additional legislation on this matter, which faced further criticism from the *Consulta*.[105]

In the judgment 24 March 2016, no. 63, the "Judge of laws" ruled on the question raised by the President of the Council of Ministers in relation to the regional law of Lombardia concerning the government of the territory[106] regarding its conflict with arts. 2, 3, 8, 19, and 117, para. 2, (c) and (h), Const.

This law – the so-called anti-mosque law[107] – distinguished three different categories of entities for the purposes of constructing places of worship and

103 TAR, Lombardia, order 4 December 2001, no. 88.

104 Constitutional Court, judgment, 16 July 2002, no. 346, "*Considerato in diritto*", para. 2.

105 Cf. the parallelism that can be drawn with the affair concerning the regional *anti-burqa* provisions mentioned *supra*, para. 3.2.

The term "*Consulta*", alongside "Judge of laws" (*Giudice delle leggi*), is commonly employed to indicate the Constitutional Court. The name is derived from the building it is housed in, known as *Palazzo della Consulta*.

106 Arts. 70, paras. 2, 2 *bis*, 2 *ter*, and 2 *quater* and 72, paras. 4, 5, and 7, (e) and (g), Lombardia regional law 11 March 2005, no. 12, "Law for the government of the territory", as amended by art. 1, para. 1, (b) and (c), Lombardia regional law 3 February 2015, no. 2 (https://normelombardia.consiglio.regione.lombardia.it/).

107 Cf. A. Fabbri, "La pronuncia della Corte costituzionale sulla 'legge anti-moschee' della Lombardia, tra riaffermazione del principio di laicità e riparto di competenze Stato – Regioni", *Cultura giuridica e diritto vivente*, vol. 3, 2016, p. 1, available at https://journals.uniurb.it/index.php/cgdv/article/view/593/545.

facilities intended for religious services. More precisely, the Court differentiated between entities that are part of the Catholic Church, those that belong to other religious denominations and have signed an *intesa* with the State, and entities that are connected with denominations without an *intesa* and which are therefore subject to the legislation of 1929–1930. Thus, the latter group found themselves in a particularly disadvantaged position given the requirements for the religious organisation to have a widespread and consistent presence in the territory and statutes reflecting institutional religious purposes and adhering to constitutional principles and values.

It is apparent that these regulations, although falling within the regional competence of territorial government, have a direct impact on the religious denominations' legal equality before the law (art. 8, para. 1, Const.) and the exercise of individual and associated religious freedom (art. 19, Const.). As a result, a portion of the legislation was pronounced unconstitutional.

Another measure, which also stems from a constitutional judgment initiated by the Government, pertains to the Veneto Region and its legislation on territorial governance.[108] In this case as well, it is assumed that this measure was contradictory to the aforementioned arts. 3, 8, 19, and 117, para. 2, (c) and (h), Const. The Constitutional Court, judgment 7 April 2017, no. 67, upheld the censures with regard to the provision that mandates, among the requirements for the establishment of the urban planning agreement,

> the commitment to use the Italian language for all activities carried out in the facilities of common interest for religious services, which are not strictly related to the ritual practices of worship.

In this case, for the Court the regional provision at issue

> lends itself to determining broad limitations of fundamental personal rights of constitutional importance, in the absence of a clear relationship of strict instrumentality and proportionality in relation to other constitutionally relevant interests included in the perimeter of regional powers.[109]

In 2019, the Constitutional Court once again had to rule on a question concerning the Lombardia Region, albeit incidentally.[110] The judgment of 5 December 2019, no. 254,[111] upholds part of the constitutionality complaints brought to its attention.

108 Arts. 31 *bis* and 31 *ter*, Veneto regional law, 23 April 2004, no. 11, "Rules for the government of the territory and landscape". Provisions implemented by Veneto regional law, 12 April 2016, no. 12.

109 Constitutional Court, judgment no. 67/2017, "*Considerato in diritto*", para. 3.3.

110 Questions raised by the TAR Lombardia, orders 3 August 2018, no. 159 and 8 October 2018, no.172.

111 It declared art. 72, para. 2 and para. 5, second sentence, of the Lombardia region law 11 March 2005, no. 12, unconstitutional as amended in 2015.

In particular, the ruling recalled its own previous case law on religious freedom and the supreme principle of *laicità*, stating that

> the religious freedom guaranteed by art. 19 Const. is an inviolable right (judgments no. 334 of 1996, no. 195 of 1993 and no. 203 of 1989), protected "to the highest degree" (judgment no. 52 of 2016) by the Constitution. The constitutional guarantee also has "positive" value, since the principle of *laicità* that characterises the republican order is "to be understood, according to the meaning that constitutional case law has given to it (judgments no. 63 of 2016, no. 508 of 2000, no. 329 of 1997, no. 440 of 1995, no. 203 of 1989), not as the State's indifference to religious experience, but rather as the protection of pluralism, in support of the maximum expansion of everyone's freedom, according to criteria of impartiality" (judgment no. 67 of 2017).[112]

Regarding the corollaries of freedom of religion and the rulings made on this subject, the Court emphasised how

> the freedom of worship also translates into the right to have adequate space to be able to concretely exercise it (judgment no. 67 of 2017) and therefore entails, more precisely, a twofold duty on the public authorities responsible for regulating and managing the use of the territory (essentially regions and municipalities): on the positive side – in application of the aforementioned principle of *laicità* – it implies that the competent administrations provide and make available public spaces for religious activities; on the negative side, it requires that no unjustified obstacles be placed in the way of the exercise of worship in private places and that no discrimination be imposed on denominations in accessing public spaces (judgments no. 63 of 2016, no. 346 of 2002 and no. 195 of 1993).[113]

The most recent ruling concerning places of worship again concerns the Veneto Region and specifically addresses the regional law 12 April 2016, no. 12.[114] As with previous cases,[115] this case was initiated as main proceedings by the Government alleging a violation of arts. 2, 3, 8, 19, and 117, para. 2, (c) and (h), Const.

The issues surrounding the problematic exercise of freedom of worship by Islamic denominations, and others as well,[116] go beyond. For example, the sub-

112 Constitutional Court, judgment no. 254/2019, "*Considerato in diritto*", para. 6.

113 Constitutional Court, judgment no. 254/2019, "*Considerato in diritto*", para. 6.

114 "Amendment of regional law 23 April 2004, no. 11 bearing 'rules for the government of the territory and in the matter of landscape' and subsequent amendments". Available at www.consiglioveneto.it/leggi-regionali.

115 Cf. Constitutional Court, judgments nos. 63/2016 and 67/2017.

116 For a reconstruction of the problematic access to places of worship for the new Evangelical and Pentecostal Churches in Italy, see A. Pace, "Le nuove Chiese evangeliche e pentecostali

ject of changing the use of buildings has been the focus of several administrative and jurisprudential interventions. The practice of employing *escamotage* to gain access to places of worship is frequently observed among minority religious denominations, with the Muslim community being a prominent example.

This issue arises primarily not in relation to newly constructed buildings that meet certain architectural criteria defining them as mosques[117] but rather in relation to prayer rooms found in various locations across the country, such as commercial premises, garages, and industrial warehouses, and the process of seeking a change in the building's designated use.

The endeavours to alter the building's designated use, stigmatised by the competent administrative jurisprudence, resulted in findings of building regulation violations and the prohibition of religious use of the premises.[118]

4.3.2 *The two most recent cases involving existing places of worship*

Two very recent cases concerning existing places of worship deserve further attention. The first concerns the Municipality of Cantù (CO) and the Assalam Islamic Cultural Association and particularly the change in use of a building that is still in the process of being built (changing from an industrial warehouse to a place of worship). This is an especially complex and articulated case on which the TAR Lombardia, Section IV, Judgment 21 February 2024, no. 483, ruled. The focus of the discussion was not primarily on the requested change of use but rather on the Cantù Municipality's failure to acknowledge the Assalam Association as an "entity of other religious denominations" according to the Lombardia regional law on land management.

The TAR Lombardia censures the restrictive interpretation of the rule, which hinders access to the benefits for constructing and opening a place of

---

in Italia, senza fissa dimora, esposte a ragionevoli discriminazioni", *Stato, Chiese e pluralismo confessionale*, Rivista telematica (www.statoechiese.it), no. 13, 2021, p. 151.

117 Furthermore, these also align with the previously discussed forecast. In Italy there are just over a dozen mosques registered. Only a select few of these edifices feature domes and minarets, and they were purposefully built *ex novo*, without any reliance on pre-existing structures. Notable examples include the mosque in Segrate in the province of Milan (1988); the largest mosque in Italy, which is located in Rome (1995); the mosque in Colle Val d'Elsa in the province of Siena (2013), which is equipped with a small crystal minaret; and the mosques in Ravenna (2013), Forlì (2014), and Brescia (2018). These constructions have always been accompanied by controversy.

118 For administrative jurisprudence, see Council of State, Section IV, judgment 28 January 2011, no. 683; TAR Veneto, Section II, judgment 27 January 2015, no. 92; Council of State, Section V, judgment 15 January 2013, no. 181; Council of State, Section VI, judgment 19 July 2021, no. 5437. The latter judgment is currently under consideration by the ECtHR, Section I. Cf. appl. no. 4311/22, lodged on 12 January 2022 and communicated to the Italian Government on 1 February 2024.

Regarding the criminal jurisprudence, see SCC, Section III Criminal, judgment 17 July 2017, no. 34812 and judgment 30 August 2019, no. 36689.

worship, including those intermediate social formations of religious inspiration.[119] The TAR assumes this restrictive interpretation to be in conflict with the constitutional right to freedom of worship, the exercise of which, as the Constitutional Court has repeatedly affirmed, "finds in the availability of dedicated places an essential condition".

The second case involve the Municipality of Monfalcone (GO) and two distinct Islamic prayer venues located within the municipal territory. First, the Darus Salaam Islamic Cultural Centre was ordered to cease its worship activities because the available premises lacked a proper building permit.[120] Second, the Baitus Salat Islamic Cultural Association was prohibited from using its premises due to ongoing renovations.[121]

As the Ramadan period approached, precautionary measures were requested, and challenges were presented to the municipal ordinances in both cases.[122]

We highlight only the most significant aspects here. The Council of State, Section II, order 21 March 2024, no. 1024,[123] is a particularly relevant ruling since, in addition to reaffirming the need to balance the conflicting interests (pending definition of the judgment), it pronounced the need to "adopt alternative interim measures that allow believers to be able to observe religious

119 For a comment, see L. Decimo, "Associazioni culturali islamiche e edifici di culto: il TAR Lombardia torna sull'applicazione della legislazione regionale sulle attrezzature religiose", March 2024, p. 1, available at www.rivistadirittoereligioni.com.

120 Municipality of Monfalcone, ordinance 15 November 2023, no. 3, concerning the *Centro Culturale Islamico Darus Salaam*. On this point, M. Croce, "Sull'ordinanza del Comune di Monfalcone per assenza di destinazione d'uso dell'immobile", December 2023, p. 1, available at www.rivistadirittoereligioni.com.

The case proceeded through a sequence of requests, with particular emphasis on precautionary measures aimed at securing a broad acknowledgment of the right to religious freedom. Cf. the following rulings: TAR Friuli Venezia Giulia, Section I, decree, 17 January 2024, no. 7; TAR Friuli Venezia Giulia, Section I, order 10 February 2024, no. 14; Council of State, Section II, decree 29 February 2024, no. 736; Council of State, Section II, decree 10 March 2024, no. 856; Council of State, Section II, order 21 March 2024, no. 1024, and Council of State, Section II, order 23 April 2024, no. 3726.

121 Municipality of Monfalcone, ordinance 7 December 2024, no. 5, concerning the *Circolo Culturale Islamico Baitus Salat*. For the relevant measures, see TAR Friuli Venezia Giulia, Section I, decree, 17 January 2024, no. 8; TAR Friuli Venezia Giulia, Section I, order 10 February 2024, no. 13; Council of State, Section II, decree 29 February 2024, no. 725; Council of State, Section II, decree 10 March 2024, no. 857; TAR Friuli Venezia Giulia, Section I, judgment 20 March 2021, no. 110, and Council of State, Section II, order 23 April 2024, no. 3727.

122 These measures are primarily parallel in relation to the two associations, as evidenced by the list provided in the preceding notes.

123 Council of State, Section II, order, 21 March 2024, no. 1024, Islamic Cultural Centre Darus Salaam. On this topic, see M. Croce, "Doppio stop per l'indirizzo politico 'anti-moschea' del Comune di Monfalcone da parte del giudice amministrativo", April 2024, p. 1, available at www.rivistadirittoereligioni.com.

prescriptions (including those related to the Ramadan period)". To this end, the Council of State asserted that

> the Administration is obliged to identify, in dialogue with the interested parties and in a spirit of reciprocal and loyal cooperation [. . .], accessible and dignified alternative sites to allow believers to pray, taking into careful consideration the critical remarks made by the Association with respect to the sites identified in the meantime by the Police Headquarters [since, it is said, they are "in the open and located in out-of-the-way and peripheral areas"].[124]

Similarly, the TAR Friuli Venezia Giulia, section I, short judgment 23 March 2024, no. 110,[125] complained firstly of the compression of the constitutional rights of assembly (art. 17), association (art. 18), and profession of worship (art. 19), and secondly of the illegitimacy of the contested measure extending the prohibition of access to an open-air area no longer affected by the renovation works. The TAR upheld the grievance and concurred with the appellants' considerations, "considering that there were no grounds for preventing the use of the building in its entirety, also in the light of its use – as known to the Municipality – for the exercise of rights of primary rank, such as freedom of assembly, association and worship"; rights that "while not enjoying unconditional prevalence over opposing public interests, would have justified a more careful balancing of the respective positions".[126]

On the other hand, the issue of the lack of suitable places of worship in which to celebrate rites, services, and ceremonies, during the main religious festivities also came to the forefront of the national news in 2024 with respect to Ramadan celebrations, which often require the availability of further places in addition to those already available to individual local communities.

This is the case of the Municipality of Tubirgo, located in the metropolitan city of Milan, where the mayor first failed to respond to repeated requests for a place to celebrate *Id al-Fitr*, the end of Ramadan, proposed by the Essa Mosque Association (*Associazione Moschea Esse*). In response to the administration's silence, the association sought recourse with the appropriate administrative justice body.

The TAR Lombardia responded, in the President's one-court injunction, by ordering the Municipality to expeditiously conclude the administrative procedure regarding the application submitted by the applicant association and,

124 Council of State, Section II, order, 21 March 2024, no. 1024, "*Ritenuto*", para. 2.

125 TAR Friuli Venezia Giulia, section I, short judgment 23 March 2024, no. 110, Baitus Salat Islamic Cultural Association.

126 TAR Friuli Venezia Giulia, Section I, short judgment no. 110/2024, "*Fatto e Diritto*", para. 5.4.

in the case of a negative response, "to indicate any potential spaces (covered or uncovered) that would be suitable for the use represented by the applicant association and the reasons for their unavailability".[127]

Following the Municipality's refusal on 5 April 2024 for unspecified and unproven reasons of public safety or security, the Esse Mosque Association proposed a new grievance that ended with the issuance of a new precautionary decree.[128] This decree charges the Prefect of Milan with "initiat[ing] a discussion between the parties [. . .] also through a special meeting by 8 April, the day before the celebrations begin". The Prefect, per the decree, successfully secured the designated sports ground in the city for the purpose of organising and hosting the end of Ramadan events on April 9–10.[129]

The Municipality of Turbigo rejected a new application submitted by the same association on 6 May 2024 for the celebration of the Feast of the Sacred (*Eid al-Adha*),[130] as stated in resolution 27 May 2024, no. 15.[131] The TAR Lombardia, Section V, decree dated 10 June 2024, no. 587, once again issued a positive response to the interlocutory application. This decision took into consideration the previous ruling regarding the *Eid al-Fitr* holiday and was based on the observation that

> at this stage, priority must be given to constitutionally guaranteed freedoms (of assembly and worship), albeit with due regard for the equally overriding requirements of public safety and security.

Despite some negative episodes, there are also many initiatives that demonstrate a favourable attitude towards sharing and inclusion, as exemplified by the sixth edition of the *Iftar Street* in Bologna.[132] Under the patronage of the Municipality of Bologna, the event received greetings from Mayor Matteo

127 See TAR Lombardia, Section V, decree 31 March 2024, no. 320. For a commentary, see A. Micciché, "Between Administrative Silence and Religious Freedom: The End of Ramadan in Front of the Lombardy Regional Administrative Court", April 2024, p. 1, available at www.rivistadirittoereligioni.com.

128 TAR Lombardia, Section V, decree 6 April 2024, no. 324.

129 For the settlement of the main judgment, see TAR Lombardia, Section V, judgment 22 April 2024, no. 1233.

130 *Eid al-Adha* is celebrated yearly on the 10th day of the month of *Dhul-Hijjah*, which is the final month of the Islamic calendar. *Eid al-Adha* is a commemoration of Prophet Abraham's (Ibrahim in Arabic) obedient act of sacrificing his son Ishmael (Ismail) per God's command, who was later substituted by a ram provided by God. This event is a powerful symbol of faith and complete surrender to the divine.

131 The association sought approval for the use of a space to hold the aforementioned celebration on June 17, 2024, between 6:00 a.m. and 11:00 a.m., with an estimated attendance of 200 people or fewer.

132 To explore the Muslim perspective, visit the website https://comunitaislamica-bo.it/news/iftar-street/ where you will find videos documenting both past and present events.

Lepore and Cardinal Matteo Zuppi,[133] the archbishop of the city and president of the Italian Bishops' Conference (CEI).

Equally noteworthy is the proclamation made by President of the Italian Republic Sergio Mattarella on 10 April 2024 to mark the conclusion of Ramadan.[134] In addition to offering well wishes to both citizens and non-citizen residents of the Islamic faith, he underlined that "the promotion of mutual respect between faiths and cultures, an element of the social cohesion of our community, calls for the exercise of shared responsibility for the common good".

It is worth recognising the commendable efforts seen in various local contexts where Muslims receive proactive support from select Catholic communities, who generously offer their parish facilities and resources. One example of this was in Renate, a small municipality located in the province of Monza and Brianza, where the initiative "An evening of Ramadan together" was arranged. The event, organised by the La Pace Association, occurred in the courtyard of the San Giovanni Bosco oratory on Friday, 5 April 2024. Unfortunately, the event led to discontent among certain political leaders,[135] prompting the parish priest in question to issue a written statement.[136]

Other countries and religious denominations orchestrate similar initiatives, such as the *Grand Iftar* event held at Anglican Bristol Cathedral in spring 2024 to celebrate the month of Ramadan.[137]

133 For the note from the diocese, see https://ecumenismo.chiesadibologna.it/zuppi-alliftar-street-2024/.

134 Available at www.quirinale.it/elementi/110635.

135 News available at www.avvenire.it/attualita/pagine/polemiche-della-lega-per-una-cena-di-fine-ramadan-in-oratorio-a-renate.

136 Cf. C. Borghi, "Alcune evidenze non sempre evidenti. Pensieri peregrini per avviare una riflessione", 5 April 2024, available at www.cprenateveduggio.it/wp-content/uploads/2024/04/2024-04-06_EvidenzeNonSempreEvidenti.pdf, where an integrated community and an oratory also attended by many Muslim children is mentioned.

For another example, see the organisation of a meeting to pray and eat together at the Church of *San Bernardino delle Monache* in Milan, planned for Sunday 7 April 2024, organised by the Community of Sant'Egidio and various Muslim associations. This was also attended by several refugees who had come to Italy via humanitarian corridors. Cf., N.A., "Milano, Ramadan della pace nella chiesa di San Bernardino: musulmani e cristiani pregano insieme", 6 April 2004, available at www.ilgiorno.it/milano/cronaca/ramadan-islamici-cristiani-preghiera-pe4ue9tk.

137 The event took place on 4 April 2024 and was organised by Muslims4Bristol in partnership with Bristol Cathedral and Bridges for Communities (N.A., "Grand Itfar at Bristol Cathedral. Communities Share a Meal Together to Share Unity", 3 April 2024, available at https://bristol-cathedral.co.uk/news/grand-iftar-at-bristol-cathedral-communities-share-a-meal-together-to-share-unity/).

In another, not entirely positive, example, consider the debates regarding the lighting arrangements for Ramadan on the streets of London (A. Tait, "Ramadan Lights on Display in Central London Over Easter. Islamic Holy Month Celebrated in West End During Christian Festival", 27 March 2024, news available at www.telegraph.co.uk/news/2024/03/27/ramadan-lights-on-display-in-central-london-over-easter/) or in Cologne (M. Trzeciak, "Heftige Ramadan-Diskussion. 'Ich finde es wunderbar' – 'Keine Toleranz gegenüber unseren Werten'", 13 March 2024, available at www.express.de/koeln/ramadan-beleuchtung-ich-ueberlege-mir-koeln-zu-verlassen-1-756508).

4.3.3 The issue pertaining to art. 71, para. 1, Third Sector Code

The Code of the Third Sector presents a multitude of issues relevant to scholars in Law and Religion. In the present context, our scope is limited to outlining a specific situation; a thorough understanding of all the implications of the subject necessitates reference to the abundant literature on the matter.[138] Nevertheless, it is important to underscore one legal provision that led to the discovery of an unforeseen loophole to address the long-standing lack of Islamic places of worship.[139]

The Third Sector Code represents an important reform aimed at regulating and promoting the non-profit sector – which subsumes the set of private entities that pursue civic, solidarity, and socially useful purposes – by ensuring greater transparency, efficiency, and regulatory consistency. Put simply, it reinforces the implementation of the principle of horizontal subsidiarity. This principle is rooted in the belief that citizens, whether on an individual or collective level, possess a superior ability to recognise and address their own needs compared to central or peripheral public authorities.

The comprehensive identification of activities of general interest are exhaustively listed in art. 5, para. 1, Third Sector Code.[140] Activities that must be exercised exclusively or principally encompass a wide range of sectors, such as education, cultural heritage preservation, scientific research, charitable endeavours, sports, international collaboration, and more.

The disputed provision is located in art. 71, para. 1, pursuant to which

> the premises of third sector organisations and the premises in which their institutional activities are carried out, provided that they are not of a productive nature, are compatible with all the homogeneous uses provided for by the decree of the Ministry of Public Works of 2 April 1968 no. 1444 and similar, regardless of the urban destination.

This provision is frequently employed, albeit in a forceful manner, by Muslim associations established in accordance with the provisions of the Third Sector Code. These associations utilise the aforementioned premises to carry out activities of general interest, primarily of a cultural nature, as well as for the

The City of Cologne had already witnessed a sharing and welcoming event in 1965 where Turkish workers celebrated the end of Ramadan in the cathedral (M. Opitz, "Ein Bild und seine Geschichte: Als Muslime zu Ramadan im Kölner Dom beteten", 11 March 2024, available at www.geo.de/wissen/weltgeschichte/ramadan-1965–als-muslime-im-koelner-dom-beteten-34535372.html).

138 Adopted by d.lgs. 3 July 2017, no. 117. For an all-round examination of the topic from the perspective of Law and Religion scholars, see A. Fuccillo – L. Decimo (eds.), *Gli enti religiosi tra diritto speciale, diritto comuni e mercati*, Editoriale Scientifica, Napoli, 2022, *passim*.

139 Most recently, see A. Fabbri, *Il diritto allo spazio di preghiera tra laicità e pluralismo religioso*, Giappichelli, Torino, 2024, *passim*.

140 This is a list that can be updated pursuant to art. 5, para. 2, Third Sector Code.

performance of religious rites and gatherings that would require compliance with quite different urban planning and security measures.

In fact, the rule has always been commonly interpreted as implying recognition of the primacy of social value in the use of public spaces by third-sector entities. Recognition intended to have precedence over measures regarding the urban use of these spaces, even it unrelated to the religious factor.[141]

Nevertheless, several questions have arisen in practice, first and foremost concerning the possibility of including worship activities among those activities that art. 6, Third Sector Code defines as "different activities", i.e. distinct from those typified in art. 5. Activities are permitted

> on condition that the memorandum or statutes of the association allow it and that they are secondary and instrumental with respect to activities in the general interest, according to defined criteria and limits.

The negative answer, however, seems to be suggested by the Code itself. Art. 4, para. 3, provides that the promotional rules apply to civilly recognised religious entities and are limited to the performance of the activities set forth in art. 5, as well as any other activities set forth in art. 6, on the condition that they adopt autonomous regulations and earmarked assets for these activities. In other words, in addition to carrying out the activities of worship that distinguish them, religious organisations may also carry out activities of general interest, provided they do so by setting up an autonomous associative branch specifically dedicated to this purpose.

From this reading of the legislation, it seems clear that the *favor legis* towards activities belonging to the third sector, "regardless of urban destination" does not extend *tout court* to activities of a religious nature, regardless of the religious denomination concerned.

The Ministry of Labour and Social Policies conveyed this stance in its note 15 April 2019, no. 3734,[142] clarifying that social promotion associations are obligated to conduct worship activities in buildings that meet town planning regulations. By doing so, it also referred to the same jurisprudence of the Council of State.[143] According to this jurisprudence, art. 71, Third Sector Code, which allows the establishment of the headquarters of a social promotion association in buildings of any use, does not authorise "the establishment of a non-occasional or precarious place of worship in in non-eligible

141 In this sense, see TAR, Abruzzo, Section I, judgment 25 October 2019, no. 519, and TAR, Lombardia, Section II, judgment 1 July 2020, no. 1269. Both cases pertain to matters that are not related to the practice of religion.

142 Ministry of Labour and Social Policies, note 15 April 2019, no. 3734, available at www.lavoro.gov.it/documenti-e-norme/normative/Documents/2019/Nota-prot-3734-del-15042019-relativa-alle-attivita-di-culto.pdf.

143 Council of State, Section VI, order 18 December 2018, no. 6176.

municipal areas or territories".[144] In the hypothesis under consideration for the Council,

> the aggregative purpose typical of third sector entities [. . .] fades from the factual data that also demonstrate the purpose of worship pursued, but in an incorrect manner in terms of urban planning.[145]

A group of deputies tried to remedy this interpretative problem by means of a parliamentary proposal to amend art. 71, Third Sector Code, submitted to the Chamber of Deputies, on 17 March 2023 under no. 1018.[146]

The introductory report promptly outlined what the *ratio* of the proposal is, namely, to remedy to the

> widespread proliferation of social promotion associations that, in fact, have as their exclusive or prevalent function that of running places of worship for Islamic communities in buildings lacking the urban, structural and safety requirements necessary for such use.[147]

In other words, the aim is to

> fill the legal vacuum that has been created in this matter by explicitly providing that all associations cannot avail themselves of the favourable regulations applicable to social promotion associations for the purposes of allocating premises to be used for worship.[148]

The text specifically provides for the insertion in art. 71, para. 1, Third Sector Code of the following sentence:

> [T]he provisions of this paragraph do not apply to associations for social promotion that carry out, even occasionally, activities of worship of religious denominations whose relations with the State are not regulated on the basis of agreements, within the meaning of article 8, para. 3, of the Constitution.[149]

144 Council of State, Section VI, order no. 6176/2018, "*Considerato*", para. 4.
145 Council of State, Section VI, order no. 6176/2018, "*Considerato*", para. 5.
146 Draft law no. 1018/2023, "Amendment to article 71 of the Code of the Third Sector, referred to in legislative decree 3 July 2017, no. 117 on the subject of urban planning compatibility of the use of headquarters and premises used by social promotion associations for their activities". Draft law available at www.camera.it/leg19/126?leg=19&idDocumento=1018.
147 What follows is the "practice, now common throughout the country [. . .] of submitting a request to the municipal administration for public premises to be used as a cultural centre. Once the concession has been obtained, without the need for a change of use and in the absence of changes to urban plans, the premises are used as places of worship, in accordance with the regulations in force".
148 Draft law no. 1018/2023, XIX Legislature, "Introductory report", in the final part.
149 Draft law no. 1018/2023, XIX Legislature, art. 1.

The Draft, approved with amendments by the Chamber of Deputies on 7 May 2024, was forwarded to the Senate.[150] It should be noted that the current version appears to be more constitutionally oriented. It no longer targets mere occasional activities of worship but rather those involving an exclusive or prevalent use for worship if they "do not comply with the defined requirements of safety and accessibility, also taking into account the impact of the activities on the surrounding urban fabric". It remains to be seen whether there will be final approval.

4.4 The ongoing lack of a general law on religious freedom and the wide margin of state decision-making in the negotiation of *intese*

One of the key symbolic questions concerns the survival of the legislation dating back to 1929–30 for religious denominations that have not been granted the benefits of art. 8, para. 8, Const.

As partially anticipated,[151] a considerable number of *intese* have now been signed between the State and various religious denominations that have requested them,[152] starting with the first signed with the Methodist Waldensian Table in 1984.[153] This *intesa* has been amended twice by consensus.[154]

Since then, the following religious denominations have entered into an *intesa* with the State: Union of Seventh-Day Adventist Christian Churches (29 December 1986, law 22 November 1988, no. 516);[155] Assemblies of God in Italy (29 December 1986; law 22 November 1988, no. 517);[156] Union of Jewish Communities in Italy (27 February 1987, law 8 March 1989, no. 101);[157] Evangelical Baptist Christian Union of Italy (29 March 1993, law 12 April 1995, no. 116);[158] Evangelical Lutheran Church in Italy (20 April 1993; law 29 November 1995,

150 Bill no. 1134, transmitted by the President of the Chamber of Deputies to the Presidency of the Senate on 8 May 2024. Text accessible at www.senato.it/service/PDF/PDFServer/BGT/01417904.pdf.

151 *Supra*, para. 1.4.

152 The procedures and texts of the *intese* can be found on the *Presidenza del Consiglio dei Ministri – Servizio per i rapporti con le confessioni religiose* webpage, located at https://presidenza.governo.it/usri/confessioni/intese_indice.html.

153 *Tavola Valdese Metodista* (https://chiesavaldese.org/). *Intesa*, 21 February 1984 (law 11 August 1984, no. 449), already evoked *supra* para. 1.4.

154 *Intese*, 25 January 1993 (law 5 October 1993, no. 409) and 4 April 2007 (law 8 June 2009, no. 68).

155 *Unione delle Chiese Cristiane Avventiste del Settimo Giorno*, available at https://chiesaavventista.it/. Text amended by the *intese* 6 November 1996 (law 20 December 1996, no. 637) and 4 April 2007 (law 8 June 2009, no. 67).

156 *Assemblee di Dio in Italia* (ADI – www.assembleedidio.org/). *Intesa* unrevised.

157 *Unione delle Comunità Ebraiche in Italia* (UCEI – www.ucei.it/). Amended by *intesa* 6 November 1996 (law 20 December 1996, no. 637).

158 *Unione Cristiana Evangelica Battista d'Italia* (UCEBI – www.ucebi.it/). Text amended by the *intesa* 16 July 2010 (law 12 March 2012, no. 34).

no. 520);[159] Holy Orthodox Archdiocese of Italy and Exarchate for Southern Europe (4 April 2007, law 30 July 2012, no. 126);[160] Church of Jesus Christ of Latter-Day Saints (4 April 2007, law 30 July 2012, no. 127);[161] Apostolic Church in Italy (4 April 2007, law 30 July 2021, no. 128);[162] Italian Buddhist Union (4 April 2007, law 31 December 2012, no. 245);[163] Italian Hinduist Union (4 April 2007, law 31 December 2012, no. 246);[164] Italian Buddhist Institute Soka Gakkai (27 June 2015, law 28 June 2016, no. 130);[165] and Association "Church of England" (30 July 2019, law 29 December 2021, no. 240).[166]

The first effect of entering into an *intesa* is to remove the applying entity from falling within the unilateral state law no. 1159/1929 and its implementing r.d. no. 289/1930.

As partially anticipated, the purpose of the *intesa* instrument was to devise a mechanism for negotiating customised treatment for every religious group, resulting in the formulation of specific regulations. However, religious denominations, wishing to have easy access to the instrument provided for in art. 8, para. 3 Const., have used the texts of previous signed *intese* as a foundation for negotiations with the State, extending and generalising related provisions.

The reason for this was also the Italian Legislator's struggle to pass a comprehensive law on religious freedom that could effectively replace the existing legislation on the so-called admitted cults in a constitutional manner. However, Italian doctrine does not reach a unanimous consensus on this matter. Some argue that the Italian State – by virtue of art. 8, para. 3, Const. – is not entitled to regulate the subject matter unilaterally.[167]

Numerous efforts have been made to initiate reform, beginning with the 1990 endeavour led by the Council of Ministers. This initiative resulted in the proposal titled "Regulations on religious freedom and abrogation of legislation on admitted cults", which was approved on 13 September 1990 but never formally introduced in Parliament.[168] This bill has the dual purpose of repealing previous legislation and establishing provisions for the protection of religious freedom, while also regulating the procedure for the stipulation of *intese*.

159 *Chiesa Evangelica Luterana in Italia* (CELI – www.chiesaluterana.it/). *Intesa* unrevised.

160 *Sacra Arcidiocesi Ortodossa d'Italia ed Esarcato per l'Europa Meridionale* (https://ortodossia.it/).

161 *Chiesa di Gesù Cristo dei Santi degli ultimi giorni* (www.churchofjesuschrist.org/).

162 *Chiesa Apostolica in Italia* (www.chiesapostolica.it/).

163 *Unione Buddhista Italiana* (UBI – https://unionebuddhistaitaliana.it/).

164 *Unione Induista Italiana* (www.induismo.it/).

165 *Istituto Buddista Italiano Soka Gakkai* (IBISG – www.sgi-italia.org/).

166 *Associazione "Chiesa d'Inghilterra"* (www.chiesadinghilterra.org/).

167 The Italian doctrine of Law and Religion has cast doubt on this thesis, especially concerning certain aspects. Cf. G. Dalla Torre, "Libertà di coscienza e di religione", *Stato, Chiese e pluralismo confessionale*, Rivista telematica (www.statoechiese.it), March 2008, pp. 18–21.

168 Bill published in the journal *Il Diritto ecclesiastico*, no. 1, 1991, pp. 474–483.

Another bill of governmental origin that was instead presented to the Chamber of Deputies on 3 July 1997 is bill no. 3947 (XIII Legislature),

> under the same title as the previous project.[169] Despite undergoing extensive debate, it was not successfully enacted into law.

It is no coincidence that d.lgs. 1 December 2009, no. 179, "State legislative provisions prior to 1 January 1970, the permanence of which is considered indispensable"[170] provided in art. 1, para. 1, annex (a) the ongoing validity of the rules regarding "admitted cults".

There is one additional initiative that deserves mention due to the individuals responsible for its development.[171] The proposal "Freedom of Conscience and Religion" was formulated by a group of scholars and overseen by the ASTRID Foundation. It was officially introduced to the public and institutions on 6 April 2017.[172] However, as of 2024, there are no discernible solutions in sight.

This particular circumstance further complicates the situation surrounding the status of specific religious denominations, particularly that of the Jehovah's Witnesses. They entered into *intesa* with the State in both 2000[173] and 2007,[174] but these *intese* have not been successfully implemented into law.[175]

An application was introduced by the Italian Congregation of Jehovah's Witnesses on 22 August 2016 and is currently pending before Section I of the EctHR.[176] The Italian Government was formally notified of the application and asked to provide comments on 3 November 2019.[177]

The main concern revolves around unequal treatment that the Congregation purportedly receives in comparison to other religious confessions that

169 Available at www.senato.it/leg/13/BGT/Schede/Ddliter/4149.htm.

170 Under art. 14, law 28 November 2005, no. 246, "Simplification and Reorganisation of Legislation for the Year 2005".

171 To gain insight into this matter, see L. De Gregorio, "Laicità e progetti per una legge generale sulla libertà religiosa", *Stato, Chiese e pluralismo confessionale*, Rivista telematica (www.statoechiese.it), no. 21, 2020, p. 67.

172 Of the drafters of the proposal, see R. Zaccaria et al. (eds.), *la legge che non c'è. Proposta per una legge sulla libertà religiosa in Italia*, il Mulino, Bologna, 2017, *passim*.

173 *Congregazione Italiana dei Testimoni di Geova*, available at www.jw.org/it/testimoni-di-geova/contatti/italia/. To access the text of the *intesa* dated 20 March 2000, see www.cesnur.org/testi/geova_it99.htm.

174 The *intesa* signed on 4 April 2007 is available at https://presidenza.governo.it/USRI/ufficio_studi/normativa/Intesa_Congregazione_cristiana_testimoni_geova.pdf.

175 On this topic, P. Floris, "Intorno all'intesa con i Testimoni di Geova", *Stato, Chiese e pluralismo confessionale*, Rivista telematica (www.statoechiese.it), no. 13, 2021, p. 119 ff.

176 Application no. 49687/16. To access the state of proceedings online, visit https://app.echr.coe.int/SOP/index.aspx?lg=.

177 The communication's content, accessible on the ECtHR's database through the "Communicated Cases" option, emphasises the additional efforts made to reach agreements in both 2014 and 2015.

have entered into an *intesa* with the Italian State, pursuant to art. 8, para. 3, Const. Thus, the application accuses the Italian Government of violation of art. 14, ECHR, in combination with art. 9.

According to the communication sent to the Italian Government on 3 November 2019, the legal basis of the application stems from the inadequacy of remedies available within the national legal system. In order to achieve the objective of reaching an *intesa* that is implemented by law, the Congregation referred to the Constitutional Court's judgment 27 January 2016, no. 52, which pertains to the UAAR case.[178] The ruling asserted that the Government holds the political discretion to reach agreements and explicitly states that such decisions are not subject to judicial scrutiny.

The various Islamic denominations mentioned at the beginning of the para. 4.3. are also still subject to the legislation of the years 1929–1930. Some of these entities have been recognised[179] or are on their way to being recognised[180] as bodies under the 1929/1930 legislation, a circumstance that represents a step forward and gives hope for the opening of possible future negotiations under art. 8, para. 3, Const.

This is an issue that introduces the topic of government discretion, as also highlighted by the issue of the UAAR's request for an *intesa*.[181]

4.4.1 The denial of an intesa *to the Union of Atheists Agnostics Rationalists*

The request made by an atheistic organisation to enter into an *intesa* may have been poorly presented by the UAAR itself. Although it is correct that freedom of religion under art. 19, Const. also includes negative freedom – i.e. the freedom not to believe – it is not automatically true that the provisions of art. 8, Const. can also refer to exponential entities of atheism and agnosticism given that it only specifies religious denominations.[182]

178 *Infra* subpara. 4.4.1.

179 See the case of the Islamic Cultural Centre of Italy that oversees the Grand Mosque in Rome, which has legal personality under d.P.R. 21 December 1974, no. 712.

180 Also in the wake of the dialogue with the institutions mentioned, *supra* para. 4.3.

181 With regard to the correlation between secularism and bilateralism, taking into consideration the challenging coexistence with *favor religionis*, see F. Alicino, "Laicità e bilateralità a trent'anni dalla sentenza madre. I test dell'Islam italiano e dell'ateismo militante", *Stato, Chiese e pluralismo confessionale*, Rivista telematica (wwww.statoechiese.it), no. 1, 2021, p. 27 ff.

182 Cf. art. 8, para. 1, Const., for all religious denominations (*"confessioni religiose"*), while in the context of art. 8, paras. 2 and 3, Const., only for religious denominations other than Catholic. On this topic, see F. Alicino, "Atheism and the Principle of Secularism in the Italian Constitutional Order", *The Italian Law Journal*, no. 1, 2021, p. 15 and R. Bottoni – C. Cianitto, "Is Nonreligion a Religion? The Italian Legal Experience", in A.L. Zwilling – H. Årsheim (eds.), *Nonreligion in Late Modern Societies. Institutional and Legal Perspective*, Springer, Cham, 2022, p. 49.

European Union law has diverged in its decision-making approach by establishing a parallel between churches and religious associations on the one hand and philosophical and non-confessional organisations on the other in art. 17 of the Treaty on the Functioning of the European Union (TFEU).[183] In line with the principle of vertical subsidiarity, this parallelism duly acknowledges the legal status of the mentioned entities as defined by the relevant national law.[184]

The ongoing case being investigated is of a highly intricate nature and dates back to the early 1990s when the UAAR initially requested the Italian Government to initiate negotiations for the purpose of reaching an agreement, per art. 8, para. 3, Const.[185] The first refusal of this request was carried out in an unceremonious manner in 1996,[186] and it was then formally rejected again in 2003.[187]

The grounds for the refusal were based on the reasoning that

> the profession of atheism, certainly to be admitted on a par with religious profession as regards free exercise in any form [. . .] cannot be regulated in a manner analogous to what is explicitly provided by art. 8 of the Constitution only for religious confessions.[188]

The term "religious confession" is to be interpreted strictly as "a fact of faith addressed to the divine and lived in common by several persons who make it manifest to society through a particular institutional structure", with the exclusion of any extensibility to different situations.[189]

This was followed by a claim to the TAR Lazio, Section I, judgment 31 December 2008, no. 12539, which declared its absolute absence of jurisdiction, recognising that the determination made by the Government in this matter was in nature a political act.

183 For EU law and case law, see https://eur-lex.europa.eu/, offered in the different languages of the European Union.

184 Cf. art., 17, para. 3, TFEU, according to which the Union, by virtue of the recognition of the specific identity and contribution, maintains "an open, transparent and regular dialogue" with these churches and organisations.

185 Cf. M. Croce, "An Agreement Denied: How Philosophical Associations Are Discriminated Against by Italian Law", in A. Orioli (ed.), *Non Believers' Europe. Models of Secularism, Individual Statuses, Collective Rights*, Nessun Dogma, Roma, 2019, p. 72 ff.; and more generally: S. Baldassarre, "The Legal Position of Non Believers under Italian Law", in A. Orioli (ed.), *Non Believers' Europe. Models of Secularism, Individual Statuses, Collective Rights*, Nessun Dogma, Roma, 2019, p. 253.

186 The text can be accessed at www.uaar.it/laicita/ateismo_e_legislazione/17e.html. Denial against which the UAAR lodged an extraordinary appeal to the Presidency of the Republic (www.uaar.it/laicita/ateismo_e_legislazione/17b.html), winning it. For an accurate reconstruction, see the Association's website at www.uaar.it/laicita/ateismo-legislazione-italiana/#04.

187 The text of the "Risposta del Consiglio dei Ministri sulla richiesta d'intesa" of the 5 December 2023 is available at www.uaar.it/laicita/ateismo_e_legislazione/17e.html.

188 Risposta del Consiglio dei Ministri sulla richiesta d'intesa" of the 5 December 2023.

189 Risposta del Consiglio dei Ministri sulla richiesta d'intesa" of the 5 December 2023.

The judgment rendered by the Council of State, Section IV, on 18 November 2011, no. 6083, reached a contradictory conclusion. It argued that the present case does not involve an indisputable political act, but rather a decision – to initiate the procedure for the conclusion of an *intesa* embodying the typical traits of discretionary assessment and open to review by the administrative judge. The Council of State overturned the first-instance judgment with a referral.

Following this, the Supreme Court of Cassation issued its decision in response to the appeal made by the Council of Ministers and its President.[190] This judgment was delivered in the United Civil Sections, 28 June 2013, no. 16305,[191] and it aligns with the conclusion reached in the Council of State ruling no. 6083/2011.

Nonetheless, the ultimate decision fell under the jurisdiction of the Constitutional Court, which was tasked with considering an appeal regarding a conflict of authority between state powers following the United Civil Sections judgment. The Court was required to examine the legitimacy of the decision to refuse negotiations for an *intesa* in accordance with art. 8, para. 3, Const., as political act immune to judicial challenge.

Constitutional Court, judgment 10 March 2016, no. 52,[192] reiterates that

> agreements are not a condition imposed by the public authorities for the purpose of allowing religious confessions to enjoy freedom of organisation and action, or to benefit from the application of the rules, intended for them, in the various sectors of the legal system. Regardless of the stipulation of understandings, equal freedom of organisation and action is guaranteed to all confessions by the first two paragraphs of art. 8, Const. (judgment no. 43 of 1988) and by art. 19, Const., which protects the exercise of religious freedom also in associated form. Indeed, the jurisprudence of this Court is constant in affirming that the Legislator cannot discriminate between religious denominations on the sole basis of whether or not they have regulated their relations with the State through agreements or *intese* (judgment no. 346 of 2002 and no. 195 of 193).[193]

190 Arguing that the UAAR's original application before the TAR Lazio was inadmissible.

191 Viewable at www.eius.it/giurisprudenza/2013/060.

192 The English translation prepared by the Court is accessible at www.cortecostituzionale.it/documenti/download/doc/recent_judgments/S52_2016_en.pdf. Nonetheless, this translation does not appear to be completely accurate.

It is worth mentioning, among other things, the inappropriate utilisation of the term "concordat" in translating the Italian "*intese*", a bilateral agreement that exclusively impacts national law and not international law, unlike the concordat with the Catholic Church.

For a comment, see V. Pacillo, "La politica ecclesiastica tra discrezionalità dell'Esecutivo, principio di bilateralità e laicità/neutralità dello Stato: brevi note a margine della sentenza della Corte costituzionale n. 52 del 10 marzo 2016", *Lo Stato*, vol. VI, 2016, p. 245.

193 Constitutional Court, judgment no. 52/2016, "*Considerato in diritto*", para. 5.1.

Considering the existing state of positive law, particularly for the Court,

> it cannot be affirmed, in fact, that the failure to conclude an *intesa* is, in itself, incompatible with the guarantee of equality between religious confessions other than the Catholic one, protected by art. 8, para. 1, Const.[194]

Regarding the central point of the dispute, namely, whether a justiciable claim to the commencement of negotiations can be configured in the Italian legal system, the Court considered that "institutional and constitutional reasons preclude the configurability of such a claim".[195] The judgment states that this is precluded firstly by

> the reference to the method of bilaterality, immanent in the *ratio* of para. 3 of art. 8, Const., which [. . .] requires a concordant will of the parties, not only in conducting and concluding negotiations, but also, before that, in initiating them. The affirmation of the possibility of judicial review of the refusal to initiate negotiations – with the consequent possibility of coercive enforcement of the recognised "right", and of the correlative obligation of the Government, to initiate them – would, instead, insert a dissonant element with respect to the method of bilateralism, derivable from the constitutional provision under examination.[196]

Secondly, "an autonomous justiciable claim to the commencement of negotiations is not recognisable precisely in the light of the non-configurability of a subjective demand for the successful conclusion of those negotiations".[197] For the Government,

> the identification of those who may be admitted to the negotiations, and the subsequent actual commencement of them, are important determinations, in which its political discretion is already engaged, and the responsibility that normally follows in a parliamentary form of government.[198]

That is, the Government can only be held politically accountable for the decision to initiate or decline negotiations but cannot be judged legally in court.

194 Constitutional Court, judgment no. 52/2016, "*Considerato in diritto*", para. 5.1.
195 Constitutional Court, judgment no. 52/2016, "*Considerato in diritto*", para. 5.2.
196 Constitutional Court, judgment no. 52/2016, "*Considerato in diritto*", para. 5.2.
197 Constitutional Court, judgment no. 52/2016, "*Considerato in diritto*", para. 5.2.
198 Constitutional Court, judgment no. 52/2016, "*Considerato in diritto*", para. 5.2.

Moreover, the Constitutional Court maintained that the act of refusal itself cannot produce, within the legal system, effects beyond those for which it is intended and

> does not lead to further negative consequences, other than the failure to enter into negotiations, on the legal sphere of the applicant association, by virtue of the principles expressed in arts. 3, 8, 19 and 20, Const.[199]

In other words, it cannot affect the legal sphere of the association itself. Indeed,

> an eventual damaging act, adopted in contexts obviously distinct from the one now at issue, may be subject to judicial review, in the procedural forms permitted by the legal system, for the purpose of reviewing the failure to qualify as a religious confession that would claim to be based on the governmental act.[200]

Additionally,

> in the delicate sphere of religious pluralism designed by the Constitution, there are in fact no "enclaves" that can be configured as "free zones" from the judge's review, which is placed to safeguard the equality of all confessions guaranteed by arts. 3, 8, 19 and 20, Const.[201]

Based on these points, the Constitutional Court asserted that it was not within the jurisdiction of the Court of Cassation to judge the Council of Ministers' decision regarding the denial of negotiations for the agreement mentioned in art. 8, para. 3, Const. Consequently, the Constitutional Court annulled judgment no. 16305/2013.

The pronouncement rendered by the Judge of Laws, though agreeable and meticulously reasoned, failed to conclusively resolve the claims of the UAAR, prompting the organisation to seek recourse through an appeal to the ECtHR.[202]

Incidentally, the question of whether atheism can be recognised as a religion has not only arisen in Italy.[203] For instance, in France, the Council of State

199 Constitutional Court, judgment no. 52/2016, "*Considerato in diritto*", para. 5.3.
200 Constitutional Court, judgment no. 52/2016, "*Considerato in diritto*", para. 5.3.
201 Constitutional Court, judgment no. 52/2016, "*Considerato in diritto*", para. 5.3.
202 Application no. 55861/16 was filed on 9 September 2016 and communicated to the Italian Government on 7 September 2020.
203 For an examination of the issue from a comparative standpoint, see G. Laneve, "Atheism as Part of Religious Phenomenon: Questions and New Challenges to Secularism", *Rivista di diritto pubblico, comparato, europeo*, Rivista telematica (www.federalismi.it), no. 25, 2020, p. 154.

also denied the qualification of the Union of Atheists[204] as a religious association for the purpose of accepting a bequest. In decision 10 June 1988, no. 63912, the Conseil of State, III and X Chambers United, held that it could not be considered a religious association within the meaning of the provisions of the Law of 9 December 1905,[205] on account of the purpose stated in its statutes, namely, that of tending "to bring together those who consider God to be a myth".

Recently, the Canada Federal Court of Appeal ruling 29 November 2019, *Church of Atheism of Central Canada v. Canada (National Revenue)*, 2019 FCA 296,[206] focused on whether or not religion qualifies as a charity for the purpose of applying the Income Tax Act 1985.[207] As the Courts did not previously recognise atheism, the Minister of National Revenue searched for three fundamental characteristics in common with previously recognised religions fulfilling charitable purposes. In other words,

> it must have the same fundamental characteristics as those recognised religions. These fundamental characteristics are not set out in a clear "test". A review of the jurisprudence shows that fundamental characteristics of religion include that the followers have a faith in a higher power such as God, entity, or Supreme Being; that followers worship this higher power; and that the religion consists of a particular and comprehensive system of faith and worship (*Syndicat Northcrest v. Amseleum*, 2004 SCC 47, at para. 39).[208]

The Court, while agreeing with the appellant that

> the requirement that the belief system have faith in a higher Supreme Being or entity and reverence of said Supreme Being is not always required when considering the meaning of "religion".[209]

It is also noted that

> [it] is with respect to the third element that the appellant's submissions must fail. It did not demonstrate that its belief system is based on a particular and comprehensive system of doctrine and observances.[210]

204 *Union of Atheists* (www.athees.fr/).

205 Cf. Title V, *loi séparation*, arts. 18–24.

206 2019 FCA 296. The decision can be accessed through the database of the Canadian Legal Information Institute, located at https://canlii.ca.

207 Available at https://laws-lois.justice.gc.ca/eng/acts/i-3.3/.

208 Canada Federal Court of Appeal, judgment 29 November 2019, para. 10.

209 Canada Federal Court of Appeal, judgment 29 November 2019, para. 21. In accordance with the Court's observation, the appellant rightly emphasised Buddhism as a recognised religion that rejects the concept of a Supreme Being or any form of entity.

210 Canada Federal Court of Appeal, judgment 29 November 2019, para. 22.

Thus, in the Court's opinion,

> the record does not support the appellant's request [. . .] to recognise the Church of Atheism as a religion in the charitable sense. The Minister's decision to refuse to register the appellant is reasonable and does not violate sections 2 *(a)*, 15 and 27 of the Charter.[211]

There are non-theistic religious denominations which lack belief in transcendent and creative deities and yet are grounded in philosophies of life, ethics, and morality, such as Buddhism.[212] Buddhism was founded in India by Siddhartha Gautama, known as the Buddha, around the 5th century BC and is based on the practice of meditation to achieve enlightenment.[213]

A similar argument could be made for the religions of human potential, which are generally non-theistic. They focus on individual, personal development and exploration of inner potential rather than on the worship of personal deities or omnipotent creators, though they still use concepts of energy or cosmic forces.[214] However, these entities are not universally recognised as religions in the proper sense in various legal systems.[215]

Furthermore, the argument that does not consider the presence of a belief system and faith in a higher Supreme Being as an essential requirement for the definition of religion has gained widespread acceptance. This occurred not only on the part of the UAAR but also in notable cases such as the landmark decision of the United State Supreme Court, judgment 19 June 1961,

211 Canada Federal Court of Appeal, judgment 29 November 2019, para. 28. The Constitution Act of 1982 (*Canadian Charter of Rights and Freedoms)* can be accessed at https://canlii.ca/t/ ldsx). The provisions of articles 2 (a), 15, and 27 pertain to the fundamental rights of freedom of conscience and religion, equality under the law, and the safeguarding of multicultural heritage.

212 For other examples of nontheistic religions, see Jainism, Confucianism, and certain sects of Taoism and Hinduism.

213 Within Buddhism, the concept of reincarnation is upheld as an essential component of the continuous cycle of existence, encompassing birth, death, and rebirth, commonly known as samsara. Living beings continue to be reborn in different forms until they reach enlightenment and nirvana, a time when they are released from the cycle of reincarnation.

214 As an example, consider Scientology, the New Age Movement, and the Human Potential Movement.

215 Take, for instance, the case of the Church of Scientology in France, which has been repeatedly labelled as a movement exhibiting characteristics of sectarianism. Cf. M.C. Ivaldi, "Alcune considerazioni sulla regolamentazione dei movimenti a carattere settario nell'ordinamento francese", *Stato, Chiese e pluralismo confessionale*, Rivista telematica (www.statoechiese.it), 8 October 2012, p. 1.

The recent law 10 May 2024, no. 2024–420, aimed at reinforcing the combat against sectarian aberrations and improving support for victims (*visant à renforcer la lutte contre les dérives sectaires et à améliorer l'accompagnement des victimes*), intervenes to regulate the matter with new provisions after it was initially regulated by law 12 June 2001, no. 2001–504, intended to reinforce the prevention and repression of sectarian movements undermining human rights and fundamental freedoms (*tendant à renforcer la prévention et la répression des mouvements sectaires portant atteinte aux droits de l'homme et aux libertés fondamentale*).

Torcaso v. Watkins.[216] This is a legal case concerning the rejection of a public office appointment in Maryland due to the refusal to profess belief in God. The proceedings unanimously determined a violation of the Religious Freedom Clause of the First Amendment and the Equal Protection Clause of the Fourteenth Amendment.

Significant the decision states that

> neither a State nor the Federal Government can constitutionally force a person "to profess a belief or disbelief in any religion". Neither can constitutionally pass laws or impose requirements which aid all religions as against non-believers, and neither can aid those religions based on a belief in the existence of God as against those religions founded on different beliefs.

This concept is further detailed in a note referring to case law and doctrine that specifies that

> among religions in this country which do not teach what would generally be considered a belief in the existence of God are Buddhism, Taoism, Ethical Culture, Secular Humanism and others.[217]

Apart from the diverse range of militant atheist organisations like the UAAR in Italy, it is noteworthy to mention the phenomenon of the Sunday Assembly. Established in London in 2013 by comedians Sanderson Jones and Pippa Evans, this movement rapidly expanded to multiple cities in the United States and Australia. It is often described as a "church for people who don't believe in God".[218]

4.5 The latest questions concerning the crucifix

A final case concerning the issue of religious symbols in institutions concerns the Municipality of Mandas, a small town located in the southern part of Sardinia. The case arises from an ordinance issued on 23 November 2009,

216 367 U.S. 488 (1961), available at https://caselaw.findlaw.com/court/us-supreme-court/367/488.html. For a parallel with the Italian situation concerning oaths in trials, see *supra* para. 1.2.

217 367 U.S. 488 (1961), nt. 11. In terms of doctrine, see R. Dworking, *Religion without God*, Harvard University Press, Cambridge, MA, 2013, *passim*. In essence, the author posits that religiosity can exist without the necessity of believing in a personal deity. Therefore, he asserts that many people, including some atheists, may have a deep sense of wonder and respect for the universe and moral values, which can be considered *sensu lato* religious.

218 Cf. www.sundayassembly.org. Sunday Assembly gatherings encompass musical performances, motivational speeches, volunteer initiatives, and social interaction. The main emphasis is on leading a better life, actively contributing to others' lives, and embracing a sense of curiosity.

no. 21/2998, by the mayor *pro tempore*,[219] which provided for the immediate posting of crucifixes in all public buildings, punishing any transgression with a fine.[220] The measure, which was subsequently withdrawn without prior notice after the billposting had already occurred, was purportedly intended to

> preserve the current traditions, i.e., to maintain in the public buildings of this municipality the presence of the crucifix as a fundamental symbol of the civil and cultural values of our country.

The ordinance was challenged through an appeal to the TAR Sardegna, Section II, 31 May 2017, no. 383, which rejected the grievance by referring to the *Lautsi II* ruling and in part declared it inadmissible due to a supervening lack of interest.[221]

However, a different perspective emerged in Council of State, Section II, judgment 18 March 2024, no. 2567. This judgment overturned the initial verdict and declared the Mayor of Mandas' ordinance as unlawful by exceeding the mayor's legally attributed powers.[222]

Referring to the judgment of the Supreme Court of Cassation, no. 24414/2021,[223] the Council of State also emphasised how the mayor did not, among other things, carry out any reasonable balancing of the interests at stake in the administrative decision before issuing the contested measure.

With regards to educational institutions, recent press reports have brought attention to a middle school in Carpi (MO) where, after undergoing renovation work, the crucifixes previously affixed in the classrooms were alleged to have disappeared upon the start of the 2023/2024 school year. As a result of parents' complaints and the subsequent controversy, as well as the clarifications from the school authorities, the crucifixes were restored to their original positions in the renovated spaces.[224]

219 Mayor of the Union of the Centre, a Catholic-inspired party that draws on the tradition of Christian Democracy.

220 Measure taken pursuant to arts. 50, para. 5 and 54, para. 4, Consolidated text of laws on the organisation of local authorities (TUEL), adopted by d.lgs. 18 August 2000, no. 267, which allow the mayor to adopt contingent and urgent ordinances in the event of particular conditions.

221 Text available at www.salvisjuribus.it/si-al-crocifisso-negli-edifici-pubblici-a-proposito-della-sentenza-tar-sardegna. The applicant association (Union of Atheists Agnostics Rationalists) was interested in obtaining a ruling on the merits, which the Council of State later recognised, despite the revocation of the ordinance.

222 Specifically, it was alleged that the mayor used the power to issue contingent and urgent measures outside the statutory requirements limiting the use of *extra ordinem* powers. Cf. art. 54, para. 4, TUEL. The Constitutional Court had previously intervened to narrow the applicability of the provision through its ruling on 7 April 2011, no. 115.

223 *Supra* para. 4.1.

224 Cf. Pazzaglia, "Carpi. Il crocifisso torna in aula alla scuola media Focherini", 12 March 2023, available at www.avvenire.it/attualita/pagine/carpi-il-crocifisso-torna-in-aula.

The same Municipality also gained national attention due to an exhibition that was authorised by the relevant ecclesiastical authorities but deemed blasphemous by numerous individuals. The exhibition took place at the Diocesan Museum, which is located within the Church of Saint Ignatius of Loyola.[225] The conflict arose due to the sacrilegious quality of artworks produced by an openly atheist artist, with specific emphasis on a piece featuring a man positioned above the crotch of the dying Christ. The depiction resulted in the bishop, Msgr. Castellucci, the artist, and the exhibition organisers being charged with contempt under art. 403, Criminal Code, and a request for the exhibition to be suspended. The proceedings concluded with a formal request for dismissal by the Public Prosecutor. However, the artist was injured by an unidentified individual wielding a knife,[226] which led to the early closure of the exhibition.[227]

From a comparative standpoint, it is worth mentioning the recent orders of the Federal Administrative Court of Leipzig (*Land* Bavaria) at the end of 2023 intervening on the "crosses decree" or the General Rules of Procedure of the Free State of Bavaria (*BayAGO*).[228] The orders specifically address art. 28 and the wording introduced following the amendment of 1 June 2018, which provides for the posting of a cross in every institutional building.[229]

Two appeals lodged by the Federation for Freedom of Thought in Bavaria and the Munich Association for Freedom of Thought[230] on the grounds of alleged violation of the State's ideological and religious neutrality and of arts. 4[231] and 5[232] of the German Basic Law were dismissed by the Federal Admin-

225 Exhibition realised by artist Andrea Saltini. For doctrine, see C.M. Pettinato, "La mostra pittorica 'Gratia plena': in odor di blasfemia la Diocesi di Carpi", March 2024, p. 1, available at www.rivistadirittoereligioni.com.

226 A. D'Agostino – A. Beltrami, "Carpi. La mostra (non blasfema), le accuse, l'artista accoltellato: cosa è successo", 28 March 2024, available at www.avvenire.it/attualita/pagine/accusato-di-blasfemia-artista-accoltellato-in-chiesa.

227 The exhibition closed early on 18 April 2024 at the request of the artist. Official press release available at https://diocesicarpi.it/comunicato-stampa-della-diocesi-sulla-chiusura-anticipata-della-mostra-gratia-plena.

228 Cfr. *supra,* para. 2.5.

229 *Allgemeine Geschäftsordnung für die Behörden des Freistaates Bayern*, available at www.gesetze-bayern.de/Content/Document/BayAGO. Art. 28 ("Affixing crosses in official buildings") – "In the entrance area of every office building, a cross must be clearly visible as an expression of Bavaria's historical and cultural character". On this topic, see S. Testa Bappenheim, "La croce nello spazio pubblico bavarese: corsi e ricorsi storici", January 2024, p. 1, available at www.rivistadirittoereligioni.com.

230 Resp. *Bundes für Geistesfreiheit Bayern* (bfg Bayern – https://bfg-bayern.de) and *Bundes für Geistesfreiheit München* (bfg München – https://bfg-muenchen.de).

231 Art. 3 ("Equality before the law") – "All persons shall be equal before the law. Men and women shall have equal rights. The state shall promote the actual implementation of equal rights for women and men and take steps to eliminate disadvantages that now exist. No person shall be favoured or disfavoured because of sex, parentage, race, language, homeland and origin, faith or religious or political opinions. No person shall be disfavoured because of disability".

232 Art. 4 ("Freedom of faith and conscience") – "Freedom of faith and conscience and freedom to profess a religious or philosophical creed shall be inviolable. The undisturbed practice of

istrative Court Tenth Senate in its judgments of 19 December 2023, no. 10 C 3.22[233] (declaring the first grievance inadmissible) and 19 December 2023, no. 10 C 5.22[234] (declaring the second complaint unfounded).

The significance of the second judgment lies in its reconstruction of past German and European jurisprudence,[235] as well as its examination of the State's obligation to maintain ideological and religious neutrality. With regard to the latter, the judgment stated that it

> should not be understood as a distancing in the sense of a strict separation of church and state, but rather as an open and comprehensive attitude that equally promotes freedom of belief for all faiths.[236]

It further stated that the judgment

> may merely not exert any targeted influence in the service of a particular political, ideological or ideological direction or identify itself explicitly or implicitly with a particular faith or ideology through measures emanating from it or attributable to it and thereby jeopardise religious peace in a society of its own accord.[237]

This pertains to a conception of neutrality that "does not necessarily exclude the use of religious symbols and the participation of the state and its representatives in religious customs" as

> the principle of neutrality does not impose a complete renunciation of religious references in the sense of strict secularism, but rather obliges it to be open to the diversity of ideological and religious convictions.[238]

However, the affair continues as the Munich Association for Freedom of Thought filed an appeal to the Federal Constitutional Court in April 2024.[239]

---

religion shall be guaranteed. No person shall be compelled against his conscience to render military service involving the use of arms. Details shall be regulated by a federal law".

233 *BVerwG*, judgment 19 December 2023, no. 10 C 3.22, available at www.bverwg.de/191223U10C3.22.0.

234 *BVerwG*, judgment 19 December 2023, no. 10 C 5.22, available at www.bverwg.de/191223U10C5.22.0.

235 *BVerwG*, judgment no. 10 C 5.22, para. 22.

236 *BVerwG*, judgment no. 10 C 5.22, para. 26.

237 *BVerwG*, judgment no. 10 C 5.22, para. 26.

238 *BVerwG*, judgment no. 10 C 5.22, para. 27, which states that the very "renunciation by the Basic Law of strict secularism and thus of the fundamental admissibility of religious references in state action means that the violation of the principle of neutrality is only taken into account if it is of (a certain) intensity".

239 News accessible at https://bfg-muenchen.de/node/2239. Appeal catalogued under no. 1 BvR 927/24 (cf. www.bundesverfassungsgericht.de/ under "Selected new arrivals 2024").

In Italy, the recent Italian draft law titled "Provisions concerning the display of crucifixes in schools and public administration offices" is notable. This legislative proposal was introduced by centre-right representatives and officially presented to the Chamber of Deputies on 6 September 2023, bearing the no. 1384.[240] The proposed text, similar to the Bavarian example, would not only establish a legal foundation for the display of crucifixes in schools but would also allow for their affixing in all other public administrative structures.

As assumed in the introductory report, the purpose of the measure is to ensure "that the symbols and founding values of our community are not called into question". The proposal refutes that

> the image of the Crucifix in school classrooms, or more generally in public offices, courtrooms and other places where the Crucifix or the Cross is to be displayed, may constitute grounds for constraining individual freedom to manifest one's beliefs in religious matters.

In essence, "[W]hile noting the State's current non-confessionalism and religious neutrality", the proposal maintains that "the principle of secularism must be transposed according to formulas attentive to the cultural tradition and customs of the life of each people".

The articles that follow are enlightening. Art. 1 ("Principles") defines the crucifix as "an emblem of universal value of Christian civilisation and culture" and "as an essential and constitutive element of Italy's historical and civic-cultural heritage". Art. 2 ("Purposes") contemplates the display of the crucifix in all public administration offices "in order to bear witness, by making its symbols known, to the country's permanent reminder of its historical and cultural heritage rooted in Christian civilisation and tradition", all with respect for arts. 7, 8, and 19, Const. Art. 3 ("Display of the Crucifix") details the contexts and methods for displaying the symbol, which must be "in an elevated and conspicuous place" and in "all public administration offices", thereby reinforcing the indication given in the preceding.[241]

With this proposal, there would be an increase in the number of locations where crucifixes must be displayed compared to current regulations.[242] This

240 XIX Legislature. The text of the draft law is available at https://documenti.camera.it/leg19/pdl/pdf/leg.19.pdl.camera.1384.19PDL0051400.pdf. It merely reproduces proposal no. 387, presented on 26 March 2018, during the previous Legislature (XVIII), on the initiative of deputies S. Saltamartini and others. (https://documenti.camera.it/leg18/pdl/pdf/leg.18.pdl.camera.387.18PDL0008140.pdf). For a commentary, see S. Baldassarre, "Brevi considerazioni a margine della proposta di legge n. 387 del 2018", *Stato, Chiese e pluralismo confessionale*, Rivista telematica (www.statoechiese.it), no. 12, 2019, p. 1 ff.

241 Draft law, assigned to the I Committee on Constitutional Affairs, in referral 27 November 2023. The procedure can be followed at www.camera.it/leg19/126?tab=&leg=19&idDocumento=1384&sede=&tipo=.

242 See art. 3, para. 1, draft law no. 1384/2023, where reference is also made to prison establishments, stations, ports, airports, diplomatic and consular premises, etc.

provision would hold legislative nature and, if approved, would be subject to constitutional review by the Judge of Laws,[243] unlike current measures.

Furthermore, the proposal envisions the imposition of administrative sanctions[244] in two distinct cases. The first concerns the behaviour of "whoever removes the emblem of the Cross or the Crucifix from the place where it is displayed or vilifies it".[245] The second and more articulated case pertains to the conduct referable to the Public Administration. This relates to individuals who hold positions of responsibility, such as public officials and those in similar capacities, who fail to meet the obligation of displaying the emblem, neglect to supervise its display, or outright refuse to do so.[246]

243 See *supra* para. 2.2.
244 Cf. art. 4 ("Sanctions"), which provides for a fine of between EUR 500 and EUR 1,000.
245 Art. 4, para. 1, draft law no. 1384/2023.
246 Art. 4, para. 2, draft law no. 1384/2023.

Conclusion

The observations in this analysis paint a mixed picture concerning the implementation of the constitutional framework regulating religion factor within a progressively diverse society like Italy. Nevertheless, despite the existing legal tensions, a bottom-up model of social integration is emerging and yielding positive results in different areas, beginning with the education system. Considering the prominent role of multiculturalism in society, is there any other possible outcome?

Religions – most notably the Catholic Church, which remains the dominant faith among the Italian population – have documented experiences of engaging in inter-faith dialogue and cooperation. These interactions often involve acts of hospitality, especially towards marginalised categories such as migrants, some of whom may lack regular status in Italy. Particularly worthy of note are the various instances of facilitating premises for worship necessities[1] or services for minors, exemplified by the oratory activities undertaken by numerous parishes.

It is crucial to highlight the existence of local-level collaborations that consciously tackle issues rooted in the imperative to protect the environment and preserve our common home.[2] As an example, the 13 March 2023 pact between the Pontifical Antonianum University and the Islamic Cultural Centre, the overseeing authority of Great Mosque of Rome, established the first inter-religious energy community in Italy.[3] This community seeks to generate renewable energy through solar panels, benefiting the participants and supplying any surplus energy to the public grid.[4]

1 This was frequently observed within the numerous orthodox Romanian communities.

2 In the context of Catholicism, see also Francis, *Encyclical letter* Fratelli tutti *on fraternity and social friendship*, 3 October 2020, available in English at www.vatican.va. For a comprehensive understanding from an Islamic standpoint, consult the recent document *Al-Mizan. A Covenant for the Earth* was introduced during a meeting held on the sidelines of the VI Session of the *United Nation Environment Assembly* (UNEA-6), which took place in Nairobi, Kenya, from 26 February to 1 March 2024. The paper (V-99 pp.) is available at www.almizan-earth.

3 A. Di Bussolo, "Patto energetico tra Università Antonianum e Moschea di Roma", March 2023, available at www.vaticannews.va/it/vaticano/news/2023-03/comunita-energetica-pace-universita-antonianum-moschea-roma-papa.html.

4 Regarding the dialogue between Catholicism and Islam on a global level, it is noteworthy to mention the Document on Human Brotherhood for World Peace and Common Coexistence.

DOI: 10.4324/9780429242953-6

The recent amendment of art. 9, Const.,[5] which is the first and currently the only modification to a norm in the "Fundamental Principles" section, provides additional evidence of the importance of this potential ground for convergence. The amendment prioritises safeguarding of the environment, biodiversity, and ecosystems, in addition to the preservation of the landscape and historical and artistic heritage for future generations.

Additionally, a multitude of integration initiatives are being implemented in private work settings. For example, the CEO of a reputable mechanical engineering company in the province of Modena chose to celebrate the end of Ramadan with a breakfast featuring Arab tea and biscuits on Friday, 12 April 2024, with the intention of promoting diversity and inclusion within the company.[6]

However, one aspect that appears to be missing is the search for a legislative solution seeking a genuine and tangible legal equilibrium for safeguarding the religious factor while both appreciating Italian cultural identity and embracing diversity.

This circumstance can also be attributed to the political exploitation of religion, which assumes various forms, such as the conspicuous exhibition of religious symbols during public speeches and the utilisation of cultural and religious traditions to promote exclusionary identities.[7]

Indeed, urgent concerns regarding Islamic terrorism, beginning with the terrorist attacks on 11 September 2001, have shaped international and national politics as well as influenced the *ius conditum* in religious matters, particularly within legal frameworks such as France.[8]

Although the matter of displaying religious symbols holds unquestionable "symbolic" importance, it does not appear to pose the most challenging situation with regards to upholding constitutional principles of religious freedom and managing the relationship between the State and religious denominations, as argued in the preceding pages.

This document was signed in Abu Dhabi on 4 February 2019 by Pope Francis and the Grand Imam of Al-Azhar Ahmad Al Tayyeb. It can be accessed at www.vatican.va.

5 Cf. Constitutional law, 11 February 2022, no. 1, addressing the "Amendments to Articles 9 and 41 of the Constitution concerning environmental protection".

6 On this topic, see N.A., "Fine di Ramadan festa in azienda: 'un momento di condivisione interculturale'", 3 April 2004, available at www.ilrestodelcarlino.it/modena/cronaca/fine-ramadan-festa-azienda-kulbovbc.

7 A notable occurrence took place at the Northern League's election rally in Milan on 18 May 2019, where the Party Secretary kissed a rosary and invoked the blessings of Our Lady during his speech. The episode elicited strong expressions of outrage from senior Catholic prelates and other individuals. Cf. N.A., "Il caso di Milano. Rosario in piazza, voci e critiche dal mondo cattolico", 20 May 2019, available at www.avvenire.it/attualita/pagine/rosario-in-piazza-salvini-le-voci-cattoliche.

8 Regarding the correlation between the exercise of freedom of religion or belief and national security, please refer to the essays in T. Pagotto – J.M. Rose – G.P. Markar (eds.), *Security, Religion and Rule of Law. International Perspectives*, Routledge, Abingdon – Ney York, 2024, *passim*.

Yet the presence of crucifixes – especially in classrooms – confronts the interpreter with several paradoxes. These paradoxes are the outcome of solutions that may not always be convincing, and not only for those who have faith in these symbols. In other words, the proposed remedy – such as confirming the significance of the crucifix as a passive symbol of cultural value – may be worse than the evil. Preserving the crucifix as a cultural symbol is unlikely to satisfy those who interpret it differently and do not support its enforced association as genuine faith requires witnesses, not mere formal representations.

Justifying the presence of crucifixes based on outdated regulations, rooted in the idea of using religion to legitimise power, is anachronistic. If it is indeed accurate that the Constitutional Court with order no. 389/2004 has not assumed the duty of ruling on regulatory rules in this particular instance in a formal sense, it is exceedingly challenging to uphold their complete efficacy and not deem them nullified by the principle of *laicità* itself.[9] The Supreme Court of Cassation's 2021 ruling has probably taken a step forward by affirming – precisely on the basis of the principle of *laicità* – that there can no longer be an obligation to display the crucifix but, at the same time, neither can there be a ban.[10]

In Italy, the absence of specific restrictions on individuals' expression of religious freedom,[11] provides the country with the chance to embrace diversity while promoting mutual respect and a fair balance of rights. This pertains to both individuals in public roles, who are obligated to act impartially, as well as individuals using public services, such as schools, which have the freedom to express their religious or philosophical beliefs.

In Italy no particular limits are placed on individuals[12] – not even on those entrusted with public functions, who are only called upon to act impartially – regarding representing their philosophical or religious convictions. Individual users of public services, including schools, represent the possibility for the country to bring diversity together through mutual respect and a balancing of rights.

Despite the previous positive observation regarding the 2021 ruling of the Supreme Court of Cassation, we are compelled to recognise the growing complexity surrounding the display of crucifixes in classrooms.

The theorised "negotiation" of the symbol's presence in classrooms, with educational institutions assuming the role of "arbiters" (under which heading? On the basis of which competences in the field of fundamental rights?) appears destined to fail.

9 *Supra* subpara. 2.2.1.

10 *Supra* para. 4.1.

11 However, see the significant exception represented by certain provisions regarding the *burqa* that have been introduced by regional legislations (*supra* para. 3.3.).

12 In contrast, there are certain provisions regarding the *burqa* that have been introduced by regional legislations (*supra* para. 3.3.).

In the same vein, the implementation of specific legislation is challenging, to say the least. How could any political majority reasonably envisage such a measure?[13] In the event that a legal requirement for the display of crucifixes is enacted, the Constitutional Court has the authority to deem it unconstitutional solely on the basis of its inconsistency with the fundamental principle of *laicità*.

Finally, allow us to present a practical observation. The presence of crucifixes in schools is quite limited for various reasons. In my personal experience, I have only rarely encountered this form of "furnishing"[14] in any of the schools I have attended or had access to, such as during temporary usage of classrooms as polling stations. Far more relevant is the possibility, for those who choose to avail themselves of it, to benefit from Catholic religious instruction, which the State is obliged to provide and bear the costs of.[15]

However, it is important to consider that also the teaching of other disciplines – especially those related to literature, history, and the arts – carries great significance. These disciplines provide a tangible representation of cultural and religious heritage that persist even without a crucifix in every classroom.

It is evident from the preceding pages that the battle to remove religious symbols from institutions, especially in Italy, has been primarily advocated for by individuals who identify as non-believers[16] rather than by members of religious minorities, except in rare instances.[17]

The circulation of legal models aimed at regulating the presence of religious symbols in public space holds some utility, especially for scholars studying the phenomenon, as well as for judges and legislators. Nonetheless, the solutions considered in this analysis[18] only pertain to Western societies.

Further substantial issues of "symbolic" significance remain. The lack of *intese* with specific religious denominations, which are still regulated by authoritarian-origin regulations, and the simultaneous failure to establish comprehensive legislation on religious freedom are areas of concern.

Problems primarily arise at the institutional level rather than with individual believers. However, these issues have far-reaching consequences for the freedoms of individuals, as exemplified by the issue of Islamic places of worship.

Both Italian society and Western societies more generally are marked by multiculturalism and religious pluralism. It is a fact that cannot be avoided. It is therefore imperative to make concerted efforts to minimise the politicisation of religious matters. The Italian Constitution, along with international

13 Lastly, consider the draft law no. 1384/2023, *supra* para. 4.5.

14 Based on the expression utilised in the regulations of the 1920s (*supra* para. 2.2.).

15 This topic is also addressed in the 1984 Revision Agreement between the State and the Holy See (*supra* para. 1.3.). It pertains to a specific opportunity reserved solely for the Catholic faith.

16 *Supra* para. 2.4. and subpara. 4.4.1.

17 Consider the case surrounding the so-called crucifix of Ofena, *supra* para. 2.2.

18 Esp. paras. 2.5. and 4.2.

and supranational instruments protecting human rights, guarantees religious freedom to all individuals; this applies to not just citizens but also to migrants, regardless of their lawful presence in the Republic's territory, as well as asylum seekers.[19]

Consequently, the pursuit of a harmonious coexistence between the religious factor, the cultural heritage of the Italian people,[20] and the diversity the nation hosts necessitates focused endeavours in the legal and socio-cultural realms. This is to be achieved for the common good. Indeed, art. 4, para 2, Const., places on the citizen – even the citizen of tomorrow – "the duty to perform, according to his or her own ability and choice, an activity or function that contributes to the material or spiritual progress of society".

19 The CJEU has also addressed the issue of asylum seekers based on religious grounds in a preliminary reference question, following the judgment of 5 September 2012 in Joined Cases C-71/11 and C-99/11. For an analysis, see M.C. Ivaldi, *Il fattore religioso nel diritto dell'Unione europea*, p. 173 ff.

20 From the writer's perspective, an example of promoting cultural identity in a positive manner, with significant economic benefits, can be seen in the establishment of religious pathways. In accordance with the provisions set forth in the 2022 budget law (law 30 December 2021, no. 234), the "religious pathways" are defined as "hiking itineraries with a religious or spiritual theme, which can be covered exclusively or predominantly on foot or by other forms of slow and sustainable tourism, at interregional and regional level" (art. 1, para. 2, Ministry of Tourism decree 23 June 2022, available at www.ministeroturismo.gov.it/wp-content/uploads/2022/07/DM_fondoLdB_art1_c963_signed.pdf).

Bibliography

Albisetti Alessandro, *Il diritto ecclesiastico nella giurisprudenza della Corte costituzionale*, Giuffrè, Milano, V ed., 2014, VIII–154 pp.

Alenda Salinas Manuel – Matilde Pineda Marcos, *El símbolo religioso en el Estado laico español*, Tirant Lo Blanch, Valencia, 2016, 376 pp.

Alicino Francesco, "Atheism and the Principle of Secularism in the Italian Constitutional Order", *The Italian Law Journal*, no. 1, 2021, pp. 15–34

Alicino Francesco, "*Ceci n'est pas une pipe*: The Crucifix in Italian Schools in the Light of Recent Jurisprudence", *Canopy Forum*, 30 November 2021, pp. 1–11.

Alicino Francesco, "Laicità e bilateralità a trent'anni dalla sentenza madre. I test dell'Islam italiano e dell'ateismo militante", *Stato, Chiese e pluralismo confessionale*, Rivista telematica (wwww.statoechiese.it), no. 1, 2021, pp. 21–42.

Alicino Francesco, *Constitutional Democracy and Islam. The Legal Status of Muslims in Italy*, Routledge, Abingdon – New York, 2023, X–210 pp.

Andreescu Gabriel – Liviu Andreescu, "The European Court of Human Rights's Lautsi Decision: Context, Contents, Consequences", *Journal for the Study of Religions and Ideologies*, vol. 9, no. 26, 2010, pp. 47–74.

Anello Giancarlo, "Colonialismo giuridico italiano. Archeologia della subalternità legale nei contesti multiculturali", *Stato, Chiese e pluralismo confessionale*, Rivista telematica (www.statoechiese.it), November 2009, pp. 1–45.

Annicchino Pasquale, "Is the Glass Half Empty or Half Full? Lautsi *v* Italy before the European Court of Human Rights", *Stato, Chiese e pluralismo confessionale*, Rivista telematica (www.statoechiese.it), May 2010, pp. 1–19.

Annicchino Pasquale, "Winning the Battle by Losing the War: The *Lautsi* Case and the Holy Alliance between American Conservative Evangelicals, the Russian Ortodox Church and the Vatican to Reshape European Identity", *Religion & Human Rights*, vol. 6, 2011, pp. 213–219.

Arcopinto Antonella, "L'utilizzo delle religioni nel marketing d'impresa. Profili di tutela giuridica", *CALUMET – Intercultural Law and Humanities Review*, Rivista telematica (www.calumet-review.it), 15 April 2019, pp. 1–20.

Astengo Francesca, "Freedom of Religion Crucified? Secularism and Italian Schools Before the European Court of Human Rights", *Politique européenne*, no. 41, 2013, pp. 12–39.

Azienda Sanitaria Locale Roma E et al., "L'accoglienza delle differenze e specificità culturali e religiose nelle strutture sanitarie ospedaliere e territoriali della Regione Lazio. Raccomandazioni per gli operatori sanitari da parte delle comunità religiose", 14 December 2010, pp. 1–42, available at https://tavolointerreligioso.org/wp-content/uploads/2015/12/Opuscolo_Santo_Spirito-1.pdf

Baldassarre Silvia, "Brevi considerazioni a margine della proposta di legge n. 387 del 2018", *Stato, Chiese e pluralismo confessionale*, Rivista telematica (www.statoechiese.it), no. 12, 2019, pp. 1–26.

Baldassarre Silvia, "The Legal Position of Non-Believers Under Italian Law", in Adele Orioli (ed.), *Non Believers' Europe. Models of Secularism, Individual Statuses, Collective Rights*, Nessun Dogma, Roma, 2019, pp. 253–262.

Baldassarre Silvia, "Campagne pubblicitarie ateiste: un'applicazione asimmetrica del principio di laicità", in Andrea Cardone – Marco Croce (eds.), *30 anni di laicità dello Stato: fu vera gloria?* Nessun Dogma, Roma, 2021, pp. 367–382.

Barbier Maurice, *La laïcité*, L'Harmattan, Paris, 1995, 320 pp.

Baubérot Jean, *Laïcité 1905–2005, entre passion et raison*, Le Seuil, Paris, 2004, 288 pp.

Baubérot Jean, *Les 7 laïcités françaises*, Éditions de la Maison des sciences de l'homme, Paris, 2015, 176 pp.

Berg Thomas C., "Can State-Sponsored Religious Symbols Promote Religious Liberty", *Journal of Catholic Legal Studies*, vol. 52, no. 1&2, 2014, pp. 23–48.

Bin Roberto et al. (eds.), *La laicità crocifissa? Il nodo costituzionale dei simboli religiosi nei luoghi pubblici*, Giappichelli, Torino, 2004, 360 pp.

Boniolo Giovanni – Enrica Maritinelli (eds.), *La cura del paziente e la diversità spirituale. Per una medicina interculturale*, Mimesis, Milano – Udine, 2024, 242 pp.

Botti Federica, "Oltre i culti ammessi. Prime note sulla gestione giuridica del pluralismo religioso nella legislazione coloniale italiana", *Stato, Chiese e pluralismo confessionale*, Rivista telematica (www.statoechiese.it), July 2011, pp. 1–20.

Bottoni Rossella, *Il principio di laicità in Turchia. Profili storico-giuridici*, Vita e Pensiero, Milano, 2012, 288 pp.

Bottoni Rossella – Cristiana Cianitto, "Is Non Religion a Religion? The Italian Legal Experience", in Anne Laure Zwilling – Helge Årsheim (eds.), *Nonreligion in Late Modern Societies. Institutional and Legal Perspective*, Cham, Springer, 2022, pp. 49–69.

Calvès Gwénaële, *La laïcité*, La Découverte, Paris, 2022, 113.

Caputo Giuseppe, *Il carattere sacro di Roma*, Giuffrè, Milano, 1971, 218 pp.

Cardia Carlo, *La riforma del concordato. Dal confessinismo alla laicità dello Stato*, Einaudi, Torino, 1980, XIV–281 pp.

Cardia Carlo, "Stato laico", in *Enciclopedia del diritto*, Giuffrè, Milano, 1990, vol. XVIII, pp. 847–890.

Carmignani Caridi Settimio, "Ostentazione di simboli religiosi e porto di armi od oggetti atti ad offendere. Il problema del *kirpan* dei fedeli Sikh", *Il Diritto ecclesiastico*, no. 3–4, 2009, pp. 739–766.

Carobene Germana, "Problems on the Legal Status of the Church of Scientology", *Stato, Chiese e pluralismo confessionale*, Rivista telematica (www.statoechiese.it), no. 21, 2014, pp. 1–15.

Cavagion Giovanni, "Gli enti locali e le limitazioni del diritto alla libertà religiosa: il divieto di indossare il velo integrale", *Stato, Chiese e pluralismo confessionale*, Rivista telematica (wwwstatoechiese.it), no. 28, 2018, pp. 1–44.

Ceccanti Stefano, "E se la Corte andasse in Baviera?", in R. Bin et al. (eds.), *La laicità crocifissa? Il nodo costituzionale dei simboli religiosi nei luoghi pubblici*, Giappichelli, Torino, 2004, pp. 1–26.

Cilardo Agostino, *Il diritto islamico e il sistema giuridico italiano. Le bozze di intesa tra la Repubblica Italiana e le associazioni islamiche italiane*, Edizioni Scientifiche Italiane, Napoli, 2002, 384 pp.

Codevilla Giovanni, *Chiesa e impero in Russia. Dalla Rus' di Kiev alla Federazione russa*, Jaka Book, Milano, 2011, XXI–683 pp.

Colaianni Nicola, "Il presidente Macron e la libertà di blasfemia", 29 September 2020, pp. 1–14, available at www.questionegiustizia.it/articolo/il-presidente-macron-e-la-liberta-di-blasfemia

Colaianni Nicola, "Propaganda ateistica: laicità e divieto di discriminazione", 10 Juin 2020, pp. 1–12, available at www.questionegiustizia.it/articolo/propaganda-ateistica-laicita-e-divieto-di-discriminazione_10-06-2020.php

Colaianni Nicola, "Dal 'crocifisso di Stato' al 'crocifisso di classe' (nota a margine di Cass., SS.UU., 9 settembre 2021, n. 24424)", *Stato, Chiese e pluralismo confessionale*, Rivista telematica (www.statoechiese.it), no. 17, 2021, pp. 18–25.
Condorelli Mario, "*Scherz und Ernst* sul nuovo Concordato", *Il Diritto ecclesiastico*, pt. I, 1984, pp. 363–373.
Consorti Pierluigi, "Nuovi rapporti tra la Repubblica e le confessioni religiose? Sui riflessi ecclesiasticistici della riforma del Titolo V, parte seconda della Costituzione", *Quaderni di diritto e politica ecclesiastica*, no. 1, 2003, pp. 13–36.
Coppola Raffaele (ed.), *Il nuovo accordo tra l'Italia e la Santa Sede*, Milano, Giuffrè, 1987, XX–844 pp.
Costa Jean Paul – Guy Bedouelle, *Les laïcité à la française*, PUF, Paris, 1998, 266 pp.
Council of Europe, European Court of Human Rights, "Guide on Article 9 of the European Convention on Human Rights. Freedom of Thought, Conscience and Religion", 29 February 2024, 114 pp. available at https://ks.echr.coe.int/documents/d/echr-ks/guide_art_9_eng
Cretu Vasile, "The Presence of Religious Symbols in Romanian Public Schools: Ethical Disputes and Legislative Interpretations", in Victoriţa Trif (ed.), *Anlayzing Paradigms Used in Education and Educational Psychology*, IGI Global, Hershey, PE, 2020, pp. 267–284.
Crisafulli Vezio, Crisafulli, "Art. 7 della Costituzione e 'vilipendio della religione dello Stato'", *Archivio penale*, pt. II, 1950, pp. 415–423.
Croce Marco, "La 'sana laicità' capitola a Strasburgo: la Corte europea diritti dell'uomo giudice di costituzionalità sulle fonti non primarie?", *Il Foro italiano*, pt. IV, 2010, cols. 67–70.
Croce Marco, "Sulla laicità dello Stato nelle aule giudiziarie: il caso della praticante velata", 1 February 2018, pp. 1–3, available at www.forumcostituzionale.it/wordpress/wp-content/uploads/2018/02/croce.pdf
Croce Marco, "An Agreement Denied: How Philosophical Associations Are Discriminated by Italian Law", in Adele Orioli (ed.), *Non Believers' Europe. Models of Secularism, Individual Statuses, Collective Rights*, Nessun Dogma, Roma, 2019, pp. 72–98.
Croce Marco, "Sull'ordinanza del Comune di Monfalcone per assenza di destinazione d'uso dell'immobile", December 2023, available at www.rivistadirittoereligioni.com
Croce Marco, "Una storica condanna antidiscriminatoria a tutela della propaganda dei non credenti (Corte d'appello di Roma, II sez., 9 febbraio 2023, n. 1923)", *Quaderni di diritto e politica ecclesiastica*, no. 3, 2023, pp. 919–930.
Croce Marco, "Doppio stop per l'indirizzo politico 'anti-moschea' del Comune di Monfalcone da parte del giudice amministrativo", April 2024, available at www.rivistadirittoereligioni.com
Croce Marco, "Potere di ordinanza del Sindaco e ostensione del crocifisso: il Consiglio di Stato si allinea alle Sezioni Unite della Cassazione?", March 2024, available at www.rivistadirittoereligioni.com
Dalla Torre Giuseppe, "Libertà di coscienza e di religione", *Stato, Chiese e pluralismo confessionale*, Rivista telematica (www.statoechiese.it), March 2008, pp. 1–21.
D'Amico Marilisa, "Constitutional Secularism and Religious Fundamentalism in Italy and Europe: Considerations Stemming from Judicial Decisions", *Italian Review of Legal History*, vol. 3, no. 10, 2017, pp. 1–38.
D'Angelo Giuseppe, "Nuovi movimenti religiosi tra (pretesa) uniformità di qualificazione e (reale) diversificazione dei relativi profili disciplinari: la Chiesa di Scientology nella più significativa giurisprudenza", *Il Diritto ecclesiastico*, no. 1, 2003, pp. 710–761.
D'Arienzo Maria, "L'Università di Napoli e la prima cattedra di Diritto ecclesiastico in Italia, L'insegnamento di Francesco Scaduto", *Stato, Chiese e pluralismo confessionale*, Rivista telematica (www.statoechiese.it), no. 27, 2012, pp. 1–19.

D'Avack Pietro Agostino, "Confessionismo", in *Enciclopedia del diritto*, Giuffrè, Milano, vol. VIII, 1961, pp. 929–945.

Decimo Ludovica, *Le organizzazioni religiose nel prisma costituzionale dell'art. 20*, Editoriale Scientifica, Napoli, 2017, 138 pp.

Decimo Ludovica, "Associazioni culturali islamiche e edifici di culto: il TAR Lombardia torna sull'applicazione della legislazione regionale sulle attrezzature religiose", Marzo 2024, available at www.rivistadirittoereligioni.com

De Gregorio Laura, "Laicità e progetti per una legge generale sulla libertà religiosa", *Stato, Chiese e pluralismo confessionale*, Rivista telematica (www.statoechiese.it), no. 21, 2020, pp. 67–87.

Delgrange Xavier – David Koussens, "Quelles laïcités en salle d'audience? A propos de quelques arrêts canadiens et européens sur le port de symboles religieux dans les prétoires", *Revue trimestrielle des droits de l'homme*, no. 2, 2019, pp. 447–475.

Della Seta Ugo, *La legge fondamentale sui Culti ammessi (Valutazione etica)*, Guanda, Modena, 1937, 237 pp.

De Oto Antonello, "Presenza del crocifisso o di altre immagini religiose nei seggi elettorali: la difficile affermazione di una 'laicità effettiva'. Osservzioni a Cass. pen. n. 439 del 2000", *Quaderni di diritto e politica ecclesiastica*, no. 3, 2000, pp. 837–854.

Di Cosimo Giovanni, "Gli spazi pubblici e la religione", *Stato, Chiese e pluralismo confessionale*, Rivista telematica (www.statoechiese.it), no. 6, 2020, pp. 20–33.

Di Iorio Tiziana, "Luci e ombre della benedizione nella scuola tra libertà religiosa e laicità dello Stato", *Stato, Chiese e pluralismo confessionale*, Rivista telematica (www.statoechiese.it), no. 24, 2017, pp. 1–30.

Domianello Sara, *Giurisprudenza costituzionale e fattore religioso. Le pronunce della Corte costituzionale in materia ecclesiastica*, Giuffrè, Milano, 1999, XII–908 pp.

Donovan Mark, "The Italian State: No Longer Catholic, No Longer Christian", in Zsolt Enyedi – John T.S. Madeley (eds.), *Church and State in Contemporary Europe. The Chimera of Neutrality*, Routledge, Abingdon – New York, 2003, pp. 95–116.

Edigati Daniele – Alessandro Tira (eds.), *Le minoranze religiose nel diritto italiano ed europeo. Esperienze del passato e problematiche contemporanee*, Giappichelli, Torino, 2021, XX–255 pp.

Ervas Elena, "The Agreements Between Church and State: The Italian Perspective", *BYU Law Review*, no. 4, 2017, pp. 869–894.

Fabbri Alberto, "Il Patto nazionale per un islam italiano come condizione preliminare per la stipula di intese con l'islam, le fasi costitutive", *Rivista di diritto pubblico, comparato, europeo*, Rivista telematica (www.federalismi.it), no. 10, 2017, pp. 1–15.

Fabbri Alberto, "Le intese alla prova: nuovi attori e vecchi contenuti", *Cultura giuridica e Diritto Vivente*, vol. 7, 2020, pp. 1–17.

Fabbri Alberto, *Il diritto allo spazio di preghiera tra laicità e pluralismo religioso*, Giappichelli, Torino, 2024, 224 pp.

Falco Mario, "Accordi lateranensi", in *Nuovo digesto italiano*, UTET, Torino, vol. I, pp. 86–91.

Falzone Vittorio – Filippo Palermo – Francesco Cosentino (eds.), *La Costituzione della Repubblica italiana illustrata con i lavori preparatori*, Colombo, Roma, 1948, 295 pp.

Feliciani Giorgio, "The Presece of the Cross in Public Spaces: Italy", in P. Stanisz – M. Zawiślak – M. Ordon (eds.), *Presence of the Cross in Public Spaces: Experiences od Selected European Countries*, Cambridge Scholar Publishing, Newcastle upon Tyne, 2016, pp. 111–126.

Ferrari Alessandro, "Religion and Rethinking the Public-Private Divide: A Broken Promise in Europe?", in Silvio Ferrari – Sabrina Pastorelli (eds.), *Religion in Public Space. A European Perspective*, Routledge, Abingdon – New York, 2012, pp. 71–92.

Ferrari Alessandro, "A Besieged Right: Religious Freedom and the Italian War on the Burqa and the Niqab", in Alessandro Ferrari – Sabrina Pastorelli (eds.), *The Burqa*

Affair Across Europe Between Public and Private Space, Routledge, Abingdon – New York, 2013, pp. 37–58.

Ferrari Alessandro, *Religious Freedom in Italy. An Impossible Paradigm?*, De Gruyter, Berlin – Boston, 2023, VII–201 pp.

Ferrari Alessandro – Silvio Ferrari, "Religion and Secular State: the Italian Case", *The Cardozo Electronic Law Bulletin*, vol. 16, no. 1 special issue, 2010, pp. 431–448.

Ferrari Alessandro – Sabrina Pastorelli (eds.), *The Burqa Affair Across Europe Between Public and Private Space*, Routledge, Abingdon – New York, 2013, 290 pp.

Ferrari Silvio (ed.), *Concordato e Costituzione. Gli accordi del 1984 tra Italia e Santa Sede*, il Mulino, Bologna, 1985, 260 pp.

Ferrari Silvio, "The New Concordat between Church and State", *Italian Politics*, vol. 1, 1985, pp. 134–145.

Ferrari Silvio, "La nozione giuridica di confessione religiosa (come sopravvivere senza conoscerla)", in Vittorio Parlato – Giovanni Battista Varnier (eds.), *Principio pattizio e realtà religiose minoritarie*, Giappichelli, Torino, 1995, pp. 19–47.

Ferrari Silvio, "Individual Religious Freedom and National Security in Europe After September 11", *Brigham Young University Law Review*, no. 2, 2004, pp. 357–383.

Ferrari Silvio, "Islam and the European System of Church-State Relations: A (False) Problem?", *Derecho y Religion*, pt. I, 2006, pp. 87–115.

Ferrari Silvio, "State-Supported Display of Religious Symbols in the Public Space", *Journal of Catholich Legal Studies*, vol. 52, no. 1&2, 2013, pp. 7–22.

Ferrari Silvio, "The Christian Roots of the Secular State", in Vv.Aa. (ed.), *Droit et religion en Europe. Étude en l'honneur de Francis Messner*, Presses Universitaires de Strasbourg, 2014, pp. 425–442.

Ferrari Silvio – Sabrina Pastorelli (eds.), *Religion in Public Space. A European Perspective*, Routledge, Abingdon – New York, 2012, 406 pp.

Finocchiaro Francesco, "Art. 7", in Giuseppe Branca (ed.), *Commentario della Costituzione, Articoli 1–12, Principi fondamentali*, Zanichelli – il Foro italiano, Bologna – Roma, 1975, pp. 321–383.

Finocchiaro Francesco, "Art. 8", in Giuseppe Branca (ed.), *Commentario della Costituzione, Articoli 1–12, Principi fondamentali*, Zanichelli – il Foro italiano, Bologna – Roma, 1975, pp. 383–434.

Finocchiaro Francesco, "Art. 19", in Giuseppe Branca (ed.), *Commentario della Costituzione, Articoli 13–20, Rapporti civili*, Zanichelli – il Foro italiano, Bologna – Roma, 1977, pp. 238–301.

Finocchiaro Francesco, "Art. 20", in Giuseppe Branca (ed.), *Commentario della Costituzione, Articoli 13–20, Rapporti civili*, Zanichelli – il Foro italiano, Bologna – Roma, 1977, pp. 302–314.

Finocchiaro Francesco, *Diritto ecclesiastico*, XIII ed., update edited by Andrea Bettentini and Gaetano Lo Castro, Zanichelli, Bologna, 2020, 592 pp.

Floris Pierangela, "Ateismo e religione nell'ambito del diritto di libertà religiosa", *Il Foro italiano*, pt. II, 1981, cols. 625–633.

Floris Pierangela, "Intorno all'intesa con i Testimoni di Geova", *Stato, Chiese e pluralismo confessionale*, Rivista telematica (www.statoechiese.it), no. 13, 2021, pp. 119–149.

Fonseca Luján Roberto Carlos, "Marco constitucional de la laicidad en México", *Revista de la Facultad de Derecho de México*, vol. LXXIV, no. 288, 2024, pp. 379–400.

Fornerod Anne, "The Burqa Affair in France", in Alessandro Ferrari – Sabrina Pastorelli (eds.), *The Burqa Affair Across Europe Between Public and Private Space*, Routledge, Abingdon – New York, 2013, pp. 57–76.

Fortier Vincente – Gérard Gonzalez (eds.), "La loi confortant le respect des principes de la République", *Dossier, Revue du droit des religions*, no. 13, 2022, pp. 1–170, available at https://journals.openedition.org/rdr/pdf/1725

Freni Fortunato, *La libertà religiosa tra solidarietà e pluralismo. Analisi delle proposte sul modello di laicità "all'italiana"*, Jovene, Napoli, 2013, 190 pp.

Fronzoni Vasco, "Ramadhan: digiuno dei minori a scuola, esigenze religiose e libertà educativa", April 2024, available at www.rivistadirittoereligioni.com

Fuccillo Antonio – Ludovica Decimo (eds.), *Gli enti religiosi tra diritto speciale, diritto comuni e mercati*, Editoriale Scientifica, Napoli, 2022, 613 pp.

Gatta Gian Luigi, "Islam, abbigliamento religioso, diritto e processo penale: brevi note a margine di due casi giurisprudenziali", *Stato, Chiese e pluralismo confessionale*, Rivista telematica (www.statoechiese.it), June 2009, pp. 1–13.

Gedicks Frederick Mark – Pasquale Annicchino, "Cross, Crucifix, Culture: An Approach to the Constitutional Meaning of Confessional Symbols", *First Amendment Law Review*, vol. 13, no. 1, 2014, pp. 71–139.

Giacchi Orio, *La legislazione italiana sui culti ammessi*, Vita e Pensiero, Milano, 1934, VII–104 pp.

Giovannelli Mauro, "The Covenant between the Republic of Italy and the Vatican: A Retrospective Analysis after Fifteen Years", *Journal of Church and State*, vol. 42, no. 3, 2000, pp. 529–538.

Gravino Federico, *Migrantes. Gli esodi contemporanei tra diritto e religioni*, ESI, Napoli, 2024, 339 pp.

Guerzoni Luciano, "Note preliminari per uno studio della laicità sotto il profilo giuridico", *Archivio giuridico Filippo Serafini*, 1967, pp. 61–130.

Hirshl Ran, *Towards Juristocracy. The Origin and Consequences of the New Constitutionalism*, Harvard University Press, Cambridge – London, 2004, 296 pp.

Hoopes James (ed.), *Peirce on Sign: Writings on Semiotic by Charles Sanders Peirce*, The University of California Press, Chapel Hill – London, 1991, 294 pp.

Horváth Gizela – Rozália Bakó, "Religious Icons in Romanian Schools: Text and Context", *Journal for the Study of Religions and Ideologies*, vol. 8, no. 24, 2009, pp. 189–206.

Iglesias Vila Marisa – Camil Ungureanu, "The Conundrum of Pluralism and the Doctrine of the Margin of Appreciation: The Crucifix 'Affair' and the Ambivalence of the ECtHR", in Ferran Requejo – Camil Ungureanu (eds.), *Democracy, Law and Religious Pluralism in Europe. Secularism and Post-Secularism*, Routledge, Abingdon – New York, 2014, pp. 179–199.

Italia, Corte Costituzionale, *The Italian Constituional Court*, Colombo, Roma, 2019, 61 pp.

Ivaldi Maria Cristina, *La tutela penale in materia religiosa nella giurisprudenza*, Giuffrè, Milano, 2004, X–305 pp.

Ivaldi Maria Cristina, "Verso una nuova definizione della laicità? La recente normativa a proposito dei segni religiosi nella scuola in Francia", *Il Diritto ecclesiastico*, no. 4, 2004, pp. 1133–1172.

Ivaldi Maria Cristina, "Robert Schuman padre della riconciliazione e della costruzione europea", *Stato, chiese e pluralismo confessionale*, Rivista telematica (www.statoechiese.it), gennaio 2010, pp. 1–32.

Ivaldi Maria Cristina, "Alcune considerazioni sulla regolamentazione dei movimenti a carattere settario nell'ordinamento francese", *Stato, Chiese e pluralisnmo confessionale*, Rivista telematica (wwwstatoechiese.it), no. 29, 2012, pp. 1–31.

Ivaldi Maria Cristina, *Il fattore religioso nel diritto dell'Unione europea tra riconoscimento giurisprudenziale e codificazione normativa*, Nuova Cultura, Roma, 2012, VIII–225 pp.

Ivaldi Maria Cristina, "Discriminazione e propaganda religiosa nel diritto calcistico", *Stato, Chiese e pluralismo confessionale*, Rivista telematica (www.statoechiese.it), 2 February 2015, pp. 1–46.

Ivaldi Maria Cristina, "Law and Religion: The Peculiarities of the Italian Model – Emergin Issues and Controversies", in Stanley D. Brunn (ed.), *The Changing World Religious Map. Sacred Places, Identities, Practices and Politics*, Springer, New York, 2015, vol. II, pp. 1275–1286.

Ivaldi Maria Cristina, "The Meaning of 'Religion' in French Case Law. The Judgments of the *Conseil d'État*", *Stato, Chiese e pluralismo confessionle*, Rivista telematica (www.statoechiese.it), no. 39, 2017, pp. 110–133.

Jahier Davide, *Il 1° articolo dello Statuto e la libertà religiosa in Italia. Monografia storico-giuridica*, Lattes & C., Torino – Genova, 1925, 46 pp.

Jemolo Arturo Carlo, "Guarentigie (Legge delle)", in *Novissimo digesto italiano*, Utet, Torino, 1962, vol. VIII, pp. 34–37.

Jemolo Arturo Carlo, *Chiesa e Stato in Italia dalla Unificazione ai giorni nostri*, Einaudi, Torino, V ed., 1978, 331 pp.

Kalliny Morris et al., "Capitalizing on Faith: A Cross-Cultural Examination of Consumer Responses to the Use of Religious Symbols in Advertising", *Journal of Global Marketing*, vol. 33, no. 3, 2020, pp. 158–176.

Laneve Giuseppe, "Atheism as Part of Religious Phenomenon: Questions and New Challenges to Secularism", *Rivista di diritto pubblico, comparato, europeo*, Rivista telematica (www.federalismi.it), no. 25, 2020, pp. 154–181.

Lariccia Sergio, *Diritti civili e fattore religioso*, il Mulino, Bologna, 1978, 211 pp.

Licastro Angelo, "Il motivo religioso non giustifica il porto fuori dell'abitazione del kirpan da parte del fedele sikh (considerazioni in margine alle sentenze n. 24739 e n. 25163 del 2016 della Cassazione penale)", *Stato, Chiese e pluralismo confessionale*, Rivista telematica (www.statoechiese.it), no. 1, 2017, pp. 1–25.

Licastro Angelo, "Crocifisso 'per scelta'. Dall'obbligatorietà alla facoltatività dell'esposizione del crocifisso nelle aule scolastiche (in margine a Cass. civ., sez. un., ord. 9 settembre 2021, n. 24414)", *Stato, Chiese e pluralismo confessionale*, Rivista telematica (www.statoechiese.it), no. 21, 2021, pp. 17–44.

Lock Tobias, "Of Crucifixes and Headscarves: Religious Symbols in Germany", in Myriam Hunter Henin (ed.), *Law, Religious Freedom and Education*, Ashgate, Farnham and Burlington, 2011, pp. 347–369.

Long Gianni, *Le* confessioni religiose "diverse dalla cattolica. Ordinamenti interni e rapporti con lo Stato, il Mulino, Bologna, 1991, 324 pp.

Loprieno Donatella, "Libertà dell'arte vs. Libertà religiosa: il caso della censura cinematografica", *Stato, Chiese e pluralismo confessionale*, Rivista telematica (www.statoechiese.it), gennaio, 2009, pp. 1–33.

Lugato Monica, "The 'Margin of Appreciation' and Freedom of Religion: Between Treaty Interpretation and Subsidiarity", *Journal of Catholich Legal Studies*, vol. 52, no. 1&2, 2013, pp. 49–70.

Macron Emmanuel, "Hommage national à la mémoire de Samuel Paty", Paris, Sorbonne, 21 Octobre 2020, pp. 1–2, available at www.elysee.fr/front/pdf/elysee-module-16345-fr.pdf

Macron Emmanuel, "La Rèpublique en acte: discurs sur le theme de la lutte contre le séparatisme", Les Murreaux, 2 October 2020, pp. 1–13, available in english at www.elysee.fr/front/pdf/elysee-module-16114-en.pdf

Macron Emmanuel, "Protéger les libertés en luttant contre le séparatisme islamiste", *Mulhouse*, 18 February 2020, pp. 1–7, available at www.elysee.fr/front/pdf/elysee-module-15216-fr.pdf

Madera Adelaide, "A Brief Introduction to the Religious Symbols Debate in Italy and the United States", in Silvio Ferrari – Rinaldo Cristiofori (eds.), *Law and Religion in the 21st Century. Relations between States and Religious Communities*, Routledge, Abingdon – New York, 2010, pp. 305–312.

Madera Adelaide, "Il porto di simboli religiosi nel contesto giudiziario", *Stato, Chiese e pluralismo confessionale*, Rivista telematica (www.statoechiese.it), no. 4, 2020, pp. 39–159.

Madonna Michele, *La città di Roma nel Concordato del 1929 e nell'Accordo del 1984. Dal "carattere sacro" al Particolare significato". Un itinerario storico giuridico*, Libellula, Tricase, LE, 2014, 233 pp.

Magni Cesare, *Intorno al nuovo diritto dei culti acattolici ammessi in Italia*, Sassari, Gallizzi, 1931, 146 pp.

Mancini Susanna, "La supervisione europea presa sul serio: la controversia sul crocifisso tra margine di apprezzamento e ruolo contro-maggioritario delle corti", *Giurisprudenza costituzionale*, no. 5, 2009, pp. 4055–4083.

Mancini Susanna, "The Crucifix Rage: Supranational Constitutionalism Bumps Against the Counter-Majoritarian Difficulty", *European Constitutional Law Review*, vol. 6, no. 1, 2010, pp. 6–27.

Margiotta Broglio, *Stato e confessioni religiose, 2 Teorie e ideologie*, La Nuova Italia, Firenze, 1976, 194 pp.

Martinelli Enrica, "Una sentenza sul crocifisso: verso un nuovo modello di laicità?", *La Nuova Giurisprudenza Civile Commentata*, no. 1, 2022, pp. 121–129.

Martínez Torrón-Javier, "Institutional Religious Symbols, State Neutrality and Protection of Minorities in Europe", *Law & Justice*, 2013, pp. 21–51.

Mazzola Roberto, "State and Church in Italy", in Gerhard Robbers (ed.), *State and Church in the European Union*, Nomos, Baden-Baden, 2019, III ed., pp. 265–280.

McGoldrick Dominic, "Religion in European Public Square and in European Public Life – Crucifixes in the Classroom?", *Human Rights Law Review*, vol. 11, no. 3, 2011, pp. 451–502.

McNeil Donald, "Rome, Global City? Church, State and the Jubilee 2000", *Political Geography*, vol. 22, no. 5, 2003, pp. 535–556.

Micciché Andrea, "Between Administrative Silence and Religious Freedom: The End of Ramadan in Front of the Lombardy Regional Administrative Court", April 2024, available at www.rivistadirittoereligioni.com

Modugno Franco, "I principi costituzionali supremi come parametro del giudizio di legittimità costituzionale", in Franco Modugno – Antonio Stefano Agrò – Augusto Cerri (eds.), *Il principio di unità del controllo sulle leggi nella giurisprudenza della Corte Costituzionale*, Giappichelli, Torino, IV ed., 2002, pp. 292–303.

Molvesian Mark L., "Crosses and Culture: State-Sponsored Religious Displays in the US and Europe", *Oxford Journal of Law and Religion*, vol. 1, no. 2, 2012, pp. 338–362.

Montagnana Marcello, "Come scrocifiggere lo Stato. Processi, sentenze, polemiche sull'esposizione del simbolo cattolico nelle istituzioni statali italiane", July 2005, 361 pp., available only online at www.uaar.it/uaar/campagne/scrocifiggiamo/montagnana/Marcello_Montagnana__Come_scrocifiggere_lo_Stato.pdf

Montieri Vittorio (ed.), *La manipolazione del sacro. L'immagine religiosa nel mondo della comunicazione*, Mimesis, Milano – Udine, 382 pp.

Morelli Alessandro, "Il giuramento di fedeltà alla bandiera: 'deismo cerimoniale' o violazione della *establishment clause*? Una complessa (e irrisolta) questione al vaglio della Corte Suprema statunitense", *Diritto pubblico comparato ed europeo*, no. 1, 2005, pp. 281–288.

Moscon Giorgio, "Separa e sarai rispettato", *Il ponte*, 1965, pp. 143–145.

Nardella Carlo, *La migrazione dei simboli. Pubblicità e religione*, Guerrini Scientifica, Milano, 2015, 191 pp.

Negri Alessandro, "Sikh condannato per porto del kirpan: una discutibile sentenza della Cassazione su immigrazione e 'valori del mondo occidentale'", *Diritto penale contemporaneo*, no. 7–8, 2017, pp. 246–255.

Nicolas Valérie, "Le principe de laïcité (ré)conforté: le référé-laïcité, le juge administratif et le burkini", *Revue des droits de l'homme*, *Actualité Droits-Libertés*, Octobre 2022, pp. 1–7, available at http://journals.openedition.org/revdh/15934

Onida Francesco, *Uguaglianza e libertà religiosa nel separatismo statunitense*, Giuffrè, Milano, 1970, 409 pp.

Onida Francesco, "Nuove problematiche religiose per gli ordinamenti laici contemporanei: Scientology e il concetto giuridico di religione", *Quaderni di diritto e politica ecclesiastica*, no. 1, 1998, pp. 279–294.

Pace Alessandro, "Le nuove Chiese evangeliche e pentecostali in Italia, senza fissa dimora, esposte a ragionevoli discriminazioni", *Stato, Chiese e pluralismo confessionale*, Rivista telematica (www.statoechiese.it), no. 13, 2021, pp. 151–166.

Pacillo Vincenzo, "'Die religiöse Heimat'. Il divieto di edificazione di minareti in Svizzera ed Austria", *Quaderni di diritto e politica ecclesiastica*, no. 1, 2010, pp. 199–226.

Pacillo Vincenzo, "Stopp Minarett? The Controversy Over the Building of Minarets in Switzerland: Religious Freedom versus Collective Identity", in Silvio Ferrari – Sabrina Pastorelli (eds.), *Religion in Public Space. A European Perspective*, Routledge, Abingdon – New York, 2012, pp. 337–352.

Pacillo Vincenzo, "La politica ecclesiastica tra discrezionalità dell'Esecutivo, principio di bilateralità e laicità/neutralità dello Stato: brevi note a margine della sentenza della Corte costituzionale n. 52 del 10 marzo 2016", *Lo Stato*, vol. VI, 2016, pp. 245–260.

Pagotto Tania, Il motto statunitense 'In God We Trust' alla luce della storia e della tradizione del Primo emendamento", *Stato, Chiese e pluralismo confessionale*, Rivista telematica (www.statoechiese.it), no. 19, 2022, pp. 101–164.

Pagotto Tania – Joshua M. Rose – G.P. Markar (eds.), *Security, Religion and Rule of Law. International Perspectives*, Routledge, Abingdon – Ney York, 2024, 240 pp.

Palomino Rafael, *La religión en el espacio público: Los símbolos religiosos antes el derecho*, Digital Reasons, Madrid, 2017, 160 pp.

Papadopoulou Lina (ed.), *Islam and Human Rights in the European Union/ Islam et droits de l'homme dans l'Union européenne*, Comares, Granada, 2022, XVIII–423 pp.

Pasquali Cerioli Jlia, "La laicità nella giurisprudenza amministrativa: da principio supremo a 'simbolo religioso'", *Stato, Chiese e pluralismo confessionale*, Rivista telematica (www.statochiese.it), marzo 2009, pp. 1–24.

Pastorelli Sabrina, "Religious Dress Code: The Italian Case", in Silvio Ferrari – Sabrina Pastorelli (eds.), *Religion in Public Space. A European Perspective*, Routledge, Abingdon – New York, 2012, pp. 235–254.

Perù Ministerio de Justicia y Derechos Humanos, *Derecho a la libertad religiosa en el Perù: normativa y jurisprudencia*, Sistema peruano de información juridica, Lima, 2019, 100 pp.

Petroncelli Mario, "La Santa Sede e lo Stato Città del Vaticano", *Rivista Internazionale di Scienze Sociali e Discipline Ausiliarie*, vol. 3, no. 2, 1932, pp. 169–193.

Pettinato Cristiana Maria, "La mostra pittorica 'Gratia plena': in odor di blasfemia la Diocesi di Carpi", March 2024, available at www.rivistadirittoereligioni.com

Peyrot Giorgio, *Gli evangelici nei loro rapporti con lo Stato dal fascismo ad oggi*, Torre Pellice, Società di studi valdesi, 1977, 40 pp.

Pierik Roland – Wibren van der Burg, "The Neutral State and the Mandatory Crucifix", *Human Rights Law Review*, vol. 11, no. 3, 2011, pp. 267–272.

Pin Andrea, "Public Schools, Italian Crucifix, and the European Court of Human Rights: The Italian Separation of Church and State", *Emory International Law Review*, no. 25, 2011, pp. 97–149.

Popa Mihai – Liviu Andreescu, "Religion and Education in Romania: Social Mobilization and the 'Shadow' of the European Court of Human Rights", *Politics and Religion*, no. 12, 2019, pp. 79–102.

Puppinck Grégor, "The Case of *Lautsi v. Italy*: A Synthesis", *Brigham Young University Law Review*, no. 3, 2012, pp. 873–930.

Ratzinger Joseph, *Europa. I suoi fondamenti oggi e domani*, San Paolo, Cinisello Balsamo, MI, 2004, 105 pp.

Recchia Nicola, "Il caso Montagnana e l'affermazione del valore della laicità nell'evoluzione della giurisprudenza penale della Corte di cassazione", *Il Diritto ecclesiastico*, no. 4, 2001, pp. 262–272.

Ricca Mario, "A Modest Proposal: An Overgrown Constitutional Path to Cultural/Religious Pluralism in Italy", *CALUMET – Intercultural Law and Humanities Review*, Rivista telematica, available at www.calumet-review.it, 9 November 2016, pp. 1–46, available at SSRN: https://ssrn.com/abstract=2876809

Ricca Mario, "Don't Uncover That Face! Covid-19 Masks and the Niqab: Ironic Transfigurations on the ECtHR's Intercultural Blindness", *International Journal of Semiotics of Law*, vol. 35, no. 3, 2022, pp. 119–1143 (original paper 2020).

Ruffini Francesco, *La libertà religiosa. I, Storia dell'idea*, Fratelli Bocca, Torino, 1901, XI–544 pp.

Ruffini Francesco, *Corso di diritto ecclesiastico italiano. La libertà religiosa come diritto pubblico subiettivo*, Fratellli Bocca, Torino, 1924, XVI–429 pp.

Sabolla Luciano, *All'origine della cura. Pauper Christi. Assistenza e sanità tra Medioevo ed Età moderna*, Itaca, Castel Bolognese, RA, 2020, 151 pp.

Sabolla Luciano, *All'origine della cura. Homo viator. Dall'accoglienza dei primi pellegrini agli Ospedali Maggiori*, Itaca, Castel Bolognese, RA, 2023, 104 pp.

Schwarz Rémy, *Un siècle de laïcité*, Berger-Levrault, Paris, 2007, 204 pp.

Slaughter Anne Marie, "Judicial Globalisation", *Virginia Journal of International Law*, vol. 40, no. 4, 2000, pp. 1103–1124.

Slaughter Anne Marie, *A New World Order*, Princeton University Press, Princeton – Oxford, 2004, 368 pp.

Stanisz Piotr – Michał Zawiślak – Marta Ordon (eds.), *Presence of the Cross in Public Spaces: Experiences of Selected European Countries*, Cambridge Scholar Publishing, Newcastle upon Tyne, 2016, VIII–270 pp.

Strasser Mark P., *Free Exercise of Religion and the United States Constitution. The Supreme Courts's Challenge*, Routledge, Abingdon – New York, 2018, X–157 pp.

Stüssi Marcel, "Banning of Minarets: Adressing the Validity of a Controversial Swiss Popular Initiative", *Religion & Human Rights*, vol. 3, no. 2, 2008, pp. 135–153.

Sweet William, "Jacques Maritain and the Universal Declaration of Human Rights", in Rafael Domingo – John Witte Jr. (eds.), *Christianity and Global Law*, Routledge, Abingdon – New York, 2020, pp. 158–177.

Tedeschi Mario, *Sulla scienza del diritto ecclesiastico*, Giuffrè, Milano, 2007, XII–168 pp.

Temperman Jeroen (ed.), *The Lautsi Papers: Multidisciplinary Reflections on Religious Symbols in the Public School Classroom*, Brill – Nijhof, Leiden, 2012, XXVIII–444 pp.

Testa Bappenheim Stefano, *I simboli religiosi nello spazio pubblico. Profili giuridici comparati*, Editoriale Scientifica, Napoli, 2019, 947 pp.

Testa Bappenheim Stefano, *La croce nello spazio pubblico bavarese: corsi e ricorsi storici*, January 2024, available at www.rivistadirittoereligioni.com/wp-content/uploads/2024/01/Corsi-e-ricorsi-storici.pdf

Torfs Rik, "The Presence of the Cross in Public Spaces from the Perspective of the European Court Oh Human Rights", in P. Stanisz – M. Zawiślak – M. Ordon (eds.), *Presence of the Cross in Public Spaces: Experiences od Selected European Countries*, Cambridge Scholar Publishing, Newcastle upon Tyne, 2016, pp. 1–10.

Toscano Marcello, *Il fattore religioso nella Convenzione Europea dei Diritti dell'Uomo. Itinerari giurisprudenziali*, Edizioni ETS, Pisa, 2018, 359 pp.

Toscano Marcello, "Immagini e simboli religiosi nella comunicazione commerciale: profili giuridici", in Vittorio Montieri (ed.), *La manipolazione del sacro. L'immagine religiosa nel mondo della comunicazione*, Mimesis, Milano – Udine, 2021, pp. 343–371.

Trofaier Leskovar Valerie, "The Crucifix in the Kindergarten", *Vienna Journal on International Constitutional Law*, vol. 5, no. 2, 2011, pp. 246–250.
Valvo Paolo (ed.), *La libertà religiosa in Messico. Dalla Rivoluzione alle sfide dell'attualità*, Studium, Roma, 2020, 272 pp.
Vanoni Luca Pietro, *Laicità e libertà di educazione. Il crocifisso nelle aule scolastiche in Italia e in Europa*, Giuffrè, Milano, 2013, VIII–339 pp.
Vázquez Gómez Rebecca, "Religious Freedom and the Burqa Ban in Italy", *Canopy Forum*, 21 November 2022, pp. 1–3.
Ventura Marco, "Dirittto ecclesiastico e Europa. Dal *Church and State* al *Law and Religion*", in Giovanni Battista Varnier (ed.), *Il nuovo volto del diritto ecclesiastico italino*, Rubbettino, Soveria Mannelli, 2004, pp. 191–216.
Ventura Marco, *Law and Religion in Italy*, Wolkers Kluvers, Alphen aan den Rijn, 2013, 234 pp.
Weil Patrick, *De la laïcité en France*, Grasset, Paris, 2022, 144 pp.
Weiler Joseph H.H., "State and Nation; Church, Mosque and Synagogue – On Religion Freedom and Religious Symbols in Public Spaces", in Mary Ann Glendon – Hans F. Zacher (eds.), *Universal Rights in a World of Diversity. The Case of Religious Freedom*, The Pontifical Academy of Social Sciences, Vatican City, 2012, pp. 578–587.
Wertman Douglas A., "The Catholic Church: The Impact of Secularization", *West European Politics*, vol. 5, no. 2, 1982, pp. 87–107.
Zaccaria Roberto et al. (eds.), *La legge che non c'è. Proposta per una legge sulla libertà religiosa in Italia*, il Mulino, Bologna, 2017, 392 pp.
Zimmermann Tristan, "Le crucifix dans la salle de classe: l'arrêt *Comune di Cadro* revisité à la lumière de l'affaire *Lautsi*", *Praxis Juristische Aktuelle*, 2011, pp. 1485–1504.

Digital Media Platform

Boezi Francesco, "Sì al Ramadan, no al parroco. Il preside vieta la benedizione", 30 March 2024, available at www.ilgiornale.it/news/politica/s-ramadan-no-parroco-preside-vieta-benedizione-2303151.html
Borghi Claudio, "Alcune evidenze non sempre evidenti. Pensieri peregrini per avviare una riflessione", 5 April 2024, available at www.cprenateveduggio.it/wp-content/uploads/2024/04/2024-04-06_EvidenzeNon SempreEvidenti.pdf
Coppetti Serena, "Chiusura per Ramadan. Il provveditore avverte: 'Delibera da revocare'. Il ministro minacciato", 21 March 2024, available at www.ilgiornale.it/news/politica/chiusura-ramadan-provveditore-avverte-delibera-revocare-2299314.html
D'Agostino Andrea – Alessandro Beltrami, "Carpi. La mostra (non blasfema), le accuse, l'artista accoltellato: cosa è successo", 28 March 2024, available at www.avvenire.it/attualita/pagine/accusato-di-blasfemia-artista-accoltellato-in-chiesa
Di Bussolo Alessandro, "Patto energetico tra Università Antonianum e Moschea di Roma", March 2023, available at www.vaticannews.va/it/vaticano/news/2023-03/comunita-energetica-pace-universita-antonianum-moschea-roma-papa.html
Fiore Eugenia, "'Crocifissi vanno in ogni stanza'. Ma all'ospedale di Chivasso scoppia la polemica", 6 June 2019, www.ilgiornale.it/news/cronache/crocefissi-ogni-stanza-all-ospedale-chivasso-scoppia-1706992
Fiorentino Giovanni, "'Mostra blasfema? È libertà di pensiero'. E la procura chiede l'archiviazione", 26 March 2024, available at www.ilgiornale.it/news/cronaca-locale/mostra-blasfema-e-libert-pensiero-e-procura-chiede-2301597.html
Galici Francesca, "'Chi viene in Italia deve rispettare le nostre regole'. Scatta la stretta sul burkini in spiagge", 16 August 2023, available at www.ilgiornale.it/news/nazionale/stretta-sul-burkini-ecco-sar-nuova-legge-2197334.html

Licoys Capucine, "Paris 2024: les athlètes ont-ils le droit de porter des signes religieux au JO?", 14 Juin 2024, available at www.la-croix.com/sport/paris-2024-les-athletes-ont-ils-le-droit-de-porter-des-signes-religieux-aux-jo-20240613

Mattozzi Savin, "Muslim Women Harassed at Northern Italian Beach for Wearing Modest Clothing", 14 August 2023, available at www.euronews.com/culture/2023/08/14/muslim-women-harassed-at-northern-italian-beach-for-wearing-modest-clothing

Mitzman Dany, "The Sikhs Who Saved Parmesan", 25 June 2015, available at www.bbc.com/news/magazine-33149580

N.A., "Crocifissi rimossi dall'ospedale di Latisana e Palmanova, caso in Regione", 19 June 2024, available at www.friulioggi.it/primo-piano-5/crocifissi-rimossi-ospedale-latisana-palmanova-caso-regione-19-giugno-2024/

N.A., "Crocifisso: Smith citato in giudizio per vilipendio", 31 October 2003, available at www.corriere.it/Primo_Piano/Cronache/2003/10_Ottobre/31/smith.shtml

N.A., "Ex giudice 'anti crocifisso' rifiuta di deporre sotto croce", 29 September 2021, available at www.ladige.it/attualita/2021/09/29/ex-giudice-anti-crocifisso-rifiuta-di-deporre-sotto-croce-1.3008190

N.A., "Fine Ramadan festa in azienda: 'Un momento di condivisione interculturale'", 3 April 2024, available at www.ilrestodelcarlino.it/modena/cronaca/fine-ramadan-festa-azienda-kulbovbc

N.A., "Getto crocifisso dalla finestra: (mesi a Smith)", 13 January 2006, available at www.ilgiornale.it/news/gett-crocifisso-finestra-8-mesi-smith.html

N.A., "Gli atei premiano Franco Coppoli, l'insegnante che tolse il crocefisso in un'aula pubblica", 20 June 2024, available at https://terninrete.it/notizie-di-terni-gli-atei-premiano-franco-coppoli-linsegnante-che-tolse-il-crocefisso-in-unaula-scolastica-pubblica/

N.A., "Grand Itfar at Bristol Cathedral. Communities Share a Meal Together to Share Unity", 3 April 2024, available at https://bristol-cathedral.co.uk/news/grand-iftar-at-bristol-cathedral-communities-share-a-meal-together-to-share-unity/

N.A., "Il caso di Milano. Rosario in piazza, voci e critiche dal mondo cattolico", 20 May 2019, available at www.avvenire.it/attualita/pagine/rosario-in-piazza-salvini-le-voci-cattoliche

N.A., "In piscina, nuotano col 'burkini': scoppia il caso", 18 August 2023, available at www.polesine24.it/cronaca/2023/08/18/news/in-piscina-nuotano-col-burkini-scoppia-il-caso-226296/

N.A., "Italian School Closes to 'Celebrate' Ramadan, While Another Prevents Easter Blessing", 21 March 2024, available at https://catholicherald.co.uk/italian-school-closes-to-celebrate-ramadan-while-another-prevents-easter-blessing/

N.A., "Mattarella risponde alla scuola di Pioltello: 'Apprezzo il vostro lavoro'", 26 March 2024, available at www.ansa.it/sito/notizie/cronaca/2024/03/26/mattarella-scrive-a-pioltello-apprezzo-i-vostro-lavoro_53c6bc62-7544-4618-b590-4a0ef0431314.html

N.A., "Milano, Ramadan della pace nella chiesa di San Bernardino: musulmani e cristiani pregano insieme", 6 April 2004, available at www.ilgiorno.it/milano/cronaca/ramadan-islamici-cristiani-preghiera-pe4ue9tk

N.A., "Pioltello, i docenti: 'Indignati e offesi'. Valditara: 'Non è violazione dell'autonomia scolastica'", 22 March 2024, available at www.rainews.it/

Opitz Manuel, "Ein Bild und seine Geschichte: Als Muslime zu Ramadan im Kölner Dom beteten", 11 March 2024, available at www.geo.de/wissen/weltgeschichte/ramadan-1965-als-muslime-im-koelner-dom-beteten-34535372.html

Padoan Florian, "Après plusieurs années de polémiques, la Vierge de la Flotte-en-Ré, sur l'île de Ré, a retrouvé sa place", 8 Juin 2024, available at https://france3-regions.francetvinfo.fr/nouvelle-aquitaine/charente-maritime/ile-de-re/apres-plusieurs-annees-de-polemique-la-vierge-de-la-flotte-en-re-sur-l-ile-de-re-a-retrouve-sa-place-2983535.html

Pazzaglia Chiara, "Carpi. Il crocifisso torna in aula alla scuola media Focherini", 12 March 2023, available at www.avvenire.it/attualita/pagine/carpi-il-crocifisso-torna-in-aula

Redaelli Pierfrancesco, "A Renate. Per la cena di fine ramadan c'è posto solo in oratorio. E la Lega attacca", 28 March 2024, available at www.avvenire.it/attualita/pagine/polemiche-della-lega-per-una-cena-di-fine-ramadan-in-oratorio-a-renate

Tait Albert, "Ramadan Lights on Display in Central London Over Easter. Islamic Holy Month Celebrated in West End during Christian Festival", 27 March 2024, available at www.telegraph.co.uk/news/2024/03/27/ramadan-lights-on-display-in-central-london-over-easter/

Trzeciak Matthias, "Heftige Ramadan-Diskussion. 'Ich finde es wunderbar' – 'Keine Toleranz gegenüber unseren Werten'", 13 March 2024, available at www.express.de/koeln/ramadan-beleuchtung-ich-ueberlege-mir-koeln-zu-verlassen-1-756508

Legal Portals

(In order of appearance)

https://caselaw.findlaw.com
https://codices.coe.int/codices/documents/welcome
https://constitution.congress.gov/
https://courdappelduquebec.ca
https://curia.europa.eu
https://decisions.scc-csc.ca
https://eur-lex.europa.eu
https://hj.tribunalconstitucional.es/es
https://hudoc.echr.coe.int
https://laws-lois.justice.gc.ca
https://legiscan.com
https://ndlegis.gov
https://openjur.de
https://tc.gob.pe/jurisprudencia
htttps://www.cortecostituzionale.it
www.bger.ch/it
www.bundesregierung.de
www.bundesverfassungsgericht.de
www.bverwg.de
www.canlii.org
www.conseil-constitutionnel.fr
www.conseil-etat.fr/avis-consultatifs/rechercher-un-avis-consiliaweb (*Consilia Web*)
www.conseil-etat.fr/decisions-de-justice/jurisprudence/rechercher-une-decision-arianeweb (*Ariane Web*)
www.corteconstitucional.gov.co
www.fedlex.admin.ch
www.gesetze-bayern.de
www.law.cornell.edu
www.legifrance.gouv.fr
www.legis.quebec.gouv.qc.ca
www.normattiva.it
www.poderjudicial.es
www.ris.bka.gv.at
www.saos.org.pl
www.scj.ro
www.scjn.gob.mx
www.vfgh.gv.at
www4.ti.ch

Table of cases

Index

FSC
www.fsc.org
MIX
Papier | Fördert
gute Waldnutzung
FSC® C083411

Kolibri 360 GmbH
Ferdinand-Jühlke-Straße 7
99095 Erfurt, Deutschland
produktsicherheit@kolibri360.de